THE MOCKINGBIRD, THE NIGHTINGALE OF THE SOUTH

BIRDS OF THE SOUTH

*PERMANENT AND WINTER BIRDS COMMONLY
FOUND IN GARDENS, FIELDS, AND WOODS*

BY

CHARLOTTE HILTON GREEN

DOVER PUBLICATIONS, INC., NEW YORK

To My Mother

MARY ROSCOE HILTON

WHO HAS EVER ENCOURAGED HER DAUGHTER
IN ALL SHE HAS TRIED TO DO
THIS BOOK IS AFFECTIONATELY DEDICATED

Published in Canada by General Publishing Company, Ltd., 30 Lesmill Road, Don Mills, Toronto, Ontario.
Published in the United Kingdom by Constable and Company, Ltd., 10 Orange Street, London WC 2.

This Dover edition, first published in 1975, is an unabridged republication of the work first published in 1933. The color plates of the original edition are here reproduced in halftone. This edition is published by special arrangement with The University of North Carolina Press, Chapel Hill, publishers of the original edition.

International Standard Book Number: 0-486-21234-3
Library of Congress Catalog Card Number: 74-22555

Manufactured in the United States of America
Dover Publications, Inc.
180 Varick Street
New York, N.Y. 10014

FOREWORD

"NATURE STUDY," says John Burroughs in *Ways of Nature,* "is only science out of school, happy in the fields and woods, loving the flower and the animal which it observes, and finding in them something for the sentiments and the emotions as well as for the understanding." It is from this point of view that the writer of the present volume hopes to enlist the sympathy and the interest of her readers in bird life and to reveal to them something of the enjoyment to be had from the observation of the living bird.

It is the nature-study approach, rather than the scientific sequence of the American Ornithologists' Union Check List, that has been used. The latter would begin with the lowest form of bird life, which, incidentally, is the form least known to the child or the layman, whereas the former—the nature-study approach—begins with any bird which is familiar and which the child can observe for himself about his home or on his walks afield. The book is intended, therefore, not for the scientist, but for the child or the layman who is interested in nature's ways, and its only objective is to lead others to observe birds with their own eyes and thus develop an interest and a joy in field work.

To an earlier generation, field work in ornithology meant chiefly collecting. Today, except for scientific purposes, it means chiefly observing. Where the scientist brings home a bird for his collection or his laboratory, the writer brings home but the memory of a bird. Her laboratory is among the free birds in the woods and fields, in the garden and about the bird bath or the feeding stations. She has endeavored to be scientifically accurate, never consciously exaggerating or over-coloring facts, but she does not go so far as the scientific ornithologist; and she makes no claim of adding to the great store of knowledge of ornithology. It has been rather difficult to decide whether or not to include certain birds, such as the cat bird, the Maryland yellow-throat, and the gray-blue gnatcatcher, which are winter residents in the lower South but which are either rare in winter or known only as summer residents in the upper South. These and other migrants and summer residents will be included in the next book, "The Return of the Birds."

A number of these bird stories have appeared as Sunday features in the *Raleigh News and Observer,* and the writer is deeply indebted to that paper, and to its managing editor, Mr. Frank Smethurst, for encouragement in the writing of them. The writer is also indebted to Miss Hattie S. Parrott, Supervisor of Elementary Instruction in the State of North Carolina, for her interest in the publication of the stories in permanent form. She also appreciates the interest that many readers, teachers, students, parents, and members of the Raleigh Garden Club and other garden clubs have expressed in them.

Acknowledgment is due to Mr. T. Gilbert Pearson, Mr. H. H. Brimley and Mr. C. S. Brimley for permission to quote freely from their extensive work on *The Birds of North Carolina;* to Mr. C. S. Brimley, for his gracious *Introduction* to this volume, for reading, criticising, and commenting on the manuscript, for many timely and helpful suggestions, and for assistance generously given in many ways; to Dr. A. A. Allen, Professor of Ornithology of Cornell University, for permission to quote freely from his extensive work *The Book of Bird Life* (D. Van Nostrand and Company, Inc.); to the late Professor

Anna Botsford Comstock and the Comstock Publishing Company for permission to quote from her *The Handbook of Nature-Study;* to Doubleday, Doran and Company for permission to quote from Mr. A. Radcliffe Dugmore's *Bird Homes;* to Mr. Ernest Thompson Seton, for the "Myth of the Song Sparrow" in *Woodland Tales* published by the same company; to Houghton Mifflin Company for the use of poems by Emerson, Lowell, Frank Bolles, and the poems and selection from John Burroughs; to Archibald Rutledge for permission to quote from his writings on the mockingbird; and to the Biological Survey of the United States Department of Agriculture for various bulletins on birds; to Miss Georgia H. Faison, Reference Librarian of the University of North Carolina, for assistance in ascertaining the copyright owners of poems quoted from; to Miss F. Elvira Martin, Dr. Ruby Green Smith, Professor Anna Botsford Comstock, and Dr. Lawrence H. Snyder, who, through their courses in nature-study and ornithology inspired the writer's interest in bird life; to her husband, who has always been an interested and helpful companion in all bird study; and to Dr. Ruby Green Smith and Miss L. Pearle Green for extensive help in reading, reviewing, and preparing the manuscript. She is also deeply appreciative of the charm added to the book by the inclusion of the many poems written by various bird lovers; the colored plates, by outstanding bird artists, secured from the National Association of Audubon Societies; and the splendid black and white drawings of Mr. Paul W. Porterfield.

CHARLOTTE HILTON GREEN

Woodhaven
Raleigh, North Carolina
October 24, 1933

BLUEBIRD

INTRODUCTION

As A STUDENT of birds for many years, it is with great pleasure that I commend Mrs. Green's little book to the bird lovers and school children of the South. It contains not only descriptions of our common resident and winter land birds but also a wealth of information concerning their ways and doings. Mrs. Green does not claim to be a scientist, but, to my mind, all accurate knowledge is science, and not merely the dry and uninteresting technical side of it. Science, in fact, is merely knowledge as compared with guesswork, being a rational putting of two and two together and a dividing of two and two into ones.

Birds have always attracted more popular interest than all other groups of animals combined, for the simple reason that, being abundant in numbers and active in the daytime, they are more easily observed than rarer and nocturnal creatures. Also their roving instinct, which causes most species to winter in one locality and nest in another, adds increasing zest to their study, for we never know how nearly on time the spring arrivals will be or how long the winter birds will delay before starting north again.

Besides this, the bird population of a given locality can never be called fixed: some species will increase in numbers and others will decrease. Part of these changes will be due to alterations in the environment, for we can easily understand that if we put more land in pastures, birds that nest in pastures, such as the meadow lark, grasshopper sparrow, and killdeer, will find more places to breed, while, if we cut down all the woods, the wood-inhabiting kinds will have to find homes elsewhere.

Other changes seem to come from a natural increase in the numbers of certain kinds which tend to over-populate the territory occupied by them, so that the surplus must seek homes elsewhere. We know that the cardinal, the Carolina wren, and the mockingbird have been extending their breeding range to the northward of recent years, while the robin, the song sparrow, and the house wren have been reversing the process and extending it southward.

Never guess at your birds; and always feel very, very dubious about determining a bird on sight as one that usually does not occur anywhere near your locality. Birds do turn up far from their natural homes, but this is not a normal occurrence.

Remember also that a bird to be correctly named must not only agree reasonably well with the description but it must not disagree in any important point. A red bird with a crest could not, for instance, be a summer tanager, nor could one without a crest be a cardinal, however the particular birds might otherwise seem to fit the description.

And remember that patience and perseverance will, in time, solve all our bird problems, and I trust this book will do its turn in helping.

C. S. BRIMLEY

June 19, 1933

TABLE OF CONTENTS

ALPHABETICAL LIST OF ILLUSTRATIONS

HALFTONE PLATES

BLACK AND WHITE PLATES IN TEXT

SONG SPARROW

Order—PASSERES   Family—FRINGILLIDÆ
Genus—MELOSPIZA   Subspecies—CINEXEA MELODIA

National Association of Audubon Societies

BIRDS OF THE SOUTH

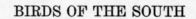

GOLDFINCH

Order—PASSERES　　　　　　　　Family—FRINGILLIDÆ
Genus—ASTRAGALINUS　　　　　　Species—TRISTIS
National Association of Audubon Societies

I

LIVING WITH THE BIRDS

WINTER is the best of all times to begin living with the birds. Being fewer then, they are less confusing to the novice; being hungry, they are more friendly and forget some of their fear of man so that, at feeding-stations, they can be brought close for observation. In winter, too, most of the shrubs and trees are bare, and the birds are more easily seen.

Attracting birds about the home is a simple matter, furnishing endless amusement and interest, and opening a window into a new and fascinating world. The companionship of birds, when once we get to know them, is more than worth the little trouble and thought involved.

Feeding birds in winter is not so important in the South as in the North; yet, even here, December, January, and February are often lean months for the feathered folks. Birds are not, as some contend, made lazy by artificial feeding. After a meal of suet, grains, nut-meats, or doughnuts, the weed warriors will enjoy a dessert of weed seeds, and the insectivorous birds will fly to the branch or trunk of a tree and diligently and joyously go insect hunting.

Though birds bathe much less frequently in winter than in summer, the hardier ones do enjoy a dip now and then, and most of them drink at the bath regularly. No matter how simple or elaborate the bath may be, whether marble, stone, or cement, there are certain important details which should be considered. The bath should be shallow, not more than two or three inches deep, and should slope towards the center. A roughened bottom prevents slipping, and fresh water is necessary the year round.

Protection against winter cold and storms is also needed, and evergreens, such as pines, spruce, cedar, and the close, broad-leaved shrubs furnish shelter for roosting places. Berry-bearing trees and shrubs, like the mountain ash, mulberry, sumac, dogwood, holly, barberry, snowberry, elderberry, silverberry, and the privets provide food for the birds, as well as attractive plantings about the grounds. No tree could add more to the appearance of a home than our native dogwood, which, with its white bloom in spring, its green foliage in summer, its flaming red leaves and scarlet berries in autumn, and the delicate tracery of its bare branches in winter, is beautiful at all seasons.

Food, water, shelter, protection! With these, one should be host to the birds throughout the year. If these are furnished the year around, birds are often induced to nest close by and to rear their young in the garden or yard.

At Woodhaven during the past summer (1933), fifteen different species brought their young to feed at our feeding-stations. These included several broods each of mockers, Carolina wrens, titmice, and chickadees; two broods each of cardinals, brown thrashers, catbirds, robins, wood thrushes, and downies; and nuthatches, pine warblers, summer tanagers, chipping sparrows, and, of course, the ever present English sparrow.

Often, during the nesting period, the brooding bird would fly to the doughnuts on the "doughnut tree" for a hurried meal, or her mate would bring her a welcome bite. Later, when the nestlings were hatched, and the young were old enough to eat something besides insects, we would see the parents take a few hungry mouthfuls themselves, and then, with beaks full, hurry off in the direction of the nest. When the young were old enough to fly, but before they could feed themselves, they were brought near the feeding-stations, and the parent birds fed them. As they grew older, they were coaxed up to the station and, in time, learned to feed themselves, though young birds demand attention as long as they can get it. Many times we have watched young mockers and cardinals awkwardly managing to feed themselves, but when the parent bird appeared, what a piteous wailing and what helpless, hungry cries issued from their wide-opened mouths!

Feeding-stations bring the birds close for observation, and here one can watch the development and change in coloration of the young. A mother chippy brings her different-looking, breast-streaked birdling to be fed. What an opportunity to know the young chippy! Particularly is this important for the child, for here he learns to observe for himself. Any detail he notes is a hundred-fold more important than that which is pointed out to him.

How better start the day than to breakfast in a jade-green and ivory nook near a window, on the other side of which a red summer tanager and his green-gold mate are feeding! The tanager is the least nervous of all the birds that feed at our window-shelf cafeteria and, unless our movements are too abrupt, will often breakfast with us.

NEST HUNTING IN WINTER

Nest hunting is a fascinating part of winter rambles. "Nest hunting in winter?" you may ask, surprised. Yes, for after the leaves are gone from most of the trees, the nests that were missed in the summer are easily found. Try it, especially after one of our rare snows, for then each nest will wear a tiny white cap and is easily found.

Nest hunting or collecting in winter is far better than nest or egg collecting in summer.

Though very popular a generation or two ago, egg collecting, except by scientists, is now more and more frowned upon. Collecting eggs and bird skins is extremely important to the scientist, who, in his analysis and research, is continuously adding new and important data to the science of ornithology. But for most of us it is far better to "name the bird without a gun"—far better to hunt birds with field glasses and camera and to collect them in "memory-chains."

A bird calendar helps in the collection of these "memory-chains." The calendar, if used by a family group or a class, may be a large placard. Sometimes children, or other members, like to keep smaller, individual calendars. Marginal sketches, water colors, or cut-outs of birds pasted on, make them attractive. We have found the form on page 7 practical.

One thing more. The bird lover must protect his winged guests from their enemies—and the greatest of these is the cat. The bird lover's enmity is not so much for the well fed, well cared for house pet, although it, too, takes its toll, but is directed mainly against the wild, half-starved stray cat and its descendants. Few people have any idea of how many of these stray cats there are about our fields and woods. Yet every night-motorist must have observed how frequently he sees their eyes shining in the dark as they skulk about on their nefarious hunting. And the more stray cats there are, the fewer birds there will be about our homes.

Birds are needed the year round, but we appreciate them especially in winter. What a dreary, lonely place a rural or suburban home would be in the long cold months without them! No blue jays flashing through the green pines, no cardinals lighting up the bare trees and calling

BIRD CALENDAR

NAME OF BIRD	DATE First	DATE Last	BY WHOM SEEN	WHERE SEEN	WHAT DOING	REMARKS
Redstart	April 20	Oct. 5	Betty Hilton	Near Stream	Flying	Found Nest Later
Song Sparrow	Oct. 15	April 20	Ronny Raynolds	In Thicket	Perched on Weed	
Brown Creeper	Nov. 2	——	Teddy Raynolds	On Trunk of Tree	Searching for Insects	Looks Like Bark

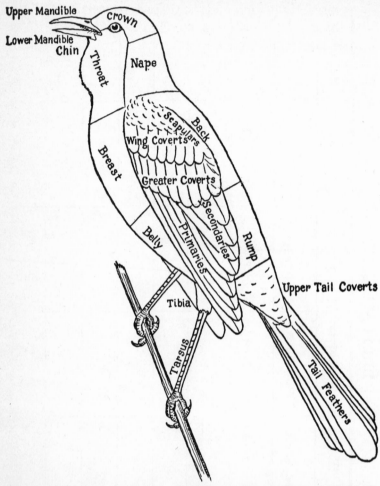

BY CONSULTING THIS CHART YOU CAN FIND OUT EXACTLY WHAT IS MEANT BY
THE NAMES USED IN DESCRIBING THE DIFFERENT PARTS OF A BIRD.

pretty, pretty, pretty, no titmice whistling cheerfully, no
wrens chattering about the dooryard, no bluebirds feeding on the scarlet berries of the dogwood, no snowbirds
bringing visions of far, free spaces or remote northern
seas, no white-throats fluting the promise of spring days
to come!

Appreciation and understanding, especially for the wild things about us, make possible an every-day life of a little less monotony, a little more interest and enthusiasm, as gradually our vision is enlarged so that we more readily see and enjoy the beauty and the charm of the world about us. With Nature as our great teacher, let us learn to live with the birds.

> And Nature spreads wide her book,
> In a temple fair and free,—
> To all who may listen she cries, ''Come, look!
>   Come and learn at my knee.
> Watch the change in the finch's vest,
> Note how the highhole carves his nest,—
> Come with light foot and loving breast,
>   And bury your ills with me!''
>   —DORA READ GOODALE.

II

CAROLINA CHICKADEE,* THE ACROBAT OF BIRDDOM

Piped a tiny voice hard by,
Gay and polite, a cheerful cry,
Chic-chickadee—dee! saucy note
Out of sound heart and merry throat,
As if it said, "Good-day, good Sir!
Fine afternoon, old passenger!
Happy to meet you in these places
Where January brings few faces."

. . . .

Flew near, with soft wing grazed my hand;
Hopped on the bough, then darting low,
Prints his small impress on the snow,
Shows feats of his gymnastic play,
Head downward, clinging to the spray.

. . . .

Here was this atom in full breath
Hurling defiance at vast death.
This scrap of valor, just for play
Fronts the north wind, in waistcoat gray!
　　　　　　　—RALPH WALDO EMERSON.

WALTER PRITCHARD EATON, who writes as delightfully—and as intelligently—of birds as he does of the theater, says that this world would be a rather dull and dolorous place without the chickadee. And "so say we all" who know and love the cheerful little gray and black ball of fluff that sings so gaily through even the bleakest, coldest days of winter.

The chickadee, a little four-and-a-half-inch gray bird with whitish underparts and a black cap and chin-bib,

* The chickadee in the colored plate is the northern form, *Penthestes atricapillus,* whereas our Carolina chickadee is *Penthestes carolinensis.* Our chickadee is similar in coloring but slightly smaller.

CHICKADEE

Order—PASSERES   Family—PARIDÆ
Genus—PENTHESTES   Species—ATRICAPILLUS
National Association of Audubon Societies

TUFTED TITMOUSE

Order—Passeres   Family—Paridæ
Genus—Bæolophus   Species—bicolor

National Association of Audubon Societies

seems a part of our winter landscape, and, perched on a bare branch against one of our rare snows for a background, he creates a living Japanese print. *Chick-a-dee-dee-dee* we hear him call.

Our Carolina chickadee, or tomtit, as he is often called, is nearly an inch smaller than his northern cousin. In some of the higher mountains of the upper South both species meet; writing of them William Brewster says: "In one place a male of each species was singing in the same tree, the low, plaintive notes of the Carolina bird contrasting sharply with the ringing notes of its more northern cousin."

Try going out for a tramp and "chickadeeing" on the first snowy day we may have. Do you remember how Uncle Remus liked to "meet up" with a chickadee? When other birds take shelter from the storm, chickadee, his black cap conspicuous in the whiteness, his feathers fluffed out by the wind, will go whirling by, just as cheerful as ever. He sings when all else in Nature is silent.

A bird's song may mean much or little to the listener; it depends on his interest. There are few who do not feel the cockles of the heart warm when they hear the gay cheery call of the tomtit.

Because of his song, his friendliness and fearlessness, and his confiding ways, the chickadee is one of our best known and best loved birds. More than any other bird he responds to friendly overtures and can be made a regular visitor by having a constant food supply within reach. Like almost all birds, the chickadee is greedy over suet; if this is placed on trees, post, or feeding-shelf near a window, it will surely bring him within reach of your observation.

A northern naturalist says that he has never seen a chickadee in or near his bird bath, but one winter day I called the man o' the house to come quickly, to see our Carolina chickadee drinking and then hopping in for a bath.

The chickadee is the acrobat of birddom, and his antics in the bath are highly amusing. Taking a step or two along the rim, he bobs up and down a bit; then, as if suddenly gaining courage, he plunges headlong in, for all the world like small bare boys in some old swimming hole. So tiny and adorable is he, as he peers over the rim of the bath, just his little black cap, bright eyes, and black bib showing, that he reminds one of a gay water sprite.

Often we have watched the chickadees feed on suet and then go to a certain branch and peck away industriously, bobbing upside down and hanging head downwards to peck on the underside. Investigation showed some sort of plant scale on that particular spot, but in a short time the chickadees had cleaned it up. They work mainly on the smaller branches and twigs.

One can hardly realize the enormous quantity of food these tiny birds require to sustain their energy, especially in winter, for most of their waking hours are spent in almost continuous search for food. Even in the South, the months of January and February are sometimes lean ones, and extra food is appreciated, and helps conserve our bird life.

During the winter months the chickadees flock together, often in company with the titmice and nuthatches. About February, listen and you will note that the male begins to sing more seductively. The love note is beginning to creep into his song.

But, although most of the year the chickadee is such a friendly mite, when it comes time for nesting, unlike many other birds, especially his cousin the tufted titmouse, which nests each year in the hollow tree beside our sleeping porch, the chickadee becomes very secretive and seems to prefer the deeper woods. Though they are about our place all the rest of the year, we have never found one of their nests at Woodhaven. They like a more quiet retreat, often near a swamp or small stream.

The nest is built in a natural cavity, in a dead or living tree, or in a hole excavated by the birds themselves in a dead limb, stump, or decayed fence-post. Occasionally they take over the abandoned hole of some other bird, particularly of the downy woodpecker.

The cavity is lined with feathers, fur, cotton, cat-tail fluff, moss, hair, strips of bark, and similar materials matted together. It is usually about six inches below the entrance hole, which may be anywhere from two to twelve feet from the ground. There are from four to eight white eggs, sprinkled with small blotches and specks of reddish brown. April is the usual month for nesting.

Young chickadees are excellent examples of the natural law that when the adult male and female are alike the young birds very often resemble them. A family of young chickadees, as soon as they are fully feathered, look exactly like the parent birds. This is in contrast to the young of the bright cardinal, which resemble the ash-washed-with-rose mother. For where there is a sexual difference in color among the birds, with few exceptions the male is the brighter.

The Carolina chickadee is one of the farmer's greatest friends, destroying winter stages of insects, eggs, and hibernating adults. Although it is also a seed eater, being particularly fond of the seeds in pine cones, and of poison ivy and other weeds, more than two-thirds of its food consists of insects, including tent-caterpillars, plant lice, scale, weevils, ants, wasps, spiders, and even grasshoppers. It has been estimated that a chickadee destroys thousands of insect eggs in one day, and orchards having these little black and gray tenants have been found freer of insect pests than others in the same locality.

The bird's beak is a sharp little pick, just fitted for taking insect eggs off from twigs and from the under side of branches where they are glued fast to the food-trees by the mother insect. Chickadee is a thorough inspector of the trees who doesn't intend any pest to be overlooked, but, neither does he believe in "all work and no play," for suddenly in the midst of his labors he will stop to send forth a happy *chick-a-dee-dee-dee!*

A CHICKADEE TRAGEDY

The chickadee is a gallant little soul, who goes down with flag flying. Once, on an early morning walk along Crabtree Creek with an ornithology class, some of the boys took an old flat-bottomed boat and paddled along the opposite shore looking for bird nests. Coming beneath an old hollow limb that extended out over the water, they noticed a hole about five feet up. One boy thoughtlessly enlarged the hole enough to see if the hollow were inhabited. Unfortunately it was, by young chickadees, almost but not quite ready to leave the nest.

Before a warning call had stopped the boy, the young birds became frightened at the intrusion and started to leave the nest. Had they turned back toward the land, they would have had strength enough to reach a tree or bush, but in their alarm they struck out straight across the water—and they were still too young to be able to fly long enough to carry them across. They could not cover the distance, and one by one the gray and black mites dropped into the water, where they struggled, instinctively trying to swim, until their feathers became water-soaked. One or two drifted downstream and across the current. Rescuing them we tried to revive them, but it was too late.

Chickadee belongs to the family *Paridae,* the titmice, small birds nearly allied to the nuthatches, but differing from them in having short, stout bills and comparatively long tails. Unlike many bird families it is largely restricted to the more northern parts of the world. Of the two hundred and forty-one known species, fifteen are in North America, where they range to the southern border of the Mexican tableland. They inhabit wooded country, where their destructiveness to insects, insect eggs and larvae, is of great value.

Edward Howe Forbush, late state ornithologist of Massachusetts, states: "My own experience for ten years, has shown that trees may be absolutely protected from leaf-eating insects by attracting chickadees through the year."

The Carolina chickadee might well be a runner-up against the Carolina wren for the honor of being the state bird of North or South Carolina or any other southern state. Like the wren, it has a southern name; and is a permanent resident (except in the highest mountains) through all seasons. It is an assiduous insect gatherer; it has no bad traits; it is cheerful and ever-present even in the bitterest weather; and, above all, it is especially beloved by children.

May no southern garden or home be without its black-capped tomtit—the winged Pippa whose gay *chickadee-dee-dee-dee* tells us

"God's in His Heaven—
All's right with the world!"

III

THE TUFTED TITMOUSE

Gay whistler of the sunny days
  Or harsh announcer of your wrath,
Gray Peto with your funny ways,
  You're always welcome in my path.
  —R. W. G.

Peto-peto-peto whistles the tufted titmouse persistently throughout much of the year. The call, especially during the winter months, is sometimes mistaken for the *pretty, pretty, pretty,* of the cardinal, but the latter has a richer tone, a more rolling cadence. Sometimes, too, it is mistaken for the *free-dom, free-dom, free-dom* of the Carolina wren.

The titmouse is well loved for this call, which some people say reminds them of a boy whistling up his dog. Easy to recognize, Peto is a trim, well-groomed bird, a little smaller than an English sparrow. He is gray above, whitish below, and the flanks, just underneath each wing, are tinged with rusty. There is a black forehead and a high, pointed gray crest and exceptionally bright black eyes that look like shining black shoe buttons. Both sexes look alike.

Peto's crest, like the wren's tail, acts as the barometer of his feelings. When excited the crest is erect; when angry it is flattened out until the bird reminds one of a crouched dog snarling.

A friendly bird, easily coaxed about dwellings, the titmouse can, by feeding, be brought close for observation. He not only feeds on our "doughnut" and "suet" tree stations, but comes regularly to the birds' cafeteria, a

[16]

shelf on the kitchen window-ledge, where we keep cracked nuts and grains, crumbs, suet, bits of rind, fruit—and, what we have found to be birds' favorite food—doughnuts.

Unlike his cousin chickadee, who makes a more leisurely, gracious call, Peto—who evidently has read no books on bird etiquette—usually snatches a bite and flies off. Somewhere near, there must be a cache where he hides his treasure, for often he is back for more before he could possibly have eaten the piece just taken. Occasionally, however, Peto pauses long enough to crack a nut by holding it firmly between his toes, and hacking at it. More often he flies up to a limb of a tree to do this.

In spite of these snatching proclivities, Peto seldom comes without making himself known. Just before or after he drops to the window-shelf, we hear a *chickadee-dee-dee,* which is more strident than the chickadee's call, or than his own whistled call of *peto.*

THE PEANUT STRING

Another feeding experiment we have found interesting is the winding of a string of raw peanuts around a small branch. What gymnastics the titmice go through to loosen and extract the peanuts! They hang and work from every possible position, but always finally manage to get the nut.

I have seen a titmouse hanging upside down to a nut on the loosened end of the string. He would work at the nut, then swing closer to the limb, where he could grasp a foothold in the bark, and straddling the space—one claw in the bark, one on the peanut—keep pecking at it until the nut came loose.

Throughout the winter, while in search of food, the titmice roam about in small flocks, probably family groups, often in company with chickadees, nuthatches, and sometimes a brown creeper or two. At the approach of spring they separate and pair off, but they do not, like the chickadees, become secretive at nesting time.

For years a pair have been nesting in the hollow oak near our sleeping porch. Sometime in April we notice them gathering the soft furry-like hair shed by the dogs, and soon we see them flying down into the cavity, and we know that once more the old tree holds the promise of bird life.

These birds do not seem to mind noise or confusion during their nesting period. The first time they built in our oak, we were having the house raised and the porches rebuilt. Piles of lumber, brick, and mortar lay right around their tree, and sawing and hammering were going on about them all day, but the birds flew in and out of their hole, apparently indifferent to it all.

But how they would scold and sputter at the dogs, which, seeing them and scenting the nest, would try to paw at the hole. For, though most titmice nests are said to be from five feet and more up, this one was less than two-and-a-half feet from the ground.

Usually the nests are in natural cavities in hollow trees, occasionally the old holes of woodpeckers being used. The birds fill these cavities with dead leaves and other material, sometimes for a depth of a foot or more, before building the nest proper, which is composed of green moss, leaves, cotton, fur, hair, and fine grasses. The five to eight eggs are pure white or creamy, profusely speckled with reddish brown. Before leaving the nest, the mother bird covers the eggs. Cairns states that if the nest is disturbed the birds will remove the eggs.

The female, a determined home-maker with a strong mother instinct, is very hard to flush from the nest, and will often allow herself to be caught rather than leave her eggs. She resents intrusion, and often, when we have tried to look down into the dusky gloom of the nest, where only a dim shape and two bright eyes were visible, she would angrily make a sort of spitted hiss.

There must have been several families of titmice raised on or near our woodland acre the past year (1933), for through the summer and fall young titmice fed almost constantly at our window-shelf cafeteria and at the "doughnut" tree. Often four or five would alight on the shelf at the same time, with several others waiting and scolding on the near-by trees. They were very quarrelsome among themselves, drawing back their heads and snarling and driving one another from the shelf.

And how angry they became if the doughnuts were missing, or if we were late in putting them out! Such peevish and strident cries and harsh calls, as they querulously tried to tell us we were late with their breakfast! A flock of angry young titmice can raise a din that is ear-splitting—as great a noise in proportion to their size, as that produced by their larger and distant cousins, the blue jays.

The young resemble the parent birds, except that they are slightly paler, the forehead is less dark, and the chestnut under the flanks may be missing, or may be just a faint trace of color.

Little has been written about this bird, for its range is south of New England and New York, where most of the bird writers have lived. But south of New York, to the Gulf coast and west to the Plains, it is a common and much loved resident. West Virginia has chosen this titmouse for its state bird.

Belonging to the family *Paridae,* the food habits of the titmouse are similar to those of its cousin, the chickadee, and it is equally deserving of protection, being listed by the Biological Survey, as an invaluable aid to the farmer.

IV

THE NUTHATCH, BIRD JACK-OF-ALL-TRADES

Head up or head down,
Like a jolly old clown,
    In and out,
    Quick about,
With many a prank,
And a lazy "Quank-quank."

Then hungry for food
In the bark or the moss;
    And who do you think
    Clipped his tail
With the shears,
Straight across?

With a cut-away coat
And a broad white vest,
And a high standing collar
He is always well dressed.
    —GARRETT NEWKIRK, in *Bird-Lore.*

IF THE Confederacy had ever had a bird mascot, the white-breasted nuthatch might well have been nominated, so nearly the same shade of gray-blue is its own military-looking uniform.

Six inches long is this nuthatch, and gray-blue above, with glossy black cap, sides of head and under parts white, wings dark blue-gray edged with black, and a few white spots showing in flight. With its black tail edged with white, and the rusty under-tail coverts, this bird is a familiar sight as it creeps about the tree trunks.

The legs are a trifle short, and the feet a trifle large, for the body. The hind toe is very strong and the claws a bit curved, which helps the nuthatch in running about the trunk of the tree. With no support from the short, bobbed tail, the bird is able to creep both up and down

WHITE-BREASTED NUTHATCH.   Upper Figures, Male and Female
RED-BREASTED NUTHATCH.   Lower Figures, Male and Female

Order—Passeres   Family—Sittidæ
   Genus—Sitta   Species—Carolinensis and Canadensis

National Association of Audubon Societies

GOLDEN—AND RUBY—CROWNED KINGLETS

Order—Passeres   Family—Sylviidæ
Genus—Regulus   Species—satrapa and calendula

National Association of Audubon Societies

the trunk of the tree, and even along the underside of branches while searching for food in the crevices of the bark.

The nuthatch is one of the most easily recognized of all birds; its habit of spiraling about the trunk, the out-thrust head, and strident call of *yank-yank-yank* quickly identify it. And once recognized, it is never forgotten.

A BIRD JACK-OF-ALL-TRADES

Dr. A. A. Allen, ornithologist, of Cornell University, says: "The nuthatch doesn't believe in specialization. He has an all around ability. He can dig out hibernating codling-moths from under bark like a woodpecker; pick canker worms from leaves like a warbler; pinch a tent caterpillar like a cuckoo; catch a moth on the wing like a kingbird; or get down on the ground and hunt weevils and spiders like a thrush."

Thus the nuthatch can find food in all places, and under all conditions. Nor is he an insect eater only. About one-half of his food is mast. He gets the name nuthatch, or nuthacker, from the manner in which he feeds upon acorns, chestnuts, chinquapins, beechnuts, sunflower, and weed seeds. Having no teeth to gnaw or crack a nut like a squirrel, he either takes it in his claws, and hacks at it with his bill, or wedges it in a crevice in the bark, and hacks, or hatches it.

The powerful bill, like the bird as a whole, is very adaptable. It is a bit long, and the lower mandible is slightly upcurved. Few crevices in bark are deep enough to hide insects from this prying bill, and, if necessary, the bird can hack out a nesting cavity from solid wood.

The birds are said to remain mated, more or less, though much of this talk of birds "remaining mated" is based upon sentimental tradition rather than scientific proof. Through the winter these nuthatches often travel in pairs, and in flocks with titmice, downy woodpeckers, chickadees, and brown creepers. In winter, especially, they are sociable birds, and come regularly to feed at our suet stations. Like the titmice, they are not strong on bird-etiquette; they snatch at a piece of suet—the bigger the better—and fly off with it. They are also extremely fond of raw peanuts, enjoying the strings of raw peanuts we wind about branches. The nuthatches, like the titmice, will furnish endless amusement, and a good opportunity for observation, as they hack away trying to extricate the nut. Sometimes shell and all come loose from the string, and off the bird flies with that.

So fond are they of suet, that if it is kept out the year around, the adult birds will bring their young, after they have left the nest, to the feeding-stations, where they proceed to feed them the delectable dainty.

Devil Downhead, as the nuthatch is sometimes called, is not a quarrelsome bird, but neither does he intend to be imposed upon. The handsome, but belligerent myrtle warbler often tries to drive other birds away from the bath and the feeding stations. Some birds are easily frightened, but the nuthatch just thrusts out his head and "gives him a dirty look," as Betsy Neale, a small visiting neighbor, once observed.

Even the matter-of-fact nuthatch feels the spring, and then he raises his voice in a peculiar monotone, a tenor *hah-hah-hah-hah,* sounding strangely like mirthless laughter.

Then it is that he becomes more attentive to his mate, tenderly feeding her tidbits, and soon he begins to think about nesting. In this locality, about April, he seeks a natural cavity, or excavates a hole himself. Often he uses the same home year after year. Having a large family, the nuthatch prefers a roomy cavity, and gathers large pieces of bark to build it up, then smoother pieces, and lastly soft strips of moss, fur, hair, and leaves. Sometimes the mate remains inside the cavity and arranges the material which the male brings. Usually there are six or more, sometimes as many as ten or even eleven eggs, which are creamy white, rosy-tinged, and speckled with reddish brown and purple.

The birds take turns sitting on the eggs, the period of incubation being twelve days. Most ornithologists state that there is one large brood; others say there are sometimes two. Dr. Delia Dixon-Carroll, of Raleigh, has had nuthatches nesting in a bird house for several years in succession, until one year some Carolina wrens got in ahead of them. That year the nuthatches nested near by, but the following year they were not caught napping and were back at the old stand. Dr. Carroll states that there are always two broods of nuthatches, and by the same pair, she believes.

The young resemble the adult birds, or rather, the female, who differs from the male only in that her cap is less glossy, and looks as if it were veiled with bluish gray.

When we stop to consider that entomologists have estimated that insects cause a loss to agriculture of $700,-000,000 every year, we realize how important the insect-eating birds are. And, as it is feeding almost continuously, the nuthatch does its full share, eating spiders, beetles, weevils, moths, caterpillars, ants, wasps, insect eggs, grubs, larvae. The nuthatch does no harm and accomplishes much good, and deserves the fullest protection man can give it.

There are some seventy species of nuthatches, belonging to the family *Sittidae,* mainly restricted to the northern parts of the Northern Hemisphere; there are four species in the New World, and three of these are in certain parts of the South.

All are small gray-blue birds with long, strong beaks,

long pointed wings, and short, square, soft tails, giving a bobbed effect. The most characteristic position of all these birds is head downward and thrust out.

The white-breasted nuthatch is the most familiar, and next to that is the smaller brown-headed nuthatch, a characteristic bird of the pine regions of the southern states. Though seen less often, it is a common resident and is more likely to be found in the upper branches of pines. The top of its head is brownish gray, and there is a whitish patch on the nape. This little nuthatch is very sociable, and as it creeps about the trees keeps up a continuous chatter.

The red-breasted nuthatch, also smaller, is an irregular winter visitor in certain parts of the South, being common some years and altogether absent in others. It usually goes in small bands, perhaps composed of the brood of the previous year. In feeding it shows a preference for the smaller branches, rather than the trunks of trees. An interesting habit claimed for this bird, in connection with its migration, according to the Audubon Leaflet, is the curious one of dropping down on ships at sea. It may be seen on such occasions traveling in its characteristic fashion up and down the masts and shrouds.

V

THE BROWN CREEPER, THE PURITAN OF BIRDS

> Beginning below, I search as I go
> The trunk and the limbs of a tree,
> For a fly or a slug, a beetle or bug;
> They're better than candy for me,
> Far better than candy for me.
>
> When people are nigh, I'm apt to be shy
> And say to myself, "I will hide,"
> Continue my creeping, but carefully keeping
> Away on the opposite side,
> Well around on the opposite side.
> —GARRETT NEWKIRK, in *Bird-Lore.*

"ALL WORK and no play makes Jack a dull boy," applies to birds as well as to people. The brown creeper is the Puritan of birds, for all his days are given to a conscientious performance of his duty of searching out insects from the crevices in the bark of trees.

No joyous caroling or acrobatic antics, such as the chickadee so thoroughly enjoys, for him! No stopping in the midst of work to sing a gay roundelay and announce that "all's right with the world." Not he! He has no time for such nonsense.

For this sober little brown bird seems to think that he bears, Atlas-like, the weight of all birddom on his shoulders. All day long you may see him as he works, methodically beginning at the bottom of a tree and climbing upwards in a spiral, now lost to sight on the opposite side of the tree, now reappearing—just where you'd expect him to—a little higher up the trunk. He peers into

[25]

the crevices, in a near-sighted, worried way, as if he feared he might overlook an insect or an egg.

When he reaches the branches, or where the bark begins to get smooth—for smooth bark conceals few insects and larvae—he usually drops, almost like a leaf, to the base of the next tree. Again he begins the weary, painstaking round. Rarely is he seen at rest.

This mottled little bird, so like the bark he creeps upon, is five-and-a-half inches long, with upper parts brown, mixed with white and buff, rump pale rufous, under parts white, tail pale grayish brown, and a band of creamy buff through all but the outer wing-feathers. The bill is long, curved, and very slender. Male and female look alike.

A bird's tail, according to Chapman, has many uses, but first of all it is a rudder. Compare the direct line of flight of a short-tailed bird, like the quail, with the darting, erratic movements of a barn swallow. Soaring birds spread the tail as an additional means of support and balance; and when it is spread and thrown downward and forward it serves as a brake for the bird when alighting.

The tail of the brown creeper, as of the woodpecker and the chimney swift, is modified for use as a prop in climbing, for when it wishes to remain still a moment, it spreads the tail, which has stiff pointed feathers, and props itself by it against the tree.

MARVELOUS MIMICRY

The brown creeper is not easily seen by its enemies, for the plumage, being nearly the same color as the brown and gray bark upon which it creeps (the white under parts are almost hidden) is one of the best examples of mimicry, or protective coloring, in Nature.

This same protective coloring is carried out in the

nest, which is usually in a half-dead tree, and is carefully concealed under a piece of loosened bark.

Except in our highest mountains the brown creeper is not a permanent resident in the South, but is fairly common in winter, coming early in October and leaving about the middle of April. The breeding range covers the eastern part of northern North America. Some nest in the northern states, but the cool climate of Canada attracts most of them.

Although often seen in company with chickadees, titmice, and nuthatches, the brown creeper is more *with* them than *of* them. For it is a lonely bird, belonging to an Old World family, the *Certhidae,* which has about twelve species, only one of them being found in this hemisphere. (The black and white creeper, which we see in summer, is not a creeper, but a warbler.) This one New World species is represented by five subspecies, ranging as far south as the southern extremity of the Mexican tableland, west to the coast, and as far north as Alaska.

Unlike the birds in whose company it is sometimes seen, the brown creeper is not easily attracted to feeding-stations. We have never seen one at our window-shelf cafeteria. For years they ignored the suet on the trees, creeping right by, sometimes even detouring to get around it.

A "SUET JAG"

And then one year a brown creeper went on a regular "suet jag." Notes taken at the time (winter, 1929) read: "For years we have never seen the brown creeper touch the suet placed on the trees. This year, after being here a couple of months, it got started and is more than feasting —it has gone on a regular "suet jag." It props itself in a comfortable position, and proceeds to stuff. Whether it is always the same bird, or not, we cannot tell."

Last year we did not see a brown creeper touch the suet until about February, and then, though frequently dining on suet, it did not go on any more "suet jags."

During the winter especially, the brown creeper is one of our most silent birds. The call is a sharp, weak, *screek, screek,* given as it winds its way up and around the tree trunk, but so faint is this call that it is hardly noticeable unless one happens to be very near.

In his northern breeding range the male has a strange, wild, lonely little song, but it is not often heard outside of his nesting range.

The nest is usually placed inside the loose bark of a tree or stump—sometimes within the rift of a tree that has been struck by lightning—and it is composed of felted material, soft feathers, moss, twigs, spider cocoons and like material. Five to eight eggs are laid; they are creamy white, spotted and speckled with reddish brown chiefly in a wreath at the larger end.

The Pearson-Brimley book on *Birds of North Carolina,* states, "According to Cairns, who reported brown creepers nesting in Buncombe County, the birds selected knot-holes and natural cavities of trees for nesting. Most ornithologists, however, report the majority of nests as being found behind the loosened bark of a tree, often a half-dead tree."

Although this cheerless, glum little worker seems to find no joy in life, it is an industrious and valuable protector of our trees. Every kind of egg and insect found in the crevices of bark is seen by its sharp little eyes— eyes that detect insects so small that other birds pass them by. And, wherever it is, it works on, day after day, summer and winter.

Its food consists of tiny insects and insects' eggs, cocoons, scales, plant lice, small wasps, small caterpillars,

spiders, and hibernating insects.   Thus the brown creeper
is one of our most important insect destroyers, and also
important is the fact that on its bill-of-fare is found no
grains or fruits raised by farmers, nor any useful insects.

BROWN CREEPER

Order—Passeres   Family—Certhidæ
Genus—Certhia   Species—familiaris americana
National Association of Audubon Societies

VI

THE KINGLETS

Oh Kinglet, in a world of falling crowns
Thy ruby crown is safe, thy reign secure,
Thy palace is a mossy, feathered nest
Where sits thy somber queen serene, intent
On hatching out new subjects for thy sway;
While thou, aperch upon a pine tree limb,
Singest thy warbling, flute-like song
That thy new hatched heirs of royal line
May learn the kingly game to carry on.

—ALBERT W. SMITH.

THE DIMINUTIVE kinglets must feel like "the old woman who lived in a shoe, and had so many children she didn't know what to do." For the kinglets, smallest of all our birds except the hummers, raise some of the largest families among the song birds.

Evidently they believe in preparedness, for they build an unusually large nest for such small birds, so that there is room for all the eggs and all the babies. Brewster, writing in *The Auk* of the nest of the golden-crowned kinglet, said that in two nests he had observed the eggs were too numerous to find room on the bottom of the nest and were piled in two layers. How does the tiny mother ever manage to keep so many eggs warm, to turn them, or to cover the young fledglings during a cold spell or a storm? It must require some sort of bird magic!

Kinglets belong to the family *Sylvidae*, or Old World warblers, which are not to be confused with our wood warblers. The kinglets are a subfamily, of which two of the seven known species, the golden-crowned and the ruby-crowned, are found in the New World—and both are in the South in winter.

Kinglets are never still, but are constantly flitting about the ends of twigs and branches, peering into tiny crevices of bark for hidden insects, eggs, or larvae. Warbler-like in appearance, they are rather hard to find with the untrained eye, and by the time one has the field glass ranged upon them, they are somewhere else.

Sometimes these kinglets are referred to as "greenlets," because of their greenish brown coloring. The male golden-crowned has an olive-green back, soiled whitish under parts, and a center crown spot of bright orange bordered by yellow and enclosed by a black line. The female and the young are similar, but, while they have the bright yellow, they lack the orange center crown spot.

Except in some of the highest mountains of the upper South these elfin feathered sprites do not summer with us, but breed mainly north of the United States. It is as winter visitors that we know them best throughout much of the South.

Muffled in a thick coat of feathers, a few of them stay in the extreme northern states, braving the coldest winters. One wonders how such tiny mites can face severe blizzards, but if a bird's food supply is plentiful, temperature seems to be a less important factor in its life. Most of the kinglets, however, winter from Virginia southward, where they are always eagerly welcomed.

TREE GLEANERS

About the time the dogwood, sourwoods, and sweet gums begin to flame in our southern forests, the kinglets come from out of the North, to add their bit of color and cheer to our autumn woods. And where you see one golden-crowned, you may confidently look around expecting to see more, for, except during the nesting season, they go in flocks. Friendly and sociable with other birds, they may also be found in the company of chickadees, titmice, nuthatches, and even the solemn brown creeper.

They do not remain in our own bit of woodland, but every winter we see them occasionally, driven in, perhaps, on the wings of a storm. For a few days they fraternize with our regular winter birds at the tree suet-stations. Like the chickadees and nuthatches, they can hang upside down in their search for insects, and they seem to be equally good as tree gleaners. Sharper-billed and finer-eyed than the chickadees, they probably gather what those birds overlook, but they are not quite so efficient as the conscientious brown creeper.

As the golden-crowned nests mainly in remote northern forests, there does not seem to be much data about its nesting habits. Dugmore, the ornithologist, claims that the nests vary greatly in form, method of support, and in material used for construction. He concludes that it is difficult to know whether birds habitually build a pensile, or a globular nest, or a combination of the two.

Other authorities claim that the nest, in general, is pensile, of green moss lined with fine strips of soft inner bark, fine rootlets, and feathers; for the babies, born in cold northern forests, need warm feather beds. The nest is usually in a coniferous tree, from six to sixty feet from the ground, and the nine or ten creamy white eggs are speckled with brown.

Though golden-crowned has a beautiful voice, strikingly powerful to issue from such a tiny throat, he is rarely heard, for he seldom sings except during his nesting season. His usual call-notes are a fine, high *li-li*, audible only to well-trained ears, the song beginning on high, shrill ascending notes, and ending in short, explosive warbles.

THE RUBY-CROWNED KINGLET

Ruby-crowned, on the other hand, who resembles his cousin golden-crowned in appearance and in some habits, and who associates with him some during migration, sings during both spring and fall migrations.

Dr. Allen, writing of birds' songs, interprets ruby-crowned's song as

> *See-see-see,*
> *Just look at me, just look at me,*
> *Just look at me, see-see-see.*

It is a mellow and flute-like song, and, it is said, can be heard several hundred yards.

Of its voice, which is powerful for such a small bird, Dr. Elliott Coues wrote: "The larynx, the bird's sound-producing organ, is not much bigger than a good-sized pin head, and the muscles that move it are almost microscopic shreds of flesh. If the strength of the human voice were the same proportion to the size of the larynx, we could converse with ease at a distance of a mile or more."

Ruby-crowned is of the same general coloring as the golden-crowned, but his ruby crest is partly hidden. The female and the young resemble him, but they lack the ruby crown patch.

There have been many interesting descriptions of the use the males make of these colorful ruby crown patches, which they seem able to conceal or uncover at will. During the mating season male rivals have been known to raise and bristle their brilliant ruby crowns at each other. At such times they hop around each other, behaving exactly as if they were comparing crowns and each was vainly praising his own. Their heads are bent forward, their tails spread, and the side feathers below the wings are fluffed out. In such manner they follow each other about among the branches, uttering their thin, shrill notes and displaying their ruby crowns to the utmost.

Apparently the ruby-crowned has a more northern range in summer than the golden-crowned, for it breeds from Maine (sparingly) north as far as Ungava and northwest Alaska. Likewise it has a more southern range in winter, for it covers territory from southern British Columbia, Iowa, and Virginia—south to Guatemala.

This kinglet's nest is usually pensile or semi-pensile, and is of moss and fine strips of bark, neatly interwoven and lined with feathers, in coniferous trees, from twelve to thirty feet from the ground. The five to nine eggs are dull whitish or pale buffy, faintly spotted with brown.

Unlike its cousin the golden-crowned, the ruby-crowned does not go in flocks and is more likely to be seen during migration than in winter. Its white eye-ring and its habit of slightly fluttering its wings when hopping from branchlet to branchlet, will help in identifying it.

VII

THE WRENS

When wintry winds through woodlands blow
And naked treetops shake and shiver;
While all the paths are bound in snow,
And thick ice chains the merry river,
One little feathered denizen,
A plump and nut-brown winter wren,
Sings of spring-time even there—
Tsip-twis-ch-e-e-e cheerily-cheerily-dare—
Who could listen and despair?
        —LYNN TEW SPRAGUE, in *Bird-Lore*.

IN THE South, this verse is much more appropriate for our common Carolina wren, than for the winter wren about which it was written, for the latter, while here, is a very quiet and unobtrusive bird.

The bird you may hear just before the dawn calling a cheery *free-dom, free-dom, free-dom,* is our Carolina wren, one of our few birds that sing at night, and through the winter. Often, from our sleeping porch under the pines, we hear him.

Others interpret his call as *jo-reeper, jo-reeper, jo-ree;* still another authority thinks it sounds like *tea-kettle, tea-kettle, tea-kettle.* In addition to his peculiar calls he also possesses a variety of loud, ringing whistles that are often mistaken for those of the tufted titmouse or the cardinal.

Indeed, such a diversity of strains has this year-round southern singer that he has been called the "mocking wren," for many people have believed he learned them by imitating other birds. But one bird authority says that of the hundreds he has heard, the songs were all too original to have been borrowed.

[35]

The Carolina wren's wide range of song and his singing at night show his apparent relationship to the mockingbird; and the manner in which he gesticulates with
his tail, would seem to show a relationship to the brown
thrasher and to the catbird. His tail, like his voice, is
an outlet for his irrepressible energy. After his emotional love-song he droops his tail, as does the catbird;
when something has caught his attention and he is alert
and inquisitive, he holds it erect. In flight the bird is unusually short-distanced, using rapid wing-beats and a
jerking motion of the tail.

Just a trifle smaller than the English sparrow, this
wren is bright rufous brown above, with a whitish throat
and bright buff-brown under parts. The wings and tail
are finely barred with black. Next to the tail, the most
conspicuous mark is the whitish streak just above the
eye, extending from the base of the bill to the nape of
the neck. The female and the young are similar, and
none of the family undergoes any change of color of
plumage. An excellent example of protective coloring
you will decide, if you watch the Carolina wren on some
autumn day, as it scuffs among the fallen leaves. At such
a time it is hard to distinguish its chestnut back from
the russet colored leaves.

The Carolina wren is the state bird for South Carolina and might well be made the state bird for North
Carolina, as Dr. L. H. Snyder, author of the bulletin *Common Birds of North Carolina,* once suggested. It bears
the state's name, and is known in all parts of the state
and in all seasons. It is a lyrical songster, singing
throughout the year; it is friendly, like all Tar Heels;
and it can easily be coaxed about the house or garden
by feeding stations, water, cover, and protection.

By some ornithologists, this wren is believed to be
constant, to be inseparable from its mate until death, in

CAROLINA WREN
(*One-half natural size*)

Order—PASSERIFORMES   Family—TROGLODYTIDÆ
Genus—THRYOTHORUS   Species—LUDOVICIANUS

National Association of Audubon Societies

BROWN THRASHER

Order—PASSERES   Family—MIMIDÆ
Genus—TOXOSTOMA   Species—RUFUM

National Association of Audubon Societies

contrast to its cousin, the house wren, which has been proved to be a regular "bird-bigamist." It is a persistent insect hunter, insects forming practically its entire diet.

The Carolina wren's nesting period usually begins early in May, and some nests are found late in June. Two broods are raised each year. The eggs, four to six in number, are white or creamy white, with numerous cinnamon-brown markings.

Truly indifferent about where and how it builds its nest, it has been known to choose a site "almost anywhere," in banks of cuts and streams; in holes in trees or stumps; in nooks and crevices about buildings; among tangled roots of upturned trees; and under brush piles. Wren families have been raised in the pockets of old coats, in old cups, broken gourds, discarded basins—and one year we found a family getting along nicely in a half-emptied box of alabastine on a shelf in the garage.

THE NEST IN A DOLL HOUSE

But most delightfully placed of the nests which have come under my observation was the one built on the shelf of a doll house belonging to my small curly-haired neighbor—Mary Louise Milam. The open-sided doll house was in an outside playroom with open windows. The wren, stealing a march on the children, had the nest built and her eggs laid before discovery. In spite of many visitors—and an egg filched by a small guest who had not yet learned "bird ethics"—the nest came to a successful fruition.

Once Mary Louise and I tried sitting quietly at one end of the room to watch the feeding. The parent birds would alight in the open window, insects in bills, and scold indignantly at us, without, however, dropping the insects. But though we sat quietly for a long time, the birds would not feed the young. One of them tried to mislead us by flitting behind some boxes and thus slip up unobserved, as it evidently thought, to the nest. But apparently it couldn't get up quite enough courage to go right to the nest, and, scolding louder than ever, it would fly back to the window and out, to return again in a few moments.

Since the birds were so upset by our presence, we left. Later the whole wren family—at least we believed it to be the same—moved over to our garden, where we heard a great deal of squeaking and *'tseep-'tseeping,* as the young were fed from our feeding-stations by the parent birds.

THE CAMOUFLAGED NEST

The nest is usually a bulky affair, composed of grasses, dead leaves, moss, cotton, rootlets, or any other convenient material. Once we discovered—and just in time—that the bundle of dead leaves, catkins, and pine needles, which looked as if it had been blown into the corner of the window-box, and which we were about to throw out, was in reality a domed nest. It had a cleverly concealed side entrance, and, with the leaves and catkins interwoven with pine needles, was a most artistic piece of camouflage. For Nature, you know, had been using camouflage long before the World War made the term familiar.

The parent bird would light in a tree at the far end of the long window-box and scold loudly, as if to frighten off any possible intruders. Then she would drop to the box, and, as if she were trying to fool anyone who might be watching, would scuttle under ferns and flowering plants until she reached the concealed entrance to the nest.

From behind the inside window draperies we could watch unobserved. After the young were born, both parents were kept busy bringing insects—and such huge insects as some of them were! One was at least half an inch long, with sharp, bristly, spike-like legs that showed as the insect passed down the semi-transparent throat of the baby bird. It seemed as if the bristly legs must pierce the tiny throat, but the nestling swallowed the insect and loudly squeaked for more.

The young birds were always hungry and ate continuously. Like Oliver Twist, they asked for more, and many a noxious insect went down their eager throats, and the garden and the trees profited thereby.

When they were almost ready to leave the nest, we were away for a day and upon our return found the nest out of place and badly torn. A bit of feather-covered skin and one tiny claw remained as mute evidence of some tragedy that had overtaken the birds. Had death come through a bird of prey, a squirrel, a snake, a rat? More likely it was a cat, for cats are responsible for the greatest number of bird deaths—one conservative estimate placing the annual number in the millions.

Nesting time is a perilous time for all birds. Storms take their toll, and squirrels, snakes, weasels, rats and birds of prey—though the latter do less damage than is generally supposed. The parent birds are likewise beset by enemies, and many young nestlings are left to starve in the nest, through the death of the parent bird.

Of the nests that we have watched closely for the past several years far less than a third have come to fruition. One day the nest is apparently safe, holding the promise of winged life and song; the next day it may be mute and empty, with little or nothing to tell of the tragedy that had taken place.

MOST INQUISITIVE OF BIRDS

Wrens are full of curiosity, and peep into every corner and hole, and investigate every possible nook or opening. Several times a wren has hopped into our kitchen porch, through a screen door left slightly ajar by the dog, and after creeping under the refrigerator, into the vegetable box and among the mops and brooms, has flown up to the clothesline, where it sang a gay roundelay to a bright December day. Again, a wren's curiosity has led it under the porch, up through a broken floor board, and into the sleeping porch. Unlike most birds, it did not become panic-stricken at finding itself confined. Instead, it proceeded to investigate the place, hopping under the bed, and then up to the springs, where it went through a series of metallic rattles and musical trills. Later, without making any fuss, it let me pick it up and carry it out of doors.

Due to this friendly curiosity, the wren can be brought close for observation, especially in winter, by feeding-stations. As this is being written, two wrens are feeding on suet on a tree near the window, and one of them just left and flew to the window-box, hopped on the sill, and peered into the glass, evidently intrigued by some bright autumn leaves on the inside window-seat.

This curiosity and love of investigating may be the reason these birds like to creep about the stones at the base of the bath, instead of going into the bath, as most birds do. For years we never saw a wren in the bath, but this past summer one occasionally did go in. Most of them, however, seem to prefer the showers of water that drip from the overhanging leaves as other birds bathe and splash in the water above.

OTHER WRENS

Belonging to the Family *Troglodytidae,* and found in both hemispheres, the majority of the two hundred and sixty known forms of wrens are American, most of them being confined to the tropics. Only fourteen species are

THE WINTER WREN IS THE "STYLISH STOUT" OF THE WREN FAMILY. IT LIKES
TO CREEP OR RUN, MOUSELIKE, ALONG THE TOP OF A FENCE, ABOUT A BRUSH-
PILE, OR DOWN A GARDEN PATH. ABOUT ONE-HALF NATURAL SIZE.

found north of Mexico, and, of these, eleven are known
in the South—several being well known, a few being rare
local residents or winter visitors.

All southern wrens are small birds, the Carolina wren
being the largest, and the only common permanent resident. All are brownish, and all are barred somewhere.

The range of the Carolina wren is the eastern United
States, breeding from the southern tier of the northern
states to the Gulf. Its center of abundance, however, is
the South. The house wren, so familiar in nature literature, is known in the South mostly as a migrant, or a
winter visitor—rare, however, in many sections. During
winter it is quiet and rather shy, frequenting low bushes
and weed patches in the fields. It is more likely to be

found in the lower South, especially the Gulf states, than in the upper South.

The winter wren, a deep reddish brown, is much shorter than our common Carolina wren, and is the "stylish stout" of the family. It breeds in the higher

THE BEWICK WREN IS AN OPERA SINGER AND LIKES TO GIVE CONCERTS FROM THE TOP OF THE ROOF, A TELEPHONE WIRE, OR A DEAD BRANCH. ABOUT ONE-HALF NATURAL SIZE.

mountains of the South, but in other sections it is a winter visitor. While here it is very quiet and retiring in its habits, frequenting brushy woodlands and, occasionally, gardens. Though quiet, it is exceedingly alert, and, with its stumpy tail up-cocked over its back, likes to creep along a fence rail, through a brush heap, or along a quiet garden path, where it looks like a mouse. In its

THE SHORT-BILLED MARSH WREN LIKES TO KEEP OUT OF SIGHT. YOU ARE MORE LIKELY TO HEAR THIS WREN THAN TO SEE IT. SLIGHTLY REDUCED.

summer home it has a wonderful song, described as a *twinkling, rippling, roundelay.*

Because of its domestic inclination, in the South the Bewick wren is sometimes known as the "house wren," but it is easily distinguished from the latter by the longer tail, which is constantly in motion. The Bewick is a small dark brown wren with a long black tail, and both wings and tail are barred. Like all wrens, the bird is active, restless, and inquisitive. A good singer—even better than the Carolina wren, many believe—it likes to mount to the pinnacle of the roof, a telephone wire, or a

THE LONG-BILLED MARSH WREN. IF YOU WALK THROUGH THE MARSHES, THIS LITTLE WREN MAY DART OUT TO SCOLD AT YOUR INTRUSION. ABOUT TWO-THIRDS NATURAL SIZE.

dead branch, and with head thrown back and tail hanging, give its whole heart and soul to song. Its breeding range is the eastern United States, mainly west of the Alleghany Mountains and south to the highlands of northern South Carolina and central Alabama. It winters from near the northern limit of its range south to the Gulf coast and Florida.

The tiny, inconspicuous Marian's marsh wren, so easily overlooked because of its habit of dwelling almost exclusively in salt marshes and hiding in dense tangles of rushes and marsh grass, winters south to South Carolina and the western coast of Florida.

The short-billed marsh wren is known in parts of the South both as a migrant and as a winter resident. In some sections it is fairly common in the marshes, but it is more likely to be heard than seen. However, it is less a species of deep-water marshes than is the long-billed, and in winter may also be found in grassy flats, either wet or dry. The long-billed marsh wren, a winter visitor along the Atlantic and Gulf coasts will make itself known by certain scolding, grumbling notes, as it darts out to know why you have intruded upon its damp retreat.

VIII

THE MOCKINGBIRD, THE NIGHTINGALE OF THE SOUTH

He wakes with dawn, this carillonneur of spring
Lifting to tulip skies a rhapsody,
Each crystal note a fluted litany
As bright as jewels sparkling on a string.
The wooded hills and smoky valleys ring
With liquid music, filled with ecstasy
Of stirring life, and April's mystery,
The new-born leaf, and brushing sound of wing.

This silver chant of pulsing loveliness,
Is but a lyric sung for hearts that need
To lift their life-bound eyes, enjoy, possess,
The miracle of beauty's golden creed;
For only those who have grown beauty-wise,
Can sing with mocking birds above the rise.

—TRAVIS TUCK JORDAN.

NOT ALL MOCKERS can mock, say authorities. Some have no other notes than their own; others seem able to imitate calls they have heard but rarely, or only once; while still others learn in addition not only the songs of the other birds, but their call-notes as well.

The mocker will often improve on a song he has learned from another bird by introducing frills of his own; and while learning a song, he is a silent, attentive listener.

Archibald Rutledge, the nature writer of the Carolina Low Country, tells of a pet mocker (though not a caged one): "I often tried to discover how many kinds of birds this particular mocker imitated; the complete list was eighty; and often in a single brief concert, as spontaneous as it was inspired, he would give the calls and songs of thirty or more birds. Most of these notes, being of birds with which I have since boyhood been familiar, were not in the least difficult to identify. But what was my astonishment one day to hear him clearly imitate the note of a rare migrant—the bartramian sandpiper—a note not native to the mocker's Southern country, one that could have been caught by him only from some high-passing migrant fleeting eerily by under the stars. I believe science should accept as authentic the mocker's repetition of a call or a song as proof that the bird imitated had been in the neighborhood, though no human eye has seen it. I have heard this superb mimic give the notes of several birds that I could not identify; doubtless they were migrants that stop rarely, if at all, on the Carolina coast.''

A TALENTED FAMILY

The mockingbird belongs to the family *Mimidae,* which includes also our familiar brown thrasher and the catbird. Though the mockingbird is distinctly a bird of the Southeast, it is known sparingly in southern New England and New York. In most parts of the South it is known and loved as a permanent resident. Loyal southerners have a saying that a city or community without mockingbirds is only ''half-southern.'' So loved is it that five southern states: Florida, Tennessee, Mississippi, Texas, and Arkansas have named it as their state bird.

Male and female mockers are not easily told apart. Both are slim gray birds with dusky-brownish wings and whitish under parts, and with large white spots on wings and tail, which are very conspicuous in flight. The males, who sing, have more white on wings and tail, than do the females, who do not sing. The nestlings are grayish brown above, and white, spotted with brownish below, showing the relationship to the brown thrasher.

Mockers are friendly birds, liking the haunts of man,

and are familiar residents of our gardens and parks, and even of public squares. A few are known even in New York City's large parks.

The nest's foundation is a rather bulky and untidy affair of interwoven twigs, weed stalks, and grasses, upon which is built a nest of softer materials such as rootlets, cotton, horse-hair. These are usually built in close thickets, or in the lower branches of trees. In the far South the birds are especially fond of nesting in orange trees. The nest is usually built somewhere between four and twelve feet from the ground.

The four to six eggs are pale greenish blue or bluish white, rather heavily spotted with reddish brown. The nesting period is from April to early July. The eggs take about two weeks to hatch, and both birds feed and care for the young. They are prolific birds, usually having two and three broods a season.

The past summer (1933) mockingbirds nesting close by came to our "doughnut-tree" to feed, and when leaving always carried a beakful home to the babies. Noticing that they always flew off in the same direction, we followed and found the nest.

Later, when the young were able to fly, the parent birds brought them to the tree. By this time they were almost as large as their parents, but were a lighter gray, and the plumage, being new and fluffy, made them appear plumper. In contrast, the parent birds were thin and worn from family cares. The young birds were white below, spotted with brown, which converged into a larger spot in the middle of the breast.

The young mockers would call incessantly for food. Such a screeching and peevish crying as they indulged in! We really began to feel sorry for the overworked parents, so imposed upon were they by their spoiled young.

Later the young birds would come to the tree alone and manage to bite off pieces of doughnut by themselves. But let one of the parents appear, and they became perfectly helpless, and would cry piteously for food.

About half the mocker's diet consists of wild berries such as cedar, holly, and myrtle. About one-fourth of his diet consists of animal matter, including grasshoppers, cotton worms, chinch bugs, rice weevils, boll worms, caterpillars, and moths. He also eats such cultivated fruits as berries of all kinds, cherries, grapes, oranges, and figs. But he pays for his thefts, with song and enchantment, and with the destruction of many noxious insects.

"The mockingbird's song makes me happy and gay," wrote a student of the Blind School, when I conducted a "Choose a State Bird" contest in *The Progressive Farmer,* a few years ago. "Even though some of us are not so fortunate as to be able to see the mockingbird, we can easily distinguish him by his song, and we take great pleasure in pointing him out to our seeing friends." Blind boys and girls make excellent bird students. Some of the most interesting, well-informed, and well-written letters received in that contest were from these children, whose trained ears are so attuned to Nature's sounds.

The most renowned singer of our western hemisphere, the mockingbird is well named "the nightingale of the South." Often, especially during the nesting season, the male sings on moonlight nights. Formerly these birds were trapped and sold for cage-birds, chiefly to Europe, which has no mockers, but today this inhumane practice has been stopped by both federal and state laws.

A pugnacious fighter and a gallant guardian of his nest, the mocker will attack cats or snakes with great ferocity. In making his attack he hovers above the enemy, striking it at the back of the head or neck. A friend told me of seeing a mocker who has lived in his garden for years, attack a neighbor's cat sneaking towards his nest. He would fly down and give the cat's tail an angry tweak, then fly back to the tree, scolding ferociously. After several such attacks the cat retreated.

During the big snow of last winter, another friend called up to say that the mockingbird was driving the blue jays away from the feeding station. Sometimes, I regret to say, the mocker is too pugnacious and tries to drive other birds away from what he considers his own sole territory. One friend has a mocker who will not let any other bird build in the garden.

COURTSHIP CEREMONY

"The courtship of the mockingbird is done with much ceremony," says Mrs. F. W. Rowe, who writes about birds. "The birds stand facing each other, with heads and tails erect and wings drooping; then the dance begins, and the two hop sideways in nearly a straight line, always keeping directly opposite each other and about the same distance apart. They chassé this way for four or five feet, then go back over the same process."

During this season the male bird sings his "mounting" and "dropping" songs, flitting up from branch to branch, singing as he goes, until finally, on the topmost branch, he sings his "Paean of Praise"—then begins to drop down from branch to branch, his song a series of soft, gurgling, liquid notes.

Sometimes at night, when the world is hushed and the air is heavy with the fragrance of syringa and honeysuckle, we are awakened on our sleeping porch under the pines by the song of the mockingbird. In a shaft of luminous moonlight we may see him, sometimes on an arm of the great pine, sometimes on the topmost spray

of the syringa. Hearts ache with the beauty and enchantment of moonlight, garden, and song—and as the bird
pours forth his song we feel indeed

"We are nearer God's heart in a garden,
Than anywhere else on earth."

IX

THE BROWN THRASHER

My creamy breast is speckled
(Perhaps you'd call it freckled)
Black and brown.

My pliant russet tail
Beats like a frantic flail,
Up and down.

In the top branch of a tree
You may chance to glance at me,
When I sing.

But I'm very, *very* shy,
When I silently float by,
On the wing.
                    —MABEL OSGOOD WRIGHT.

IT IS HIGH in a tree top, in an exposed position, that
brown thrasher likes to perch for his melodious song.
Often he is credited by some of his hearers with being
his gray cousin, the mockingbird, for his song is as clear
and joyous—and many think as beautiful—as that of his
Cousin Mocker. But there is a distinct difference, which
makes the trained listener easily recognize which bird it
is. The thrasher almost always repeats each note once,
whereas the mocker, if he repeats, does so several times.
Moreover, the mocker sings for a much longer period of
the year than does the thrasher.

Brown thrasher, like his cousins the mockers and the
catbirds, and his more distant kin, the wrens, belongs to
the family of "Long Tails." He is a large bird, over
eleven inches in length—a good inch longer than the
robin. Rusty red-brown above, darkest on the wings,
with two light bands on each wing, and with yellowish-

white under-breast heavily streaked with dark brown arrow-shaped spots, the bird is easy to identify. The throat is not spotted. The long tail is decidedly rounded at the end, with the middle tail feathers longer than the outside ones. Like the catbird and the wren, the thrasher twitches and flirts his tail, as if that extra emotional outlet were needed.

The eyes are yellow, and the long bill is curved at the tip. Although the female is said to be slightly paler than the male, it is difficult to tell them apart.

Brown thrasher breeds from the Gulf to southern Canada, and westward to the Rockies, wintering from southern Missouri and parts of North Carolina to central Texas, and sometimes farther into that state. North of North Carolina it is known more as a summer resident; south of it, as permanent. The brown thrasher is so loved in Georgia that it has been elected as the state bird.

Except when singing, thrashers frequent scrubby growths and bushy borders of wooded land, spending much of their time on the ground, foraging among the fallen leaves, which give them color protection. They are said to get the name "thrasher" from the manner in which they thrash the leaves about with their bills, sometimes tossing them overhead.

When singing—and especially for the morning and evening concert—they seem to prefer a more or less high, exposed place, and mounting a favorite perch, usually sing for rather long intervals.

NEST A TRAINING GROUND FOR YOUNG

Bulkily built, of twigs, vine tendrils, roots, bark, and leaves, and lined with horsehair or fine rootlets, the thrasher's net has a sort of platform affair extending all around the edge. This is used as a training ground for the young birds, which learn to perch precariously upon it, strengthening their legs and wings with stretching and balancing exercises.

Apparently thrashers become attached to certain nesting localities, and often return to the same nest, or spot, year after year. In our own woodland acre they have several times used the same nest, though not in succession. Occasionally they nest on the ground, but more often in low shrubs, bushes, rose arbors, trellises, and low-hanging branches of trees.

Often they seem unable to make up their minds about a nesting place. One year they looked over an old site here, and then started a nest in our Silver Moon rose. When it was about half done, they abandoned it and built and brooded in our neighbor's rose trellis, right in front of a window. The nest could not have been more favorably placed for observation, though unfortunately it received the drip from the eaves of the house. However, the mistress of the house fastened an old umbrella over the nest, and the thrashers brooded and raised their young under its protection.

My neighbor became such a bird enthusiast that in the end she had the parent birds "eating out of her hand," that is, figuratively. Literally, they did eat from the bowl of a long-handled spoon.

They must have been very modern birds; at least they had a most up-to-date diet. From orange juice to lettuce leaves, scarcely a vitamin was missing! Leaves of lettuce, sections of orange, cornbread, rolls, toasted whole-wheat bread, cherries, strawberries, cranberries, pieces of apples and of carrot were stuck on the thorns about the nest, and were greedily pecked at. And from the bowl of the long-handled spoon held out to them, raisins, puffed wheat, flies, and worms were eaten with equal relish and abandon. Perched on the platform of the nest, both parent birds would often feed simultaneously from the same spoon, then turn and give a tidbit to the young birds.

A little later, from the same platform, the young birds would reach up and peck at the corn bread, the apple, or the orange. Apparently the unusual diet had no ill effect upon them, for they grew and were normal, husky birdlings.

MANY NESTS FAIL OF FRUITION

As a rule, birds spend but little time between broods. On the same day when the young thrashers left the nest, the parent birds returned to the half-finished nest in our Silver Moon rose, examined it half-heartedly, added a few touches, and then left. Several days later we saw them busily engaged with a new nest a few feet away. It was quickly completed and one egg laid. For some reason unknown to us, this nest, also, was abandoned.

About a week later we saw them return to the first nest, the one in our rosebush, and this time both birds worked busily until dark carrying leaves and fine rootlets for interlining. Early the next morning they were busily working again, and the hen bird started laying the following day. There were three grayish white eggs closely speckled all over with reddish brown. Sometimes there are as many as four or five eggs, and they may be laid from late April to early July.

Through torrid days, with the sun beating down mercilessly, and through the cold wet spell that followed, the birds brooded. There was no place to attach an umbrella above this nest. Then, two days before time for hatching, we noticed the birds were not on, or near, the nest. Investigation showed the nest to be empty, and search about the nest, and on the ground beneath it, brought to light but one tiny bit of shell.

What had happened? Whatever it was, it must have

occurred during our absence, for we heard no disturbance, and thrasher parents are loud and vociferous in their distress when danger approaches. And the nest is seldom left unprotected for more than a few moments; one or the other of the parent birds is always on guard.

Not so fond of fruit as the mocker and the catbird, the brown thrasher consumes a much larger percentage of insect food, including grasshoppers, caterpillars, cutworms, spiders, crickets, beetles, and other insects. Only about one-tenth of its diet is derived from cultivated fruits.

Brown thrasher is also a planter, being responsible for many of our wild seedlings. He loves especially the wild cherries, and will bring the fruit to his brooding mate, so that wherever he has nested, the next year we find young cherry seedlings from the discarded seeds.

Songster, forester, insect fighter! Fortunate indeed is the garden that is host to the brown thrasher.

X

THE HERMIT, OUR ONLY WINTER THRUSH

Then on the silence falls a fluted sound,
Melodious, full and round,
  Flooding the mossy solitudes,
As from the topmost height of clustering firs,
The high priest of the woodland choristers
  Outpours his threefold chant by threefold
    interludes.
    —GRACE DENIO LITCHFIELD.

"A PROPHET without honor in his own country," is the little-known hermit thrush—the winter thrush which comes about the time our wood thrush leaves, and returns North about the time the wood thrush returns for the summer. The hermit is the hardiest of all our thrushes, the only one that winters in the states; all others go to Central or to South America.

He is, according to Walter Pritchard Eaton, the New England Nature writer, a much more skilled musician than either the nightingale or the skylark of England— both birds made famous by generations of Old World poets. His song has a more exquisite timbre than even that of the nightingale. But the hermit thrush has no classic background to sing against, and because his song reaches its perfection only in the depths of remote northern woods in June, his incomparable melody is relatively unknown, though our minor poets have celebrated his less-talented cousins, the veery and the robin.

A bird lover, writing from a camping trip in a far northern forest, said: "If I would listen to a bird song

OUR HERMIT THRUSH OF WINTER COMES AS OUR WOOD THRUSH OF SUMMER LEAVES. IN ITS NESTING PLACE IN FAR NORTHERN FORESTS THIS FINE SINGER IS CALLED "THE SPIRIT OF THE PINES." ABOUT ONE-HALF NATURAL SIZE.

for pure enjoyment of its musical beauty, my choice would be that of the thrush. First of all the hermit thrush, but the wood thrush if the hermit were not to be heard in the region I was in."

"SWAMP ANGEL"

The hermit thrush is also called the Swamp Robin or Swamp Angel. Smaller than the wood thrush, and more subdued in coloring, its upper parts are olive-brown, the throat and breast having a slight, buffy tinge, with wedge-shaped black spots which seem to run together, chain-like. Its brightest spot is the tail, which is a cinnamon-red, the hermit being the only one of our thrushes having a tail brighter than its back. It is in direct contrast to the wood thrush, whose coloring is brightest on the head and dullest on the tail.

The hermit's range is eastern North America, breeding from the mountains of our northern states northward, and wintering from Virginia southward. Though it is fairly common in yards and gardens, it seems to like heavy, damp woods or thick growths, and borders of streams, feeding to some extent on small wild fruits such as frost grapes and the berries of sumac, poison oak, holly, and dogwood.

Ever since we have had a feeding-shelf and suet-stations for birds, the hermit thrush has been one of our regular winter guests, coming unobtrusively, always jerking his tail slightly when alighting on the feeding-shelf. He is a meditative bird. I have seen him remain perched on a limb for a long period, his wings folded under his tail feathers, like some old-fashioned orator with his hands clasped beneath his swallow-tailed coat.

The hermit thrush is cousin to our better known thrushes of summer, and to the robin and the bluebird, and with them belongs to the family *Turdidae,* a large and cosmopolitan family, of which more live in the Old World than in the New.

The hermit thrush's song is his chief claim to fame, but unfortunately, all too few of us are likely to hear it, for he sings only occasionally while in the South. To hear him at his best, you must spend the summer in the mountains of our border states, or in Canada. There, during this song period, the bird is sometimes called "The Spirit of the Pines." Even then he is a cautious bird, for he never sings near his nest, trying to keep secret its location on the ground. The nest is made of moss, leaves, and pine needles, and the three to four eggs are similar in coloring to the robin's.

XI

THE ROBIN

I wonder how the robin's throat
Hath caught the rain's sweet dripping note,
That little falling, pelting sound,
Liquidly clear and crystal round,
The very heart-rune of the Spring,
Enchanted of the sky and ground,
That conjures life from everything.

. . . .

Robin and rain in mystic way
Bring life back greenly; ah, and how
One's very heart and pulse obey
That lure of music! Listen now . . .
—SARA KING.

BECAUSE our early settlers, homesick for old England, noted and loved the red-breasted bird that appeared after the long, bitter winter—apparently bringing with it "the very heart-rune of the Spring," they named it "Robin Red-breast." This was after the familiar and beloved little songbird of the old country—because it, too, had an olive-brown back, a red breast, and was friendly to man.

There the connection ends, for there is absolutely no relationship between the American and the English robin. The latter belongs to the family *Sylviidae,* Old World warblers, and is a much smaller bird, whereas our robin is a thrush, closely allied to our hermit thrush of winter, and to our more familiar and beloved wood thrush, or "quillaree" of summer, and to the bluebird.

All the members of the thrush family at some time have spotted breasts, but the robins and bluebirds have them only when they are young.

ROBIN-REDBREAST IS THE BIRD FIRST RECOGNIZED AND LOVED BY CHILDREN.
HERE HE IS SEEN HAVING A TUG-OF-WAR WITH THE EARLY WORM. ABOUT
ONE-THIRD NATURAL SIZE.

The relationship of bird families, like that of other
animals, is based, not on size or color, but upon a likeness
in the formation of their bodies—just as the tiger and the
cat are related. This likeness proves their descent, in
remote ages, from a common ancestor.

The robin is the best known of all birds, and with its
cousin, the bluebird, shares the honor of being the two
birds first recognized and loved by children. It is the
state bird of Virginia.

Robin is too familiar in song and story to need any
description; instead, we might point out a few things
that may have escaped those who have only a slight acquaintance with him: the head, black on top and sides,
the white spots around the eyes, the black and white
streaked throat. And have you noticed the white spots
on the tips of some feathers in the blackfish tail, the
white under-tail patch, and the yellow bill? The female's
coloring is slightly duller.

ROBIN'S REPERTOIRE A LARGE ONE

Few birds have a more extended vocabulary. Robin's
notes express interrogation, suspicion, alarm, despair.

During his nesting season he sings his happiest, cheeriest melody, and in it he seems to get all the blue of the sky, the warmth of the sun, the song of the brook. But he also has a scolding, fretful song, if something disturbs or angers him.

One year, before the leaves were out, a pair nested in the oak by the sleeping porch. We could lie in bed and watch them. Both birds shared in the building, and later in the incubation. Robin is not noted for any fine architectural ability, the nest being a rather crude affair of coarse grasses, leaves, and rootlets, lined with mud, which the birds bring in their beaks. The female molds the inside into shape by nestling and turning round and round, the interior of the nest taking the shape of her breast. Before this mud hardens, the nest is lined with fine grass and rootlets.

Robins have three to five eggs—there were four in our birds' nest. They are pale greenish blue, and have given the name "robin's egg blue" to the color. In our nest, incubation took thirteen days, and from then on both birds were kept busy feeding their greedy young— of which three had hatched—for a young robin's mouth seems always wide open, and it can consume a vast amount of food.

The young birds' eyes were closed until the sixth to the eighth day; all three were fairly well feathered by the eleventh day. By then the wing-feathers were moderately well developed, but the birds had no tail-feathers, only a very short stub, which made the first flight awkward and unbalanced.

Our birds left the nest on a Sunday morning. We were awakened by loud scoldings and pleadings and, hastily donning bathrobes, hurried out to follow the first flight. Two fledglings were ready to leave, but the third, the runt of the lot, could not be coaxed any farther than the next branch. Apparently in despair, the parents left "Stubby," as we named him, and flew off with the other two. The flight was in easy stages from tree to tree, until the interior of our woods was reached. There one parent remained with the two fledglings, while the other went back to look after "Stubby," who was perched exactly where they had left him. Repeated pleadings and scoldings got him up to another branch, and that was all he would do. The parent bird brought him some juicy tidbits, which quickly disappeared down his wide mouth, and then again tried to get him to fly. At last, discouraged, the parent bird again left him alone, and flew off to see how the others were getting on.

This performance lasted all day, and we managed to keep track of the three birds, the two in the back woods, and "Stubby," who clung to his home-tree. The next morning "Stubby" was still there, but during the day he disappeared, and we did not see him again. The other two birds were raised in our garden, the parents caring for them and feeding them solicitously for what seemed an unusually long time, until the ungainly birdlings equaled them in size. For a long time the two always went into the bird bath together, and had a grand time, ducking their heads and splashing water over their backs like children in a swimming pool.

Cats, crows, and squirrels seem to be the robin's chief enemies. And the birds are belligerent when it comes to protecting their eggs or nestlings. Once my father and I saw a squirrel being driven off by an angry robin. The squirrel scuttled down the trunk, but the robin reached the ground first and gave the squirrel an angry tweak, and two more before it squeezed through an opening into which the robin could not follow. But the bird remained there, scolding harshly for a few seconds, evidently giving the squirrel a piece of her mind.

Nearly half of the robin's food consists of beetles, grasshoppers, caterpillars, and other animal matter, but occasionally its fruit-eating habits bring it into disrepute. As a government bulletin points out, however, the robin has already been working during a whole season to make the fruit crop possible, and doubtless it thinks it should be entitled to a small share. Robins are also very fond of wild berries of all kinds, especially the mulberry, and if these are planted about a large orchard they will probably lure the birds away from the cultivated fruits.

GREAT MIGRATORY FLOCKS

The robin, in some form, is known throughout most of eastern North America. A few stragglers winter throughout the North, but the vast majority migrate to the Gulf states, often in enormous flocks. Once, in Georgia, we saw a flock of several thousands, and five years ago (February, 1928), the greatest migratory flock of robins ever known was seen near New Hope, Gaston County, North Carolina. Game Warden Ford estimated that there were several millions roosting in the pine woods. For over a week they wheeled about in the sky, coming to rest in the woods, and in flight they appeared like dark clouds. This great flock was the nearest approach of modern times to the flocks of passenger pigeons which, only a few generations ago, were so numerous that they darkened the earth during their migratory flights. Today, not one passenger pigeon is left to wing its way through the blue. May the day never come when our robin red-breasts will likewise fail to be numbered among the winged travelers of the skies.

XII

THE BLUEBIRD

Winged lute that we call a bluebird,
 You blend in a silver strain
The sound of the laughing waters,
 The patter of Spring's sweet rain,
The voice of the winds, the sunshine,
 And fragrance of blossoming things.
Ah! You are an April poem,
 That God has dowered with wings.
                              —REXFORD.

"WHAT PRICE English sparrows?" might be answered in terms of fewer bluebirds about our homes. Before these English sparrows became so numerous, the bluebirds nested about our homes and gardens in far greater numbers, for the bluebird, more than any other bird, is in conflict with the English sparrow over nesting sites. How to drive the sparrows out of the bird houses that one has put up for bluebirds seems an unanswerable problem to the bird lover.

Other natural enemies of the bluebird are cats, squirrels, and blizzards. Brimley tells of the great blizzard of 1895 which, covering the earth and everything with a sheet of ice for several days, killed bluebirds by thousands all over the country, until there was fear that the birds might have been exterminated. For a few years following, a bluebird was a rare sight, but by now they have regained their former numbers.

The bluebird's range covers practically all of eastern North America, from Nova Scotia and Manitoba to the Gulf. It is the state bird of Missouri. While not a migrant in the South, it is in the North, where the return of the bluebird, which is earlier than the robin, is greeted with a joy that is hard to understand in the South, which has not endured long months of snow and blizzards.

In a bleak hill-country school overlooking Lake Erie, where I once taught, when my children first heard the bluebird's soft, plaintive warble, they interpreted its song as, *tru-al-ly-spring-is-here-tru-al-ly*.

"BLUE ROBIN"

Though not realizing the relationship, the Pilgrim Fathers, who named the robin after their own loved English robin—largely because of its reddish breast—likewise called the bluebird "blue robin" because it, too, had a reddish breast, was friendly to man, and built near his dwelling places. The bluebird is cousin to the robin, both birds belonging to the family *Turdidae,* or thrushes.

There is no blue so beautiful as the cerulean blue of the upper parts, wings, and tail of the bluebird. The throat, breast, and sides are reddish, or dull cinnamon rufous, the belly whitish. The blue is tipped with rusty in the fall and winter. The female is a duller blue washed with gray, and the breast is paler. Thoreau said the bluebird carried the sky on his back; and John Burroughs added, "and the earth on his breast."

Observing the bluebird both in flight and at rest, you will note that the blue is most brilliant when the bird is on the wing, and in the sunshine. In reality there is no blue pigment in the bird world. The red feather of the cardinal would produce a red pigment, but the blue feather of a blue-colored bird produces no blue color. Under a microscope the seeming blue feather is brownish, and is overlaid with a thin film that reflects light.

Neither is there any iridescent pigment in the bird world. Blue and all the metallic or iridescent colors are due entirely to this process of refraction. Thus the iridescent throat of the male hummingbird is due to the fact that the exposed portions of those feathers are coated with a transparent colorless layer of extreme thinness (8/1000th of an inch) which breaks up the rays of light.

Once, when we were visiting in his studio, Louis Agassiz Fuertes, the bird artist, held a large tropical bird in his hand and placed two of us in different positions. "What color is it?" he asked us. "Grayish brown," said my niece. "Why, it's a bright blue," I objected. Then, just by shifting the position of his hand, so that the light reflected in a different way on the bird, Mr. Fuertes asked again. "And now?" "Bright blue," answered my niece, and "grayish brown," I insisted.

TENANTS OF OLD ORCHARDS

Bluebirds haunt open woods and meadows, cut-over fields, house premises and gardens, and especially old orchards with hollow and partly decayed trees, where they flit about in small companies until time for nesting begins. They nest in holes in trees and fence-posts, in crevices and crannies about buildings, and in bird houses. Once a pair nested in my neighbor's mail-box, and the nest came to successful fruition. The mail-man helped by being careful not to push the mail in very far, and both he and the family saw that the box was never closed.

The bluebirds also nest often in the small round tin boxes put out by various newspapers. Taking a hint from that, we last year put out a tin cookie box, and the bluebirds, scorning the sparrow-infested bird houses, nested there.

On Easter morn the baby birds were born, and no Easter gift was ever more appreciated. We had so placed the can that the opening was toward the house, and we could watch the comings and goings of the little blue tenants. They were very domestic birds, the male singing to his mate on the grass-lined nest, and feeding her, too, but he did not seem to share in the incubating. He did, however, bestir himself more when the young were born, and helped feed the ever-hungry babies.

The nest was just a few feet from the bird bath, and though the female only stopped now and then for a hurried drink, the male occasionally took time for a bath. The sight of him, settling down into the water, wings outspread, with the afternoon sunlight on his vivid blue, created another exquisite bird-memory picture.

The young birds were almost black at first, thickly spotted on throat and back; then they became a dark gray-blue, streaked with darker markings. By the time they were ready for flight, a few blue feathers began to show. After they had left the nest, they often came back to the garden to feed. One day I noticed them pecking greedily at a rotten stump, which proved to be literally covered with termites, or winged ants. As we had suffered from termites to the extent of having to raise the house and to refloor all the porches, we thought the blue-birds, in consuming thousands of these winged ants, were indeed "paying guests."

The bluebird pays in both beauty and use, consuming quantities of early grasshoppers, caterpillars, weevils, beetles, and other insects. It is evident that in the selection of its food the bird is governed more by abundance than by choice. The vegetable food consumed consists of berries of dogwood, holly, hackberry, wild cherry, pokeberry, juniper, and some weed seeds. Few, if any, cultivated fruits are eaten. Walter Pritchard Eaton tells of watching a single bluebird alternating song with caterpillar-eating—a caterpillar, then a bit of melody, then another caterpillar, and another bit of melody, and so on, unceasingly, for two hours.

During the winter, bluebirds migrate from the North in large flocks, filling our southern woods and gardens with color. Once, at Christmas time, a flock of twenty settled in the twin dogwoods by our dining room window—the bluebirds and the ruby-colored berries against gray skies creating a vivid poem in color. Dinner was forgotten, while our northern guests crept to the windows to watch the birds, which, a few weeks before, may have been about their own homes in the North.

XIII

OUR WINTER WARBLERS

Narcissus-like you sit above
The bird bath mirror, preen and gaze
   On your reflected self,
    Neglectful of your mate.
You thrill, admiring your fair image,
As vain as if you'd shared your beauty's making.
             —ALBERT W. SMITH.

KING MIDAS, who turned all he touched to gold, must have put his fingers on the myrtle warbler, for this bird has four golden spots—a large one on the rump, one on each side of the breast, and one on the crown. The golden crown, however, is not distinguishable until the spring moult.

The upper parts of the myrtle, or yellow-rumped warbler, are a dark blue-gray, streaked with black; the throat is white, the breast and upper belly heavily marked with black, the lower belly white. There are two white wing-bars, and large white spots on the outer tail-feathers. In the South, in winter, the yellow on the sides of the breast is much reduced. Only the rump remains as brilliantly yellow. The birds are about five and one-half inches in length.

The female is similar, but with less black below; the throat is less streaked with black, and the upper parts are brownish. In both the young and the adults in winter the yellow crown patch is concealed by brownish tips to the feathers. But watch this bird carefully, for it has a spring as well as a fall moult. You will observe a bit of Mother Nature's magic, as, day by day, before

MYRTLE WARBLER

Order—PASSERIFORMES   Family—COMPSOTHLYPIDÆ

Genus—DENDROICA   Species—CORONÁTA

National Association of Audubon Societies

PHŒBE

your eyes, the golden crown will slowly emerge, until, just before the bird leaves for its northern home, the crown patch is a brilliant, gleaming yellow.

The myrtle warbler, and all his 154 cousins of the wood warbler family, are exclusively American birds—real "hundred per cent-ers," for the European warblers that we read about belong to the *Sylviidae*. Our own warblers, the *Mniotiltidae*, are more brilliantly plumaged, with yellow, orange, blue, green, slate, olive, and black and white predominating, except in a few ground species, such as the ovenbird and the water thrushes. As a rule, the sexes are rather unlike, whereas the European warblers are more plainly plumaged and the sexes are usually similar.

The South has two common winter warblers, the myrtle warbler—one of the most abundant species of its family—which comes about the middle of October and leaves in May, and the pine warbler, our only permanent resident of this group. These two warblers are among the strongest, hardiest members of the species. Although warblers are almost entirely insect-eaters, spending their busy lives pursuing insects which they destroy in all stages, from egg and larva, to adult, the myrtle is also especially adept at catching insects on the wing. Unlike most of the family, it eats weed seeds, such as the goldenrod. It is also fond of frost grapes, and of the berries of sumac, poison oak, holly, red cedar, palmetto, and especially of the bay, so that it can winter farther north than most of the other warblers. In fact, the bird gets its name from this liking for wax-myrtle or bayberries.

So fond are these birds of bayberries, that their movements are largely governed by the success or failure of the crop. It is said that as far north as New Jersey, these birds always come in winter if there is an abundance of the berries, and are always absent when there are none. It was claimed by E. H. Forbush, former state ornithologist of Massachusetts, that the starling is also very fond of bayberries, devouring them before the myrtle warblers arrive. He feared, therefore, that the early wintering myrtle warblers might gradually disappear from the more northern coastal region if the starlings continued to increase at their present rate.

Toward spring, however, the birds seem to weary of their diet of berries and seeds, and eagerly pursue early flies, moths, ants, and other insects. As these birds remain until rather late in the spring, they feed also on the pests that develop with the opening foliage of trees and shrubs.

The male myrtle bird exemplifies the old adage, "Handsome is as handsome does." He is a fearless and aggressive bird, but selfish to the extent of being a sort of "bird-in-the-manger" in his attitude towards other birds. Though there is suet and food in plenty for all the birds about our place, the myrtle warbler nearly worries himself into a nervous "bird-wreck" trying to police them all and to drive other birds away from each feeding-station. He will flatten himself out and snarl like an angry dog if other birds try to stand their ground.

And he is over-fond of the reflection of his gold-bedecked self in the bird bath. Though some bird writers say this warbler delights to bathe, not only in the hot weather of summer but also in spring and autumn, we have never seen one bathe. Often he comes to drink and remains perched on the rim, gazing at himself with every appearance of calm satisfaction.

During migration myrtle warblers—or yellow-rumps, as they are sometimes called—travel in sociable flocks, and as they are fearless and aggressive, they are accompanied by their more timid warbler cousins, which gladly seek the escort of birds more courageous than themselves.

In general, warblers are not noted songsters, most of them having rather weak voices. But toward nesting time, the myrtle begins to sing a bright, cheery trill suggestive of the song of the junco.

Though the myrtle warblers are found throughout most of the South in winter, they do not nest here, but only in our extreme northern boundary states, and throughout much of the forested areas of Canada, even as far north as Alaska. They winter as far south as Panama, but are most abundant in the pine flats and palmetto hammocks of the Coast belt. During migration they seem to appear in every patch of woodland, and are so numerous and so easily identified that anyone can observe them.

During courtship it is said the males follow the females about, displaying their "beauty spots" by fluffing out the feathers of their sides, raising their wings, and erecting the feathers of the crown, so as to show to the utmost their beautiful golden markings.

The nest is composed of hemlock twigs and soft vegetable fiber, lined with grass and feathers, and sometimes hair. Usually it is within eight feet of the ground, in coniferous trees or bushes. The three to five eggs are whitish, spotted with purple.

THE PINE WARBLER, A YEAR-ROUND RESIDENT

The pine warbler is fittingly named, for it not only wears the green of our pines, but it is also most common in the great "pineries" of the South and in the pine forests of New York and New England; true to its name, it is rarely found where there are no pines, or where they have been cut.

THE PINE WARBLER, OUR ONLY YEAR-ROUND WARBLER, WEARS THE GREEN OF THE PINES ON ITS BACK.   ABOUT THREE-FIFTHS NATURAL SIZE.

Here in the South, where our "pineries" extend over large areas, it is an abundant and generally distributed bird, being found in the loblollies, the short-leaf, and the long-leaf forests.   In our mountains it is only a summer visitor, but elsewhere throughout the Carolinas and much of the South it is a permanent resident.   In winter the northern-breeding pine warblers move southward and occupy the Gulf States in company with the breeding birds of the same region.

In winter the pine warbler is often found in small flocks which frequently contain a few myrtle warblers and palm warblers.   At this time of the year it may be seen on or near the ground. In summer it stays more in the trees. Its habit of clinging to the trunk of a tree, or hopping along a limb while searching for insects in crevices of the bark, has given it the name of pine creeper, or pine creeping warbler.

This little olive-green-with-breast-of-gold warbler is easy to recognize and also easy to induce to feeding-stations. It is a friendly bird, more deliberate in its motions and less easily startled than most of the birds that come to the window-shelf to feed. It will let you approach the window-pane closely, where you can observe the faint olive-green markings on the sides of its under parts, the two whitish wing-bars, and the white patches on the outer tail-feathers. The female is similar to the male, but duller in appearance. In size the pine warbler is a trifle smaller than the English sparrow.

CURIOUS HABITS

The pine warbler has the curious habits of several other birds, creeping over trunks and branches like the creepers and nuthatches; flying about twigs and branchlets like the other warblers; darting into the air for insects like the flycatchers; and dropping to the ground and feeding on seeds and berries in winter, like the ground birds. Its song is very much like that of the chipping sparrow, but more musical.

This warbler likes a swaying aerial home in high tree-tops, especially pines, and usually on a horizontal limb, but sometimes among the outer twigs. The nest may be as high as eighty feet, and is made of strips of bark, leaves, and plant fibers. The nesting date is usually in early April, but in different sections of the South nests have been found as early as March 20, and as late as May 24. The four to five eggs are whitish, with numerous cinnamon markings.

A pine warbler's nest built in a great pine in our yard was cleverly hidden from sight by being built over a downward hanging cone, so that even with bird glasses it was difficult to detect, and if we had not watched the movements of the birds we never should have found it.

THE YELLOW PALM WARBLER

Lesser known warblers of winter are the palm warbler and the yellow palm warbler. The latter breeds mainly north of the United States, and winters in the Gulf States from Louisiana to northern Florida, and sometimes to North Carolina and farther north. It has a chestnut crown and is brownish olive above shading into green on the lower back. The under parts are bright yellow, streaked with chestnut on throat, breast, and sides. In winter it is more brownish. A noticeable trait of this bird, which helps in its identification, is the constant wagging of its tail.

Sometimes this warbler is found in company with the pine warblers, especially in the pine flats along the coastal plain. In some parts of the South, in winter, it is also common about gardens and in streets of small towns. Its call is a fine, shrill *chip, chip.*

The palm warbler, sometimes called redpoll warbler, resembles the yellow palm, but is slightly smaller and more grayish brown above, and the under parts are a more uneven yellow. It lives farther inland than the yellow palm warbler, and is occasionally found in summer in the northern Mississippi Valley. It winters from southern Florida southward.

XIV

THE AMERICAN PIPIT, OR TITLARK

The pale purple even
Melts around thy flight;
Like a star of Heaven,
In the broad daylight
Thou art unseen, but yet I hear thy shrill delight.
—PERCY BYSSHE SHELLEY.

POURED forth in the air both as he mounts to and descends from a height of as much as two hundred feet, the pipit's song, according to Townsend, sounds like the ringing of a little bell—a vibrating *che-whée, che-whée,* with the resonance on the *whee.* Others interpret the song as *pip-it, pip-it,* which gives the bird its name.

In some parts of the South this pipit, or titlark, is a locally known common winter resident, at times occurring in large numbers. It is a strictly terrestrial, or ground-dwelling bird, except during its breeding period, when, in its ecstasy, it indulges in the flight song.

Resembling somewhat the sparrows, especially the vesper sparrow, it is distinguished from them by its slender bill and its habit of walking instead of hopping. Because of its constant tail-wagging, or jerking, it is also sometimes mistaken for the water-thrushes, but the pipit is a browner bird. It has brown upper parts, and buffy under parts, with breast and sides streaked with brown. The wings and tail-coverts are olive brown, the wing-coverts being tipped with buffy or whitish, and the white ends of the outer tail-feathers showing conspicuously in flight. The pipit also has a long hind toenail.

Pipits belong to the family *Motacillidae*, the wagtails and pipits. Though a hundred species are included in this family, only ten are American and of those only two are known in eastern North America. The American

LOOK FOR THE "TAIL-WAGGING" PIPIT IN NEWLY PLOWED OR RECENTLY BURNED FIELDS. ABOUT ONE-HALF NATURAL SIZE.

pipit breeds mainly in far northern countries, including northeastern Siberia, northern Alaska, Quebec and Labrador, and the higher mountains of our Rockies; it winters from the Ohio and lower Delaware valleys south to Guatemala.

The nest is built on the ground and is of grasses lined with moss and lichens. The four to six bluish white or grayish white eggs are thickly speckled with cinnamon. The nesting date is usually in June.

While in the South, the pipit is mainly found in small flocks in cultivated fields and pastures. A recently burned or newly plowed field is a good place to go in

search of pipits. It is decidedly a "paying guest" while
here, for its bill-of-fare includes weevils, grasshoppers,
beetles, spiders, crickets, cotton boll weevils, and a few
small seeds and berries.

XV

THE PHOEBE

Phoebe is all it has to say
In plaintive cadence o'er and o'er,
Like children that have lost their way
And know their names, but nothing more.
—JAMES RUSSELL LOWELL.

THE PHOEBES are popularly credited with being the most devoted couples, and are believed by some to mate for life; yet one of the many mysteries of migration is that they do not travel together. While they are not migratory with us—(at least as a species, but may be as individuals)—they are in the North, where they are among the first of the common birds to make their appearance in the spring.

When I was teaching in the North, in a country school overlooking Lake Erie, about the time the children brought in the first pussy willows we began to look for the return of the phoebes. Near this school for several years a pair of phoebes nested on a beam under a bridge.

The male would come a week or so in advance of his dusky mate, and sit around morose and dejected until she arrived. No energetic *phoe-be* out of him at such times! Instead it was a disconsolate, heart-breaking, wailing *pho-e-bee*. Upon her arrival he was a changed bird, his whole being seeming to perk up. Once more the sky was blue, the sunshine bright, and the insects tasted, oh, so *much* better!

How happy they were to be reunited, and how cheerily and energetically they went about looking for a nesting site! At last they decided on a location next to that of the one built the previous year.

What tales the phoebes must have had to chirp to each other of their adventures and the dangers of the long way! We could imagine him saying to her, "That was a terrific storm we ran into, Phoebe-girl. Really, for the first time I was glad you were not along. I do hope you had better weather."

And like all wives she probably answered, "Yes, but I was worried about you, braving the cold of an early spring. I do think it would be better if you would wait a bit. I never did approve of your leaving earlier."

The phoebes, members of the flycatcher family, the *Tyrannidae,* are deep olive-brown above, and darkest on the head; the under parts are dull white with a grayish or yellowish tinge. The head feathers give the appearance of being slightly crested, and the bill and feet are black. The bill, like that of all flycatchers, is wide at the base and slightly hooked at the tip, with bristles about the gape. The bird is slightly longer than an English sparrow.

Phoebe, the hardiest member of the family, breeds from Canada to central Texas, northern Mississippi, and the higher regions of Georgia and Alabama, and winters from the upper part of the South to southern Mexico. In parts of the South there seem to be several times as many phoebes in winter as there are in the summer. This is probably because the birds from the more northern part of the range winter in this section.

With no pretentions to beauty of plumage or song, phoebes have won for themselves a warm place in our hearts. Their contented ways and trustworthy dispositions make them welcome everywhere, and they seem to sense that welcome. Farmers like to hear their voices in early spring and are always glad to have them nest about their buildings.

A HOUSE UPON A ROCK

Phoebes love water and are great bathers, and they like cool, wet woodland retreats. Originally the phoebe built its house upon a rock, building it under a ledge or in a protected place, and making the outside of the nest match the rock by covering it with lichens. There was one phoebe's nest I watched for a whole season. This was built upon a rock, and though "the rains descended and the winds blew and beat upon that house" yet this particular little house fell not, for it was stoutly built. Phoebe is usually a good architect.

They are adaptable birds, able to make the best of changing conditions, and therefore they may increase, while birds that are not adaptable may become extinct. With the coming of mankind, phoebe, like the chimney swift, has changed his habits somewhat, and while he still builds upon rocks and under bridges, he also likes to build about farm buildings. Nests may be found among rafters, eaves, porches, barns, wood-sheds, and pigsties. Brimley tells of a pair that nested inside an unused well near his home.

The nest is rather bulky, made mostly of moss and mud and various vegetable substances, and is lined with grasses and long hairs, and, too often, alas, with feathers. For phoebe, unfortunately has never learned not to use feathers, if they are temptingly within reach. Chicken feathers are usually infested with lice or mites or parasites, and the phoebe's nest quickly becomes infested, to the injury of the young birds, which often suffer tortures. Sometimes death is caused by these parasites, especially—which occasionally happens—if a second brood is raised in the same nest. Nests have been observed under these conditions, in which but one nestling pulled through.

Generally, however, when rearing a second brood, even though they use the same site, the old nest is torn down. Again, the birds will build another nest near by, sometimes also returning season after season, until there is a colony of nests.

And here is a warning! If collecting old nests, leave the phoebe's nest alone, no matter how it may tempt you. Once an enthusiastic city teacher, summer-schooling with me at Chautauqua Institute, put one of these nests in her trunk to take back to her classroom in an East-Side tenement district in New York. The result was—terrible. No doughboy from the trenches ever had to be deloused more thoroughly than did her trunkful of clothes! So, admire the phoebe's nest, but leave it where you found it.

The four to five eggs of the phoebe are white, usually unspotted, but sometimes showing obscure speckles near the larger end. The breeding date seems to be from the middle of April to the end of May. The male phoebe is a devoted parent, rarely being found far from home.

The young are like the adults but their upper parts are more olive, their under parts more yellow, and the wing-bars more distinct. After the young leave the nest they often stay together, generally perching close to one another on a low branch, and taking short flights in a body. Observers say that the families tend to keep in groups the greater part of the year.

Phoebes, like all flycatchers, often sit motionless on a lookout, waiting for an insect to pass by; then with a quick movement they dart down and snap it up. In this way they are among our most useful birds and should be given every protection, especially about the farm. They are said to have peculiarly constructed eyes, something like the nighthawk's, so that they can hunt late, catching insects that are not out by day. The birds are adaptable, in that they can live throughout the winter on berries, though their regular food is insects.

XVI

THE HORNED LARKS

A BIRD that, like the English skylark of the above poem, sings while it soars, is the American horned lark, our only member of the *Alaudidae*, the lark family, of which the English skylark is the best known and the best loved.

Several attempts have been made to introduce the English skylark, so loved by poets, into this country, but none of them has been very successful, though a few skylarks are said to have become established near Flatbush, Long Island.

The horned lark of America has several subspecies, consisting of slightly different geographical races. A little larger than the English sparrow, the horned lark is pinkish brown or gray above, with a large black crescent on the breast, a yellow throat, and a broad black patch extending downward on the side of the eye. A black band across the top of the head ends in tufts of feathers, or "horns" on each side of the crown and gives the lark its name. The tail is blackish, bordered on the sides by a

[85]

narrow white line, and the feet are black, the hind toenail being exceptionally long.

Similar in color, but darker, the female is also smaller, and the markings, especially those of the head, are less

DURING ITS NESTING SEASON THE HORNED LARK, LIKE ITS FAMOUS COUSIN, THE ENGLISH SKYLARK, SINGS WHILE SOARING. ABOUT ONE-HALF NATURAL SIZE.

distinct. In winter both the adults and the young have the black markings veiled by yellowish or whitish tips to the feathers. A distinguishing characteristic of the horned larks is that they do not hop, but walk gracefully.

The breeding range of the horned lark is mainly north of the United States, and it winters south to the Ohio valley and Georgia, and sometimes to Louisiana. It is usually during hard, cold winters that these birds drift south, coming in large flocks, which separate into smaller, scattered flocks. They prefer flat open tracts of land. Years ago flocks of these larks used to visit the upper South rather regularly during February and March, and large numbers of them were trapped and sold in the markets.

One especially cold winter a small flock came to the fields surrounding a country school where I was teaching. They remained several weeks, the children bringing waste grain, and gleaning weed seeds, which they scattered on the packed snow about the school yard. We could look out of the windows at almost any time and see these larks feeding.

At this time the older children were reading selections from *Lorna Doone,* and the trim, pinkish brown of the birds reminded them of the color of Winnie, the famous strawberry mare of Tom Faggus, the highwayman. This appealed to the country children, and they gleefully named the strange-looking birds, which they had not seen before, the "Winnie birds." In the sunlight the trim bodies of the pinkish brown birds did have something of the sheen of the well groomed coat of a horse.

Though for the most part a strictly terrestrial, or ground-dwelling bird, during the breeding season the horned lark, like the skylark of England, sings while soaring. Starting from the ground, the lark mounts upward in great spirals until it is almost lost to sight. There, a tiny speck in the blue, it sometimes reaches an altitude of two or three hundred feet before it hovers and sings. So far skyward it is that the eye can barely discern it, and the ear catches only a faint, far away sound. The song of the horned lark is not a great song, but the manner of its delivery is awe-inspiring. Finally, closing its wings, the lark drops headlong to earth, and for a moment it seems as if it would strike the ground, when suddenly it spreads its wings and alights. Here in the

South we do not see or hear the flight song, but hear only the call-notes, sharp, whistled notes of *tseep, tseep* as the bird takes alarm.

The greater part of the horned lark's food consists of vegetable matter, about half of which is grain and the remainder weed seeds. A few insects are also eaten.

The horned lark nests in May, on the ground, and the four to five eggs are pale bluish or greenish white, speckled with brown.

THE PRAIRIE HORNED LARK

This lark, a subspecies, is similar to the former but is slightly smaller and paler. According to Ernest Thompson Seton, it is one of the birds that has changed its range since the coming of civilization to America. Formerly a bird of the prairies and open barrens, of recent years it has extended its range more eastward to southern Missouri, Western Virginia, Ohio, and Tennessee, and winters south to Texas and Georgia. Tennessee reports it as a rare summer resident and a more common winter resident, and North Carolina, Alabama, and other southern states as an occasional common winter resident.

An earlier nesting bird than the former species, the prairie horned lark's nest is built on the ground in bare exposed places. Sometimes the bird is too eager to get at home-making, and nests have been found in which the eggs were frozen and cracked.

XVII

THE WHITE-THROATED SPARROW

Have you ever heard of the singaway bird,
　　That sings where the Runaway River
Runs down with its rills from the bald-headed hills
　　That stand in the sunshine and shiver?
"Oh, sing! sing-away! sing-away!"
How the pines and the birches are stirred
By the trill of the sing-away bird!

'Twas a white-throated sparrow, that sped a light arrow
　　Of song from his musical quiver,
And it pierced with its spell every valley and dell
　　On the banks of the Runaway River.
"Oh, sing! sing-away! sing-away!"
The song of the wild singer had
The sound of a soul that is glad.
　　　　　　　　　　—LUCY LARCOM.

THE WHITE-THROAT'S plaintive song, easily recognized, is heard throughout the winter, and especially on warm days toward spring. It is probably our most abundant winter bird, being found in fields of scrubby growth, along the edge of woodlands, in gardens, yards, farms—in fact, almost anywhere. Look out of your window and you will probably see a flock of white-throats feeding on the ground with juncos, English sparrows, and perhaps a fox sparrow or two, a towhee, and a hermit thrush.

NOT ALL SPARROWS BAD

Unfortunately, to people who know little about birds, the very name of sparrow has come to mean only the unpopular English sparrow, which has become such a nuisance everywhere. There is just enough resemblance among the sparrows to cause a person unfamiliar with birds to think that all sparrows are English sparrows and bad; whereas some of our best "weed warriors"—the best friends the farmer and gardener has in his fields—are our native sparrows. The chippy and the grasshopper sparrow of summer; the white-throat, the song, the junco, the fox, the vesper, the savannah, and the swamp sparrow of winter, and the field sparrow, a permanent resident, are included in this group of native sparrows.

A government bulletin states: "While sparrows are seed eaters, they do not by any means confine themselves to a vegetable diet. During the summer, and especially during the breeding season, they eat many insects, and feed their young largely upon the same food. The insects they eat include beetles, weevils, many grasshoppers, wasps, bugs, and potato-bug larvae. Useful predacious and parasitic insects are eaten only to a slight extent, so that as a whole the insect diet of our native sparrows is beneficial."

The white-throat is a handsome fellow—especially after the spring moult—and is about six and one-half inches in length. The back is reddish brown and black, streaked with some white markings. There are three distinct white stripes on the head, with a yellow line before the eye, and the throat has a conspicuous white patch. Rump and tail are grayish brown, and there is a yellowish bit on the bend of the wing.

Few birds are more sociable than the white-throats. In fall and winter they gather in little companies, frequently roosting together in large numbers in the depths of dense thickets or clumps of evergreens. After they have apparently retired for the night one may hear the sharp *chink* of their 'quarrier' chorus, as Chapman calls it.

The call notes while feeding are only *t'sip, t'sip;* but

WHITE-THROATED SPARROW

Order—PASSERES   Family—FRINGILLIDÆ
Genus—ZONOTRICHIA   Species—ALBICOLLIS

National Association of Audubon Societies

SLATE-COLORED JUNCO

Order—PASSERES   Family—FRINGILLIDÆ
Genus—JUNCO   Species—HYEMALIS

National Association of Audubon Societies

the song, even as heard in winter, has a plaintive soft-
ness, becoming more sweet and wistful as spring warms
the heart. New Englanders think its song sounds like
pea-body-pea-body-pea-body, and so they call it the Pea-
body bird, while loyal Canadians are certain it is trying to say *Swee-e-et Can-a-day, Can-a-day, Can-a-day*
and have named it "Sweet Canada bird." While in the
South the white-throat is generally silent through the
colder months of the winter, but commences to sing again
on warm days in February, and continues rather constantly from then until the end of its stay. White-throat
also sings at night, when disturbed, or perhaps, when it
has been dreaming.

Young white-throats begin to try their voices in the
fall, as if practising for their spring song and courtship.
We hear them when they first come, a sort of fall chorus,
and the result is singularly sweet and inspiring.

Through the winter the white-throats become very
friendly, and will peck at a dog's dish, feed on the ground
near the kitchen doorstep or barn, at suet stations, and
at window-shelf cafeterias. One year, during an early
big snow, there were sometimes as many as six to ten
of them feeding on the window-shelf at one time, and a
friend who had a much larger "bird-cafeteria" tele-
phoned that her husband had counted twenty-four feeding there at one time.

During such storms it is amusing to observe the white-
throats—and the juncos, too—alight on the tops of
slender weed stalks, and as the stalks bend beneath the
double burden of snow and bird, the bird is borne to
the ground, but holds grimly on. There, holding the
dried plant firmly under the toes, it cleverly strips off
the seeds.

The white-throat belongs to the largest of the bird
families, the *Fringillidae,* which, including sparrows,

finches, and grosbeaks, is represented in all parts of the world except the Australian region.

NESTS IN THE NORTH

The white-throat's range is eastern North America, breeding from Canada south to New York and Massachusetts, and wintering from Missouri and the Ohio valley south to Mexico and Florida. Some flocks remain all winter as far north as New Jersey, or even farther.

But the bulk of the white-throated sparrow population comes to our southern states, arriving in the upper South by mid-October and remaining well into May. Here they may be seen in suitable localities all over the South, where they thrive and grow fat.

To become familiar with the white-throat's nesting habits, however, it is necessary to go to the northern border states or into Canada, where they nest usually on the ground or in low bushes.

Built externally of coarse grasses, rootlets, moss, and strips of bark, the nest is lined with fine grasses. The four to five bluish-white eggs are speckled with pale reddish brown.

And so the cycle of the white-throat's life runs on, and when our southern trees and fields come out in their reds and golds and dull browns of autumn, the "sing-away" bird comes back again to "pierce with its spell every valley and dell."

XVIII

THE SLATE-COLORED JUNCO, OR SNOW BIRD

From out the white and pulsing storm
I hear the snow birds calling;
The sheeted winds stalk o'er the hills,
And fast the snow is falling.

On twinkling wings they eddy past,
At home amid the drifting,
Or seek the hills and weedy fields,
Where fast the snow is sifting.
—JOHN BURROUGHS.

ALTHOUGH the junco, or snow bird, comes South in late October or early November, we always think of it as being blown in with a storm, a sort of gray-clad messenger of wintry blasts.

And it is as a winter bird that we know the junco; in fact, few know it during the nesting season, for the summer home extends from the extreme northern states, north to the tree limit, and may be well within the Arctic Circle.

The juncos, like the white-throats, are among our most numerous winter birds and are found throughout the greater part of the South at that season. They are fittingly called snow birds, for they brave all weather and often seem to be virtually blown about by a storm.

Short and plump—about the size of an English sparrow, but stockier—the bird is dark slate-gray in color, with a white belly that looks like a white-bibbed apron. There are no wing bars, and the white outer tail-feathers, easily seen in flight, aid in the quick recognition of the bird. The blunt bill, fitted for seed crushing, is a flesh

[93]

pink—another distinguishing mark. The female is similar, but the upper parts are more brownish, and the throat and breast paler. The nestlings resemble the adults, but have the upper parts, throat, and breast streaked with black.

During the winter the juncos are found in open woods, along roadsides, in bushy fields, yards, and gardens, often in company with their cousins, the sparrows. They are friendly birds, feeding about doorsteps and barnyards, and during extreme cold, they frequently will eat regularly with a flock of chickens. When snow is on the ground they are often in need of food, and will respond to any friendly overture that includes feeding. They come regularly to our suet-stations, and less regularly to the window-shelf bird cafeteria. During one of our snows, we scattered grain out on the ground and soon had a flock of over thirty juncos, with some white-throats and English sparrows, feeding. Sunflower seeds, cracked wheat, grains, poppy seeds, crumbs, are all welcomed by these small gray visitors.

The juncos also belong to the Weed Warrior group and eat the seeds of harmful weeds and grasses. Some insects are also eaten by them, including caterpillars, beetles, ants, bugs, and spiders.

During cold weather these birds often creep into stacks of corn or hay, where they form burrows which afford snug quarters for the night, or even during stormy days. In the more open weather of the South, however, they prefer the green foliage of holly, cedar, or low pines for roosting.

So abundant and friendly and vivacious are the juncos, that, when they reappear again in the fall, we feel like saying, as to long absent friends, "Howdy, we're right smart glad to see you again!"

REAL SNOW BIRDS

The junco hasn't much of a song while he is with us, but his *'tsip, 'tsip, 'tsip* has a cheery, friendly sound, and it is heard throughout the winter. Before he leaves us, about the middle of April or a little later, his *'tsip* has become a low, sweet song.

Juncos are real snow birds in that, coming from a cold country, they do not mind the cold water of the bird bath, and go in, off and on, throughout the winter, and splash away, supplying cheer and action to a sometimes lonely bath.

The junco's nest is of grasses, moss, and rootlets, lined with fine grasses and long hairs, on or near the ground. The four to five eggs are white or bluish white, finely spotted with brown.

The Carolina junco, similar to the former, but with head not quite so dark, and slightly less white on the belly, breeds in the mountains from western Maryland, Virginia, and West Virginia south to northern Georgia, and winters in the neighboring lowlands.

XIX

THE SONG SPARROW, THE "SWEET SINGER"

THE MYTH OF THE SONG SPARROW

His mother was the Brook, his sisters were the Reeds,
And they everyone applauded when he sang about his deeds.
    His vest was white, his mantle brown, as clear as
      they could be,
    And his songs were fairly bubbling o'er with melody
      and glee.
But an envious neighbor splashed with mud our Brownie's
    coat and vest,
And then a final handful threw that stuck upon his breast.
    The Brook-bird's mother did her best to wash the
      stains away,
    But there they stuck, and, as it seems, are very like
      to stay.
And so he wears the splashes and the mud blotch as you see,
But his songs are bubbling over still with melody and glee.
          —ERNEST THOMPSON SETON.

THE MERRY CHANT of another sweet singer of this group has earned for it the name of song sparrow. Though it sings a little on warm days in the fall and early spring, its best song is heard only at the breeding grounds in the North. This sparrow prefers the neighborhood of brooks and ponds which are bordered with bushes, and also the hedges planted by Mother Nature along fences and telegraph lines, and it has a special liking for shrubbery about gardens. It is not so friendly a bird as the white-throat, nor does it travel in large flocks.

Characteristic are the movements and flight of this sparrow. When singing it usually perches at the very top of a shrub or low tree; when disturbed it never rises into the air but drops into a low flight and flies into a thicket with a defiant twitch of the tail which plainly says, "Find me if you can."

Its colors and markings are typical of the sparrows, the head being a warm brown with a gray 'parting-line' along the center of the brown crown, and the throat white with a dark spot on either side. The breast is white, spotted with brown with a large blotch at the very center, the blotch distinguishing this bird from all other sparrows. The tail and wings are brown and without buff or white bars or other markings; the tail is also long and rounded, and is very expressive of the bird's emotions.

Fond of insects and their larvae, through the spring and summer the song sparrows do their full share in destroying these pests of field and garden. They also eat small fruits and berries, but only in slight amounts, and those are usually wild. While these birds are in the South, seeds form the principal part of their diet. Seeming to prefer the shelter of low bushes, they are seldom seen feeding on the ground, as do the white-throats.

Though the song sparrow is found abundantly throughout much of the South in winter, coming about the middle of October and leaving early in April, it breeds mainly north of Carolina, though Brimley states it breeds in the Carolina mountains and in places along the coast and also in Virginia. Evidence seems to be that the bird is rapidly extending its breeding range southward in the Allegheny Mountains. In eastern Tennessee it is listed as a fairly common summer resident.

The nest is usually placed on or near the ground, but wherever it is, it is always cleverly concealed, and is of coarse grasses, rootlets, and dead leaves. The four to five eggs are as varied as the birds' songs and colorings, being light blue, or whitish, or greenish white, and with every imaginable sort of brown marking. The increasing abundance of this species is accounted for when we realize that a single pair may raise three broods, or twelve to fifteen birdlings, each summer. The male bird apparently believes in and enjoys family life, for he cheerfully shares with his mate the task of hatching and feeding the young, and he has been known to raise the young when his mate had been killed.

Song sparrows vary much in habits as well as size, coloration, and nest. Some forms live along streams bordered by deserts, others in swamps among cat-tails, others in timbered regions, on rocky barren hillsides, and still others in rich, fertile valleys. But wherever they are, they are greatly loved, for neither the cold of winter nor the darkness of the night discourages these little brown-feathered minstrels.

XX

THE FIELD, FOX, AND SWAMP SPARROWS

THE FIELD SPARROW

A bubble of music floats, the slope of the hillside over;
A little wandering sparrow's notes; and the bloom of the
    yarrow and clover,
And the smell of sweet-fern and the bayberry leaf, on his
    ripple of songs are stealing,
For he is a cheerful thief, the wealth of the fields revealing.

One syllable, clear and soft as a raindrop's silvery patter,
Or a tinkling fairy-bell; heard aloft, in the midst of the
    merry chatter
Of robin and linnet and wren and jay, one syllable, oft
    repeated;
He has but a word to say, and of that he will not be cheated.

—LUCY LARCOM.

SINGING best after sunset, a sort of anthem that is often expressive of the peace and quiet of eventide, the field sparrow's song is one that should be better known and loved.

A little smaller than the English sparrow, a little larger than its better known cousin, the chippy, this member of our native sparrows is too often overlooked as "just a sparrow." One of our most common birds, it is found principally in grassy fields and somewhat open country, especially pasture lands or old fields dotted with small bushes or clumps of cedars. Like many of the sparrows, it also frequents the neighborhood of houses and gardens, where it feeds on insects and weed seeds.

In winter its food seems to consist mainly of grass seeds. Like all of our native sparrows, the field sparrow is of great help to gardeners, farmers, and orchard-

THE REDDISH-BILLED FIELD SPARROW, A YEAR-ROUND RESIDENT, SINGS AN ANTHEM AFTER SUNSET. LOOK FOR IT IN OLD FIELDS AND PASTURE LANDS. SLIGHTLY REDUCED.

ists, and is a source of interest to bird and nature lovers; so it is deserving of every protection.

Because both sparrows have chestnut crowns, the field sparrow is sometimes confused with its smaller cousin, the chippy. The distinguishing points are that the field sparrow has a more reddish-brown back, a longer tail, and more buffy under parts. It also lacks the dark streak through the eye, and has a reddish, or coral bill. There are no spots of any kind on its breast.

Breeding from southern Quebec to central Texas and northern Florida, and wintering from southern Pennsylvania to the Gulf coast, the field sparrow is common throughout the South. It is only because its individuality is lost in being "just a sparrow," that the bird is not better known and loved.

KNOWN ALSO AS "BUSH SPARROW"

The nest, of rather coarse grasses, weed stalks, and rootlets, lined with fine grasses and long hairs, is found either on the ground—often in tussocks of green or dried grass—or in low bushes. Because in its more northern locality it frequently nests in low bushes, it is often known as the "bush sparrow." Though in the North the bird is pretty constant in building in bushes, I have found nests there built upon the ground without any protection, when there were bushes within a few feet that would have offered much safer nesting sites.

The three to five eggs are whitish or bluish white, marked with brownish, chiefly at the larger end. The nesting season extends from May to June or even early July, and there are often two or even three broods. As with many of the sparrow family, the nestlings have breasts streaked with black, and the young—and likewise the adults in winter—have duller colors, and the crown has a grayish edge, with sometimes a faint grayish line through its center.

The field sparrow's song, while beautiful, differs greatly both as to individual birds and in different localities. It may be heard in the early hours of morning, almost before dawn, or around sunset, and less often throughout the day. Its song is difficult to describe, consisting of a *cher-wee, cher-wee, cher-wee, chee-o, de-de-de-de*, the last notes being joined in a trill.

Always a rather shy bird, when alarmed the field sparrow has a habit of flying some distance ahead and then alighting on a bare twig near the top of a bush or small tree. From this vantage point he seems to watch

the intruder solemnly, thus giving the bird student a
good chance to look him over and note his distinguishing points—the reddish brown back, chestnut crown, long
tail, buffy breast, and reddish bill.

Along with most of our native sparrows, the field
sparrow is on the government's Agricultural Roll of
Honor of Southern Birds, for preying upon our arch
enemy, the boll weevil, together with other insects and
numerous noxious weeds.

THE RED FOX-SPARROW MAY BE BRINGING US GREETINGS FROM NORTHERN
LANDS. WATCH IT SCRATCHING AMONG THE DEAD LEAVES. IT IS AS ENERGETIC
AS ANY BUSY HEN. ABOUT ONE-HALF NATURAL SIZE.

THE FOX SPARROW

Largest, handsomest, and reddest of all his sparrow
kin, the fox sparrow is easily recognized. His name
comes from his fox-red coloring rather than from any
fox-like attributes.

The fox sparrows come to us as winter visitors in the South, about the first of November, and leave us sometime about mid-March. They are much more abundant in some years than in others. They have come to our garden in flocks, remaining for a few days, but last year we saw no flocks here, though we could always count on finding one or two birds about the yard, the garden, or the edge of the woodland. They feed with the white-throats and juncos, and are easily told apart.

As the name suggests, the fox sparrow's upper parts are reddish brown, brightest on lower back, wings, and tail. The whitish under parts are heavily streaked and spotted with reddish brown, and the lower mandible is yellowish. Measuring over seven inches, the fox is easily the largest of the sparrows.

A fine vocalist, he brings cheer to our garden, especially on damp or cloudy days of late February or early March. Perhaps he realizes that on such days his song is needed more. Though his usual note is but a feeble *'tseep*, when excited his notes are louder and sharper. The song has a fullness of power and a richness of tone that seem to hold a promise of awakening spring.

Although he feeds largely on weed and grass seeds, when it comes to scratching among the dead leaves and rubbish of a garden or woodland, the fox sparrow is as energetic a scratcher as any hen or thrasher. In this way he finds insects with which to vary his seed diet.

Breeding beyond the United States northward as far as the tree limit in northeastern Alaska, the bird is known to the South only as a winter resident, ranging at that time from the lower Ohio and Potomac valleys to central Texas and northern Florida.

The nest is said to be of coarse grasses lined with finer grasses, hair, moss, and feathers, and may be on the ground, in low bushes, or in small trees. The four to five pale bluish eggs are heavily blotched with brown.

A red-letter day, indeed, is the fall day in which we may look out among our hedges, in the garden, along the roadside, or at the edge of our woodland, and see again the colorful little red sparrow that may be bringing us woodland greetings from some remote northern field or forest.

THE SWAMP SPARROW LIKES PATCHES OF SWAMP AND WHILE IN THE SOUTH MAY ALSO BE FOUND IN FIELDS OF BROOM SEDGE. ABOUT ONE-HALF NATURAL SIZE.

THE SWAMP SPARROW

Swamp sparrows are common throughout the central and eastern portions of the southern states in winter. They like the patches of marsh containing low bushes, where, when alarmed, they can find cover quickly. They are also seen in the southern mountain regions.

The swamp sparrow may be distinguished from the song sparrow, with which it is sometimes confused, by its much darker upper parts, unstreaked breast, and entirely different notes. For the notes, quite unlike those of the song sparrow, do resemble somewhat the sharp *cheep* of the white-throat. In summer the swamp sparrow has a chestnut crown and black forehead, but while in the South in winter, the head is streaked with black, reddish, and grayish, and the breast is washed with brownish. In size it is slightly smaller than the English sparrow.

Nesting from Pennsylvania northward to Labrador, the swamp sparrow winters from the Ohio valley south to the Gulf coast, and from central Florida to Mexico. Like the nest of the song sparrow, the swamp sparrow's is generally found on the ground. The four to five eggs are white, or bluish white, with reddish brown markings, and the nesting period is in May.

XXI

THE VESPER AND OTHER SPARROWS

THE VESPER SPARROW

Upon a pasture stone,
　　Against the fading west,
A small bird sings alone,
　　Then dives and finds its nest.

The evening star has heard
　　And flutters into sight.
O, childhood's vesper bird
　　My heart calls back, "Good night."
　　　　　　—Edith M. Thomas.

This is the sparrow which conducts the evening service of the birds, and it is from the sweet, vesper-like quality of the song that the bird gets the name of vesper sparrow. For, though this bird sings in early morning and occasionally through the day, he is at his best late in the evening, when most birds are quiet. In the stillness of the twilight his songs rings out sweet and clear, *chewee, chewee, pira, lira, lira, lira*. Peace and gentleness steal into the heart on the wings of his song.

The distinguishing marks of the vesper sparrow are the white outer tail-feathers, and the reddish wing coverts, which easily make him known among his small brown cousins. The upper parts are brownish gray, streaked with black; the under parts are white, and the breast and sides are streaked with black or dark brown. The bird is almost as large as the English sparrow.

The vesper's breeding range is from the mountains of North Carolina northward and west to the plains, and

[106]

THE VESPER SPARROW CONDUCTS THE VESPER SERVICE OF THE BIRDS. ITS WHITE OUTER TAIL-FEATHERS HELP TO IDENTIFY IT. ABOUT ONE-HALF NATURAL SIZE.

in some of the higher mountains of the southern Appalachians; it winters from Virginia south to the Gulf coast and west to middle Texas.

As there is less variation in the vesper's song than in that of the field sparrow, so also is there less variation in its nesting habits. The nest is always built on the ground, usually at the foot of a small bush or weed, and is composed of grass with a lining of hair. The four to five eggs are pale bluish or pinkish white, speckled with reddish brown.

In the South, where they are known mainly as winter birds, they are likely to be found in open fields or high pasture lands, or dry fields along dusty roadsides. While walking country lanes or dirt roads, you may see a small, streaked-brownish bird running rapidly ahead of you. It does not let you get too close, and as you approach, it will spring up and off it goes, showing the distinctive white outer tail-feathers—and then you know you have seen the vesper sparrow.

Although a terrestrial bird, the vesper is by no means a ground sparrow only. For song, he generally prefers an elevated perch and then seems to forget himself entirely in his concert, which, loud and clear, can be heard for some little distance. The song resembles somewhat that of the song sparrow, but it is sweeter and more plaintive. On rare occasions you may be fortunate enough to hear the vesper during its flight-song.

The flight-song is not the gift of many of our birds. Something like only a dozen species are known as having this wing-song, or song of ecstasy. The song seems to spring from some more intense excitement and self-abandonment than the ordinary song delivered from the perch. When the point of rapture is reached the bird is literally carried off its feet, and up it goes into the air, pouring out its song as a rocket pours out its sparks. The skylark of England habitually does this, as do our own vesper, bobolink, horned lark, pipit, and occasionally a few others of our birds.

THE SAVANNAH SPARROW

The Savannah, one of the most abundant of the sparrows in its more northern range, winters in the South, and usually can be found in small numbers in almost any grassy situation. In various parts of the South, especially along the coast, it is a common winter bird.

The Savannah sparrow is a trifle smaller than the English sparrow and has brownish drab upper parts streaked with black, and whitish under parts streaked with black or reddish wedge-shaped spots. There is a pale yellow spot above the eye and another on the bend of the wing; in winter the plumage of both the adults and the young is slightly suffused with a yellow tinge.

A shy bird, hiding close in the grass until flushed, it will sometimes startle one by springing up, almost from under foot, with a whir of wings.

IN THE SOUTH THE SAVANNAH SPARROW IS A SHY BIRD, HIDING IN THE GRASS UNTIL FLUSHED. THEN IT MAY SPRING UP ALMOST FROM UNDER YOUR VERY FEET AND FLY OFF WITH A GREAT WHIR OF WINGS. ABOUT THREE-FIFTHS NATURAL SIZE.

The breeding range is from the northern states northward. The nest, built on the ground, is of grasses, sometimes of moss, lined with finer grasses or hair. Laid usually in May, the four to five bluish white eggs are thickly marked with reddish brown.

The song is an insignificant and weak little musical trill that cannot be heard unless one is close by. Towards sunset the bird sings a bit louder, the males having several favorite perches from which they sometimes sing.

BACHMAN'S SPARROW

The Bachman's, a distinctly southern species of our native sparrows, breeds throughout sections of the South, and winters from southern North Carolina south into Florida, where it is rather common, especially in pine woods undergrown with turkey oaks.

Slightly smaller than the English sparrow, it has reddish, dark streaked upper parts, with yellow at the bend of the wing, and light brownish buff under parts. The nest, usually built on the ground, is either domed or cylindrical, with the opening well hidden on the side. Grass alone is used in its construction, with grass tops for a lining. The three to four white eggs are usually laid in May.

The Bachman's sparrow is an excellent singer, the song being something like that of the cardinal. Of this song, Bradford Torrey, a northern bird lover spending his spring vacation in Tennessee in order to become familiar with southern birds, wrote: "That one dingy, shabbily clad little genius might almost have repaid me for my thousand miles on the rail."

XXII

THE CARDINAL

One bright morning, loud and clear,
Its whistle smote my drowsy ear,
Ten times repeated, till the sound
Filled every echoing niche around;
And all things earliest loved by me,—
The bird, the brook, the flower, the tree—
Came back again, as thus I heard
    The cardinal bird.
        —WILLIAM DAVIS GALLAGHER.

THERE is an old adage to the effect that "Beauty is its own undoing." In the past this has been far too true of the cardinal, our flaming redbird of the South, which used to be trapped and caged to send to Europe as a "Virginia Nightingale"; and, I am ashamed to add, was also hunted and killed because women thought his feathers used as hat trimmings added to their own adornment. Today, a more humane and thoughtful generation sees that the cardinal is protected by law.

Our redbird, whose range is the eastern United States, but which is rare except in the South, is too familiar to every southerner to need much of a description. His bright rosy coat, black throat, with black about the base of the bill, his conspicuous red crest and bill, are known and loved throughout the South. The crest, wings, tail, and bill of the female are a duller rose, and the upper parts are ashy-brown, sometimes tinged with rose. A friend recently gave the best description of her that I know: "She looks as if she wore a chiffon veil over her rose dress."

And that is exactly what she does look like. At first

one thinks of the female cardinal as being plainer than the male, but after living with them both, seeing them day by day, against gray skies, snowy landscapes, green pines, and summer bloom, I find myself delighting more and more in her delicate beauty.

CARDINALS IN A COLONIAL GARDEN

On a snowy winter day in old Williamsburg, Virginia, I saw my largest flock of cardinals. Before that, I had thought two or three, or a family group in one's garden, was bird wealth untold. Driving by an old colonial home on Nichols Street, I saw this large flock in an ancient garden. Later, walking by, I saw them again, and feeling that anyone who managed to entice such a large flock of cardinals must also be a bird lover, and would forgive intrusion, I knocked at the door. Williamsburg, under the "Restoration," must have much of that, but if so, its people are more than friendly to the stranger within its gates.

After explaining my interest in birds, I was asked to enter, and we sat in an ancient room, full of beautiful old furniture that would make any lover of antiques worshipful—and almost forgetful of birds. In front of the small-paned window was a great hackberry tree, one Japanese-like branch extending across the panes. While we sat and talked there were always from one to three or four cardinals, both male and female, on the snow-covered branch. No artist could have created a more perfect setting or background—and I added another to my bird-memory pictures.

I myself had counted fifteen cardinals in the group, but my hostess said they had often counted twenty-five. They are there the year round, for it is an old, old garden, with trees, grass, flowers, shrubbery, and many of the tangled growths so loved by birds—and is far more

CARDINAL
Upper Figure, Male; Lower Figure, Female

Order—PASSERES   Family—FRINGILLIDÆ
Genus—CARDINALIS   Species—CARDINALIS

(About one-half natural size)

National Association of Audubon Societies

TOWHEE
(Upper figure, female; lower figure, male)

Order—PASSERES   Family—FRINGILLIDÆ
Genus—PIPILO   Species—ERYTHROPHTHALMUS

National Association of Audubon Societies

picturesque than the more formal gardens that have been restored.

The birds are given every protection possible from dogs and cats; they are supplied with water, and with all sorts of berry-bearing shrubs. They are fed also with suet, grains, nuts—with all kinds of foods that are loved by birds and, what was then new to me, doughnuts!

Since my return, I, too, have put doughnuts out, and the birds love them. For that was where I first learned that doughnuts were the best possible "open sesame" to Birddom.

SCARLET WEDDING

There are always two or three cardinals in our own woods and garden. Towards spring the female accompanies the male more frequently, and we begin to hear soft murmurings of *pretty! pretty!*—and know that a little later there will be another scarlet wedding in our garden.

Several years ago our first pair of cardinals went to housekeeping in our Silver Moon rose, and the male was the most devoted one I have known. He divided his time between swaying high above the nest on the topmost spray, where he sang to his mate of his love and care, and perching on the rim of the bird bath, where, before drinking or bathing, he would pause, Narcissus-like, to gaze with an air of satisfaction at his scarlet reflection.

But it was well that he had that short time of rest, for though this cardinal was a vain spouse, he was a devoted one. Later in the season he nursed the first brood while his mate was busy with her second sitting.

He appeared most conscientious and a bit worried, apparently thinking all the world was in a conspiracy against his birdlings. The little ash-brown-washed-with-rose babies, which resembled the mother, were very beautiful in Papa Cardinal's eyes. How proud he was the first time he succeeded in coaxing them up to the rim of the bath! Forgotten then were all his own airs and graces, and throwing back his head he loudly whistled *pretty! pretty! pretty!* as if confiding to his near-by mate, "See, Mama, how smart our babies are!"

In contrast to our first nesting cardinals were this year's (1933) early nesting pair, which again built in the Silver Moon rose. They must have been different birds, for there was apparently little devotion between them. We saw the male about only occasionally, nor did he feed his mate so attentively.

The female left the nest each time the porch door was opened. Never, in all my years of bird study, have I seen a bird brood less than this one. We were unable to figure out how the eggs were ever incubated, but all were fruitful and the young nestlings throve. Later in the year there was another nest, probably by the same pair.

Shrubbery is the cardinal's chosen haunt, and the more tangled it is the better he likes it; but for his song he usually prefers a topmost branch. The nest is made of weed stems and leaves, and is usually lined with grass. It is built in a low bush, small tree, clump of bushes, or hedge, and often is but two to four feet from the ground, though all of ours have been higher, the last nest being over twelve feet up. There are usually three, sometimes four eggs, with a white ground, marked with reddish brown.

Nesting may begin as early as April and may continue until early July. More than one brood is raised, the male taking care of the first brood while the female is busy with her second. Family groups often stay together throughout the winter, and this probably accounts for the large number of cardinals in the Williamsburg garden.

TWO BROODS TO OBSERVE

We felt that we were particularly fortunate the past summer, for two broods of cardinals were raised within a few feet of the house. As there was a sufficient interval between nestings, we were sure they were by the same pair.

During the weeks that followed we watched the development of the two different age-groups. We saw the three of the first brood leave the nest. Already a bit of rose was discernible on the wings, but there was no tail, only a stub.

For over a week we were able to locate the three young birds daily in our woods, and to watch the stubs gradually develop into first a hint, then a promise, and eventually a real tail. We also observed the gradual coloring of the bill. Dark at first, slowly it lightened, and then passed into stages of purple, raspberry, and at last red.

For several weeks the crests remained ashy, with no hint of color, but toward the end of the third month a bit of rose began to appear at the base of the crest, and gradually deepened and crept up. The breasts of the young males began to show streaks of rose, until they gave promise of being as handsome Beau Brummels as their fathers.

The whistled call of *pretty! pretty! pretty!* is heard through much of the year, and is rather similar to—and sometimes mistaken for—the tufted titmouse's whistled call of *peto! peto! peto!* A more complete song begins early in March and continues, with a few interruptions, until September. James Lane Allen, who has immortalized this bird in his story, *The Kentucky Cardinal* (the cardinal is the state bird of Kentucky), calls its song "a most melodious sigh." The female is herself a charming singer; to some her song is more pleasing than that of the male.

It would seem that a bird which gives us so much of color and beauty and song need not have any other assets, but the cardinal is of decided economic importance. "This bird has a record," says a government bulletin, "of feeding on many of the worst agricultural pests, including cotton-boll worm, codling moth, cotton cut worm, cucumber beetles, grasshoppers, scale insects, rose chafers, and various weed seeds, especially smartweeds, bindweeds, bur, crab grass, thistle, plaintain." It also eats such berries as dogwood, holly, hackberries, elderberries, poke berries, wild cherries, sumac. Little, if any, attention is paid to cultivated fruits.

XXIII

THE TOWHEE, OR CHEWINK

The flirting chewink calls his dear
Behind a bush.
—VAN DYKE.

A BIRD which intrigued Thomas Jefferson when he was president, and about which he wrote to Alexander Wilson, the ornithologist, was the towhee. To Jefferson it was a "curious bird," which he had heard often, but which he had never seen clearly. "I have followed it for miles without ever but once getting a good view of it. It is of the size and make of a mockingbird, lightly thrush-colored on the back, and grayish-white on the breast and belly."

His son-in-law had a specimen which had been shot by a neighbor, and he pronounced it a flycatcher, which, of course, was entirely wrong.

From the description of the bird, it was evidently the female which Jefferson had seen. At that time the bird was familiarly called the "ground-robin," for because of its size—(though it is a trifle smaller)—its reddish sides, and its being a ground bird, it resembles the robin somewhat.

But there is no family connection, for the robin is a thrush and the towhee is a finch, first cousin to the sparrows, belonging to the same family, the *Fringillidae*. It is one of the larger birds of that family.

The male towhee is black with chestnut sides and white belly, and is tan colored under the tail, which is long and black, the side feathers being tipped with white.

The bird is about eight and one-half inches in length. The female is similar, but is reddish brown where the male is black. The iris of the eye of both birds is red— hence the name "red-eyed towhee."

For in birds the iris may be of many different colors, even red, as in the red-eyed towhee and the red-eyed vireo; or white, as in the white-eyed towhee and the white-eyed vireo. A few birds have blue, or green eyes, but the vast majority have either black, or some shade of brown or yellow.

The towhee breeds in the mountains and near the coast of Carolina, and west of Raleigh it is generally a permanent resident. North of North Carolina it is generally known as a summer bird, and south of it, as a winter bird, arriving about the first of October, and leaving in early May. It is more abundant in the South during migration.

Deriving its name from the various interpretations of its different calls, it is known as joree, joreeper, chewink, and, in the far South, especially Louisiana, it is known as grasel. Because it is so much on the ground, it is also called ground-robin. The male is more conspicuously marked than most ground birds, for though the under parts are the color of the dead leaves he scratches among, the glossy black back is rather startling. However, he seems to keep himself screened from view rather well.

The female on the nest is, on the other hand, an excellent example of protective coloring in Nature, for her brown back, matching the dead leaves and materials of which the outside of the nest is made, keeps her safe from sight. So much so, in fact, that the nest is difficult to find. Speaking of these nests, Audubon, the great naturalist, wrote: "Some of the nests of the species are so well concealed that in order to discover them one requires to stand quite still on the first appearance of the mother. I have, myself, several times had to regret not taking this precaution.'' By which he meant, probably, that he had stepped on some nests.

The nest, a rather poor affair, is made externally of dead leaves and strips of bark, lined with finer grasses, and is usually on the ground where it is within reach of dogs, cats, snakes, weasels, and other enemies that are more adept at finding it than are people. Occasionally towhee builds in a thick bush. The four to five eggs are thickly spotted with reddish brown. The back and under parts of the nestlings are streaked with black, showing their sparrow relationship, for all sparrows have streaked breasts sometime in their life history. Those that do not have streaks as adults, have them as young or in the female plumage.

Like many other birds, the towhee is imposed upon by the parasite cowbird; yet why, when the towhee is a fairly large and strong bird, it does not tumble the intruder's egg out of the nest is a question. Instead, the cowbird's egg is allowed to remain, often at the cost of the lives or development of the young towhees.

A thicket-loving bird, the towhee is fonder of second growth and scrub, or bushy pastures, than of woods. It is a most energetic scratcher and in action resembles a hen at her busiest. No other bird, unless it be the brown thrasher or the wood thrush, can so make the leaves and rubbish fly in its search for seeds and insects.

Nervous and shy, the towhee is quick to slip out of sight; but it is also a wise bird in that it never flies straight to or from its nest. Nor is it graceful in flight; rather it is hurried, jerky, and heavy, as if it were far more used to being on the ground.

However, like many other birds, the towhee grows more sociable in winter. A pair usually spends the winter in the garden or about the shrubbery, or along the edge of our bit of woodland at Woodhaven. We see them off and on all through the season, busily scratching, as if life depended on their industry, as, of course, it does.

Of this scratching habit, a government bulletin states: "In scratching for its dinner like a hen, the towhee overturns dead leaves in its search for hibernating beetles and larvae. The good it does in this way can hardly be over-estimated, since the death of a single insect at this time, before it has had an opportunity to deposit its eggs, is equivalent to the destruction of a host later in the year."

Never singing while on the ground, the towhee will flap his wings and flirt his tail and call *towhee* or *chewhee*. When ready for song he mounts a perch—almost always the topmost branch of the bush or tree—and there gives himself, heart and soul, to his song, which some think sounds like *whe-chu, weedle-deedle-de,* but which Ernest Thompson Seton interprets as *chuck-burr, pill-a-will-a-will-a.*

THE WHITE-EYED TOWHEE

Found in summer along the coastal country from southern North Carolina to southern Florida, the white-eyed towhee is similar in coloring and marking to the red-eyed. It has a little less white on its wings and tail, and the adult male has a white iris. It is a shyer bird than its more northern cousin. It is said the two species do not associate. The white-eyed is generally found in heavy growths of scrub palmetto.

XXIV

THE GOLDFINCH

Sometimes goldfinches one by one will drop
From low-hung branches; little space they stop,
But sip, and twitter, and their feathers sleek,
Then off at once, as in a wanton freak;
Or perhaps to show their black and golden wings,
Pausing upon their yellow flutterings.

—JOHN KEATS.

AFTER OUR ragged robins have begun to go to seed, they seem to burst, at times, into a miraculous second blooming. Mischievous garden elves must have been at work, for their bloom is no longer blue or pink, or white or purple, but gold and black. This bit of garden alchemy is performed by the goldfinches, or thistle-birds, which come to feed and swing airily on the swaying stalks. The golden birds fill the garden with color and song, and as we watch their peculiar, wavy flight from one stalk to another, where they settle softly down like a bit of golden fluff, we think they are rightly called "thistle-birds."

It is a bit difficult to realize that these dainty winged jewels of gold and jet are related to the plain sparrow family. Yet they, too, belong to the *Fringillidae,* the largest of all bird families, which includes, besides the sparrows, the more colorful finches and grosbeaks. This really makes such different looking and acting birds as the cardinal, the blue grosbeak, the goldfinch, the purple finch, and the plain little chippy and song sparrow, all members of the same family.

On the other hand, the cardinal and the red summer tanager, which look so much alike, have no family connection whatever, nor have the blue grosbeak and the bluebird, nor the goldfinch and the yellow warbler. Relationship, as I have said before, depends not on color or size, but on similarity in the formation of the bodies.

Like all sparrows and finches, the goldfinch has the common, distinguishing feature of the conical bill, stout at the base and pointed at the tip, with the corners of the mouth drawn sharply downward.

About an inch smaller than the English sparrow, the goldfinch is a canary yellow, with a black crown, black tail and wings with white-tipped coverts and yellow lesser wing coverts. The tail feathers also have white on the inner vanes, but this does not show when the tail is closed.

The female lacks the black crown, and is more yellowish brown above, and a lighter yellow below. Her wings and tail are less black than those of the male.

In the postnuptial moult, about October, the male loses his gay "cloth-of-gold" coat, and through the winter resembles closely his duller mate and the young. This plumage is worn until the spring, when he, like the scarlet tanager, moults the body feathers, and comes out quite a gay fellow. Then indeed

> "The thistle birds have changed their dun
> For yellow coats, to match the sun."

The goldfinch breeds from about middle Canada to northern Georgia and winters through much of its breeding range, and south to the Gulf coast. In North Carolina it is resident except in the east, where it is only a winter visitor. In Alabama it is a common migrant and winter resident over most of the state, and a moderately common breeder in the northern part.

Because of its color and food habits the goldfinch has many names, including yellowbird, lettuce-bird, thistle-bird. And because it is related to the canary, closely resembling it in color, form, song, and habits, it is often known as wild canary.

In sections of the country where thistles grow in profusion, that plant is its greatest favorite, the seeds furnishing both food and nesting material. The bird is extremely fond of the tiny seed attached to the parachute-like down, and with the down he, or rather she, makes downy beds for her babies.

It may be, as some naturalists believe, because of their love of certain seeds, and their desire for a fine down bed for the fledglings, that they wait so long before nesting. Other birds are busy feeding awkward young ones, or even with a second brood, before goldfinches think of housekeeping. Attired in gay color, and with sweet dreamy songs that last through this period, they have a long courtship and honeymoon. And when they finally do settle down to the more humdrum existence of home life and family, they seem quite happy about it. Perhaps it is because they have had such a long, care-free play-time.

The nesting period is usually from late June through August, which is much later than most other small birds breed. The nest is a dainty, compact structure of fine grasses, strips of bark and moss, thickly lined with thistledown or other plant down. It may be in trees or bushes, from five to thirty feet up. The three to six eggs are pale bluish white and are almost always unspotted, though occasionally some have obscure freckles, showing the relationship to other members of the family, for most sparrows lay spotted eggs. According to Dr. A. A. Allen, this faint spotting is a reversion, or atavism, the individual female bird having inherited the pigment-forming glands from some remote ancestor, its own mother probably not having them.

The female builds the nest, the male encouraging her

the while. During this period he is a gay little minstrel in gold and jet, singing while he flies as well as while at rest—and voicing his approval of her more prosaic labors.   But he feeds her while she is incubating and helps take care of the young.   Though it is generally conceded that the male does not incubate, one naturalist writes that she once saw a male on the nest being fed by a female, but although she observed closely, she did not see the performance repeated.   Perhaps the male bird thought he would give domesticity a trial, but finding it too confining for a gay young minstrel like himself, decided not to repeat it.

POLLYANNAS OF BIRDDOM

Except during the nesting period, the goldfinches are generally found in small flocks, and few birds seem to enjoy life more.   Each month brings them a tasty and exciting change-of-fare, from the dandelion seeds of early spring, the grass seeds of early summer; and the garden flowers, such as ragged robins, coreopsis, calliopsis, and especially sunflowers; the thistles of later summer, the zinnia and marigolds and cosmos; and the composites of fall, the goldenrods, asters, and such, many of which retain their seeds until well through the winter.

These birds also do a great service in keeping down weeds.   They are particularly fond of the "seed-sails," the tiny seeds attached to a bit of fluff which acts as a parachute, carrying the seeds of plants like the thistle or dandelion far away so that they spread rapidly.   The goldfinch also eats many insects, including canker-worms, plant lice, and beetles.

Expressive of their buoyant, joyous nature, is their wavy flight as they bound through the air calling *per-chic-o-ree, per-chic-o-ree,* which some children interpret as *wait-for-me, wait-for-m*e. Goldfinches do not fly straight, but jerkily, constantly dropping down and lifting up. The song, as well as the call-notes and the alarm-notes, has a canary-like character, with a wilder ringing, though less varied, quality.

They even sing merrily at times through the fall and winter, as they fly in flocks about gardens and fields gathering seeds. Even though their gleaming yellow coats are gone, they are easily recognized by their wavy, dipping flight.

In our own garden we feel Croesus-like when we see four or five of these golden birds, but recently, in a friend's garden in Chapel Hill, we saw a flock of over thirty feeding on poppy and ragged robin seeds. But the best memory picture of all is on a northern country road, where, as a child, I was driving with my father. We passed a field taken over by thistles, and as something startled the horse, it neighed loudly. Up from the thistle-sown fields, on both sides of the road, rose a veritable golden, black-flecked cloud, as several hundred goldfinches mounted in the air, singing. I think that picture and experience started my interest in birds. I had not realized before that birds could be so beautiful, or so plentiful. Later, in a book by a New England naturalist, I read about "collecting" birds in the memory instead of specimens in the bag. And that picture, of a northern field sun-flecked with goldfinches rising on wings of song, ranks first of my many "memory-chain" pictures.

Nor are our goldfinches beautiful to us alone. Years ago, when the distinguished Scotch ornithologist, the Duke of Argyll, published his impressions of this country, he wrote he had "hardly been more interested in the 'glories of Niagara' than in the golden finch which I first saw while looking out of my hotel window at the great cataract."

XXV

THE PURPLE FINCH AND SOME COUSINS

In winter time he comes and goes;
　　Defies Jack Frost
And, 'mid the hindering snows,
　　He seeks his meagre food.

In spring he flits on buoyant wings,
　　Or in his rosy coat
He sits above his nest and sings
　　Ecstatic love songs, early and late,
　　To cheer his brooding mate,
And stir the hearts of listening men.
　　　　　　　—ALBERT W. SMITH.

THE PURPLE finch isn't really purple. A mistake in coloring an early picture gave him this name. The streaked body of the male, when in full plumage, is suffused with rosy or raspberry red, brightest on the head, rump, and breast, more brownish on the back, and whitish on the belly. The wings and tail are brownish.

The female and the young birds strongly resemble some sparrows, but may be distinguished from them by the forked tail, the heavy rounded bill, and the tuft of feathers over the nostrils.

Young male finches wear this sparrow-like dress slightly diffused with rose until the second year, for the rose-suffused plumage is not acquired until then.

Sometimes the adult male finch ruffles or bristles the feathers on his crown until they resemble a crest, and because of this, and his rosy coloring, he has been mistaken by enthusiastic new bird students, for "a baby cardinal, and *in winter!*"

In spite of the bright coloring, and the fact that it is most commonly found in small flocks, the purple finch is not so well known as it should be in the South, or in any

THE PURPLE FINCH IS NOT PURPLE, BUT ITS PLUMAGE IS SUFFUSED WITH ROSY-RED, WHICH IS DEEPEST ON BREAST, HEAD, AND RUMP. ITS HEAVY ROUND BILL AND ITS HABIT OF BRISTLING THE FEATHERS ON ITS CROWN RE-MIND SOME PEOPLE OF A TINY EDITION OF A CARDINAL. ABOUT ONE-HALF NATURAL SIZE.

other part of its range. Doubtless this is because of the bird's tendency to keep largely to the tree-tops, where identification, especially if the observer is without field glasses, is difficult.

Though an irregular winter visitor in many sections of the South, the purple finch may possibly breed in the higher mountains. In central Carolina, it usually comes late in October, and may remain until mid-April or even May. In some parts of the South it is better known as a fall and spring migrant than as a winter visitor.

The range of this "rosy" finch is eastern North America, breeding from our northern states northward —with a few breeding in the higher Appalachians. Most of these birds winter from north of the southern limit of their breeding range, and sometimes to the Gulf coast and Florida.

WANDERING FLOCKS

Of a naturally roving disposition, these birds, especially the small flocks of the South, are seldom seen in the same place twice. Last winter a small flock settled in our large "Breath o' Spring" bush and began eating the flower buds, for these birds are confirmed bud and blossom eaters. However, they created such a beautiful picture, the rosy-hued birds among the dainty white blossoms, that we could not begrudge them a few buds and flowers. Moreover, this pruning of buds, blossoms, and seeds of trees is not, as a rule, excessive. On the other hand, these birds eat many of the seeds of the most destructive weeds, ragweed being a favorite. They also destroy many orchard and woodland caterpillars, and are particularly destructive to plant lice, canker-worms, and some ground beetles and cutworms. They also eat the seeds of various weeds, and of tulips, mulberries, beech-nuts, thorn apples, frost grapes, ash, elm, and sycamore.

Another time, while walking through a weed-grown field, we saw a small flock of these purple finches, in company with some dun-colored goldfinches, feeding on weed seeds. When we approached too closely, they quickly flew to the tree-tops.

While in the South, these birds often try to sing,

especially when they first come in the fall, and before they leave in the spring; but they are in the full power of their song only during the nesting period, when they take their place as outstanding song birds. At this period several males, in near-by trees, will often sing in concert, the song being somewhat suggestive of the robin's. Once, in a woodland bordering Lake George, in northern New York, I heard such a concert.

The flight call is a *creak, creak,* coming faintly from above, and only distinguishable when all is very quiet.

Resembling somewhat that of the chippy, the nest of the purple finch is usually found in coniferous trees, at a height of from five to thirty feet. It is constructed of twigs, grasses, and rootlets, thickly lined with long hairs. The four to six eggs are greenish blue spotted with dark brown, and resemble the eggs of the chippy, although they are larger.

Seeming to have a wide variety in the choice of nesting sites, these birds may be found in trees in private grounds, thus becoming familiar garden birds; or they may prefer a home in some remote mountain forest.

In the parts of the South where they are more common during migration than during the winter, they are often seen visiting blossoming shrubs and fruit, maple, and elm trees. While feeding on the buds and flowers, they indulge in a medley of music, a soft warbling that, coming from blossoming trees or tall shrubs, is the very essence of spring.

PINE SISKIN

One winter afternoon, while taking a favorite walk that leads through woods and meadows, by a winding stream and a marsh, and comes out at an old mill-stream —we were suddenly showered, from above, by tiny golden parachutes.

Looking up, we saw that we were under a tulip tree, and the tiny whirling wings were the samara-like carpels from the narrow cones of the tree. Through the glasses we could see a flock of small brownish birds—which we judged to be pine siskins—apparently busily pecking at the seeds at the end of the carpels in the cones. For each seed they extricated to eat, several were loosened and came whirling down and furnished our golden cloud.

THE PINE SISKIN IS A VISITOR FROM THE FAR NORTH WHICH LIKES THE SEEDS OF OUR PINES, CEDARS, TULIP TREES, AND BIRCHES. ABOUT TWO-THIRDS NATURAL SIZE.

Like the purple finches, pine siskins are irregular winter visitors through many parts of the South, though some probably breed in the higher mountains. They are sparrowish-looking birds, the plumage being streaked with brown, and, in the breeding season, suffused with yellow.

Their range is northern North America, breeding northward, and wintering, occasionally, to the south as far as northern Mexico. They seem to be abundant in certain sections in some winters, and very rare, or entirely lacking, in others.

And like their cousins, the purple finches, the pine siskins while here also go in flocks, feeding on various seeds and berries, including those of thistle, dandelion, ragweed, tulip, alder, pine, cedar, birch, maple, fir, and larch. Their movements are very erratic; they, too, may be here today and gone tomorrow.

The nest is said to be built in coniferous trees, about twenty-five feet from the ground, and is of grasses and pine needles lined with hair, feathers, and fine rootlets. The three or four greenish white or pale bluish eggs are faintly marked with brown.

In habit these birds resemble somewhat other cousins of theirs, the goldfinches, but they remain in more closely massed flocks and lack the cheery musical notes. They share somewhat the goldfinch's wavy flight and fondness for thistle seeds, and their song is said to resemble in some ways that of the wild canary.

THE CROSSBILLS AND THE REDPOLL

A curious bird, with crossed mandibles, which give it its name, is the American crossbill. Very erratic in its movements and habits, this bird breeds in late winter or early spring, sometimes before the snow is off the ground. Though the breeding range is in the far North—with a few breeding in the higher Appalachians of the southern states—the bird occasionally nests far south of its regular breeding range. The winter home is irregularly

South, occasionally as far as northern Texas, Louisiana, and Florida.

The male crossbill is a dull red; the female brownish washed with greenish yellow. Traveling in small flocks, these curious birds feed on various seeds, their peculiarly crossed bills being well adapted for the purpose of tearing pine cones apart to get at the seeds. One way to find these birds is to watch for the falling scales of the cones; when you see them whirling down, turn your glasses upwards and you may be fortunate enough to see the crossbills.

In general habits the white-winged crossbill resembles the other crossbill, but is somewhat duller in coloring. It is known only as a rare winter visitor in the upper South. Another occasional winter visitor from the far North is the redpoll. The male redpoll has a red crown, rump, throat, and breast, and the back, wings, and tail are reddish brown. This bird, too, wanders in flocks, and during a severe winter in the North, may drift southward in search of food. In habits, it somewhat resembles its cousin, the goldfinch.

XXVI

THE ENGLISH SPARROW, AN UNWELCOME FOREIGNER

So dainty in plumage and hue,
  A study in grey and in brown,
How little, how little we knew
  The pest he would prove to the town!
From dawn till daylight grow dim,
  Perpetual chatter and scold.
No winter migration for him,
  Not even afraid of the cold!
Scarce a songbird he fails to molest,
  Belligerent, meddlesome thing!
Wherever he goes as a guest
  He is sure to remain as a King.
          —MARY ISABELLA FORSYTH.

THE ENGLISH, or house sparrow is an excellent example of the folly of upsetting the balance of Nature by bringing into our country a foreign plant or animal without first making a scientific study of it in its natural habitat.

In England, it was claimed by some, this sparrow ate both insects and seeds, and did some good by eating certain tree-worms. This, however, was never made sure of scientifically before the bird was introduced here. On the other hand, there are many claims that the English sparrow is as great a nuisance in Europe as it is here.

It seems that just before the middle of the nineteenth century the trees in some of the eastern cities were being eaten by canker-worms, and some one suggested that English sparrows be imported to destroy them. The birds were duly brought over, introduced in Brooklyn in 1851, and it is said that for a time they did eat the worms, and they remained in or near the cities. For about twenty years there were several subsequent importations of

THE ENGLISH SPARROW IS A NOISY, FOREIGN BIRD, A STREET GAMIN WHO HAS
INVADED OUR ENTIRE COUNTRY. ABOUT ONE-HALF NATURAL SIZE.

sparrows, until, in the 1870's, people began to wake up
to the mistake that had been made.

In its European home this sparrow may be a useful
citizen—that is still a disputed question—and there it is
held somewhat in check by natural enemies, food lim-
itations, and other agents of Nature. But here, where
climatic conditions seem to favor it, where the food supply is almost unlimited, and where, apparently, it has no
natural enemies to hold it in check, it has increased to the
point where we are paying a high price for our ignorance
and indifference of the past.

WHAT PRICE SPARROWS?

For the English sparrows are driving our native song
birds from our towns and villages, and from nesting sites

about our homes. Especially are they in conflict with the bluebirds over nesting sites. At Woodhaven they have driven the bluebirds out of every bluebird house we have erected. The statement by some ornithologists that "sparrows will not build in boxes suspended by wire, nor do they like a box without a perch in front of the entrance hole" may be true in some parts of the country, but in our grounds English sparrows have taken over these boxes as quickly as any others.

Another of the great prices we are paying for the English sparrows is that we are never free from their incessant scolding. Worse still, they often drown out the exquisite chorus of our native song birds.

So familiar and commonplace has the English sparrow become, that it scarcely needs much of a description. The male has a brown, streaked-with-black back, the lower breast and under parts grayish white, with a large black patch on breast and throat, the top of the head gray with a chestnut patch on each side. In winter the gray tips of the feathers nearly conceal the black on throat and breast; by spring these tips wear off, showing the black beneath. The female is an insignificant, bleached-out looking creature, the back being brown, streaked with black and dirty yellow, and the breast, throat, and under parts grayish white.

Many years ago a few observing bird lovers predicted that the English sparrow, being hardy, prolific, and not easily discouraged, would become a serious problem. No successful way of keeping it in check has yet been devised.

Not only are they more prolific and persistent, more quick-witted and aggressive than our native birds, but they seem also to be better able to resist diseases. So prolific are English sparrows that no one seems to know definitely how many broods a year they may have. Often they begin breeding almost before winter is over, and continue into late fall.

NO OUTWITTING THEM

Nothing seems to discourage English sparrows. At least that has been our experience. We have persistently destroyed their nests for years, and yet each year we have several large broods. They like to build in the protected space on each side of our front entrance. One spring day, when I was spending the whole day working in the yard, I determined to war it out with them. As fast as they would begin bringing in nesting material I would tear it down. They would move to the other side and begin again. As I would destroy that, back they would come to the first place, and start all over. This performance was kept up all day, until I had pulled down the beginnings of twenty nesting attempts. For the next three days they kept trying to build there, though I only got out two or three times during the day to destroy their efforts.

I hate to admit it, but in the end it was I who was outwitted. For though eventually the birds gave up trying to build in the entrance porch, they cleverly chose an inaccessible site in the tall pine by the front door. Though the nest was out of reach, it was an untidy structure in plain view and the birds' incessant scolding and chatter could be heard all over the house and garden.

Nests are built in any available place and of any available material, such as grasses, weed stems, trash, and hen's feathers, all mixed together without form or fashion. The four to seven eggs vary from plain white to almost uniform olive brown, but are more likely to be white, finely marked with olive.

Not only are these birds noisy, dirty, and destructive about the place, but they defile buildings with their droppings; and they usurp other birds' nesting sites and drive them out. An even greater count against them is that they destroy the nests and eggs of other birds, at times even thrusting the fledglings out of the nests.

Yet noisy, dirty, and destructive as they are, we must admire their persistence. Had mankind the persistence and determination of the English sparrow, the top rungs of the ladder of success would be crowded for space.

NOT WEED WARRIORS

During the nesting season, and then only, do the English sparrows prey on insects, including weevils, to any extent. Some ornithologists credit the birds with devouring the cabbage-worm. Nor can it be said in their favor that they are weed warriors as are our native sparrows. Instead, they prefer cultivated grains to weed seeds, eating the latter only during periods of scarcity. They flock to grain fields and steal the seed after sowing, and later strip the new grain in the "milk" stage, and even the ripened grain in the sheaf.

As bud and blossom eaters they are also very destructive. Often I have seen them stripping the buds from branch after branch of early blossoming shrubs. If you drive them away, they are back before you are again in the house. They are also destructive of the buds and blossoms of fruit trees.

The range of this sparrow seems to be almost world wide. It is said to be a familiar bird to travelers in Europe and in upper Egypt, as well as in many parts of the Orient, and it has been introduced into Australia and New Zealand. Some idea of how prolific it is may be gained by quoting from a government bulletin which states that the progeny of a single pair might, in ten years, amount to 275,716,983,689.

We must admit that the introduction of the English

sparrow was a grave mistake; that it has overrun the whole country, at the expense of the beauty and the usefulness of our native birds; and that it should be discouraged from nesting around our homes and gardens, and exterminated wherever possible.

The bird is not protected by law. Shooting and trapping seem to be the only safe methods of controlling the pest, but, before starting on any such campaign, make sure that you know the English sparrow and his mate and young. Avoid the danger and high cost of making warfare on our own valuable native sparrows, each and every one of which is a distinct economic asset.

XXVII

THE STARLING, ANOTHER UNWELCOME FOREIGNER

Here's to the stranger, so lately a ranger,
  Who came from far over the seas:—
Whatever the weather, still in high feather,
  At top of the windy trees!

Here's to the darling—brave English starling,
  Stays the long winter through;
He would not leave us, would not bereave us,—
  Not he, though our own birds do!
                              —Edith M. Thomas.

The starling is far from being as popular as when this poem was written, back in the first years of its introduction.

Rapidly extending its range, by now (1933) the starling has spread well over the eastern seaboard, as far north as Quebec, south towards Texas, and westward to the plains. It is confidently expected that this bird will soon be everywhere as commonplace as its unwelcome forerunner, the English sparrow, and with the same disastrous results.

There had been several attempts to introduce the starling at various points in the United States and Canada prior to 1890, but until then none had been successful. That year, sixty birds were released in Central Park, New York City, and the following year, forty more. From these one hundred birds have descended the millions of starlings now inhabiting a large part of the eastern half of the country.

About eight and one-half inches in length, the adult

bird has, in summer, a metallic, or iridescent, purplish, greenish, or bluish plumage. The feathers of the upper parts are tipped with cream-buff spots; those of the under parts are marked only on the sides; and the lower

THE STARLING IS AN UNWELCOME BIRD-FOREIGNER, AND IN SOME SECTIONS OF THE COUNTRY IS EVEN MORE UNPOPULAR THAN THE ENGLISH SPARROW. ABOUT TWO-THIRDS NATURAL SIZE. (WINTER PLUMAGE.)

belly, wings, and tail are a dark brownish gray, edged with creamy buff. The bill is yellow. Aside from their color, the starlings may be known by their long pointed wings and short square tail, and by their jerky walk, instead of hop.

Adult starlings have a single, full, annual moult in late summer, which is complete by the middle of September, leaving the starling a much changed bird. The nuptial plumage of early spring is acquired by wear and fading.

The late summer moult leaves both adults and immature birds looking rather similar, the upper parts being heavily spotted with buff, and the entire under parts with white. After the breeding season, and at the same time as the moult, the yellow bill of summer darkens until it is nearly black.

Belonging to the family *Sturnidae,* the starlings are the only representative of their family in America, and that, as we have said, is by artificial introduction. The sixty species of true starlings are distributed throughout the eastern hemisphere, with the exception of Australia and New Guinea.

The starling has many economic factors in its favor, a government bulletin listing it in the ranks of birds most beneficial to agriculture. "It is an effective destroyer of terrestrial insects, including such pests as cutworms, caterpillars, grasshoppers, weevils, crickets, locusts and army worms." It has been discovered recently that it is the most efficient natural enemy of the Japanese beetle. In spite of all this, most bird lovers feel that any bird which takes the place of our native birds is unwelcome.

And the starling, like the English sparrow, does just that. Moreover, its enormous increase and rapid spread, its quarrelsome nature, gregarious habits, and large, noisy filthy roosts—often in the heart of cities—make it unpopular. Its conflict over nesting sites with other birds—especially the beloved bluebird, the purple martin, the crested flycatcher, and the flicker—and its destructiveness to fruit crops, more than outweigh any good it may do.

ALREADY A PROBLEM IN FRUIT-GROWING SECTIONS

For starlings are destructive to small fruits, particularly cherries, strawberries, and grapes. Arriving in flocks, they sometimes strip whole cherry trees of fruit in a few minutes. They also ruin many apples, pears, and peaches by pecking a small hole in them. Recently, while driving past a vineyard in the famous grape-belt of Chautauqua County, New York, we saw a flock of several hundred settling down among the grapes. They eat some green corn in the ear, pull sprouting corn, and sometimes eat young sprouting plants such as peas, beans, lettuce, spinach, and radishes. It is, of course, only when they come in large numbers, that their depredations may become serious.

The bulky and loosely constructed nests, especially when placed in recesses about buildings, are not only unsightly, but often become foul with the excrement of the young. These nests are of grasses, straw, weeds, and trash, lined with feathers and moss, either in the crevice of a building, in a hollow tree, or in some other species' bird-house. The four to six, sometimes seven or eight eggs are pale bluish or whitish. In some sections there is but one brood; in others, two or three. The incubation period is about twelve days, and the young remain in the nest from two to three weeks.

Young starlings have a harsh, rasping, or hissing note, which seems partly a sort of feeding call, but which is given for some time after leaving the nest. On leaving the nest young starlings are well feathered, being dark brown on the back, with under parts at first slightly streaked with lighter markings, but soon becoming a solid color. The throat is white or buff.

The call of the male is a high, clear, drawn-out whistle, and the bird is also credited with being a clever mimic. Of these powers of mimicry, the government bulletin on starlings states that the bird already has the notes of a number of our native birds in its repertoire. The bird said to be most frequently imitated, is, oddly enough, the wood pewee. Had I not myself but recently heard this imitation, I should find it difficult to believe that such a large, awkward bird as the starling could imitate the plaintive *pee-ah-wee* of the dainty little flycatcher.

Besides the pewee, the bird is credited with imitating, though less frequently, the following birds: bluebird, redwinged blackbird, grackle, field sparrow, flicker, blue jay, Carolina wren, and the English sparrow. It is claimed by some that the notes of the bob-white have been imitated so perfectly that hunters have been fooled. E. H. Forbush, in his *Birds of Massachusetts,* gives a list of thirty-eight species that are more or less imitated by the starling, and adds that it can also bark like a dog, and mew like a cat.

Soon after the moulting period, young and old begin to flock in great numbers. As late as 1925 flocks numbering between three and four thousand were roosting in small shade trees along Pennsylvania Avenue, in Washington, D. C. And while we were motoring along the upper Niagara River in Canada, we once saw a flock of several thousand starlings settling like a dark cloud upon a vast grain field, where the grain was already in sheaves.

Just a few years ago starlings settled in such numbers on the cornices of New York buildings that action had to be taken by city authorities. At the Metropolitan Museum of Art they had to be driven away by a large force of men armed with long sticks, from which fluttered pieces of cloth.

The history of the starling in America is the history of the English sparrow repeating itself, and it may have the same disastrous results. Some observers claim that they are in conflict with the English sparrows over food and nesting habits, and that first one, and then the other, is the master of the situation.

If that is true, it is too bad that, like Eugene Field's "gingham dog and calico cat" they cannot "eat each other up" and then our problem of two unwelcome bird-foreigners would be solved.

XXVIII

THE CEDAR WAXWING

You come with flashing gleams of gold
  Before spring bids the leaves unfold;
With hood of black and crested head,
  With wings adorned with gems of red,
You perch, or flit on joyous wing;
  With color usher in the spring.
                    —ALBERT W. SMITH.

"MADE-IN-JAPAN" seem the waxwings, those artificial looking birds whose soft silky plumage suggests a fine Japanese water-color painting.

Our cedar waxwing is soft cinnamon-brown of body, with the breast lighter than the back and shading into yellow underneath; there is a yellow band across the end of the tail, and each secondary feather in the wing ends in a red tip, like a drop of ruby sealing wax, which gives the bird its name. There is a velvety-black chin and a conspicuous crest, with a velvety-black line running through the eye and back of it.

Expressive of every emotion is this erectile crest. When the bird is at ease and calm, the crest may lie loose upon the head; when he is angered, or excited, it is very erect; and in fear, it is flattened, which, with the black frontlet, gives a serpentine look to the bird's head.

The female is slightly duller than the male, and the red "sealing wax tips" may be missing both on her and on the immature birds. The plumage of the waxwings always seems to appear the same, beautifully neat and full-feathered, not showing the ragged appearance that most birds do through the moulting season.

[145]

Waxwings belong to the family *Bombycillidae,* and of the three known species one, the Bohemian, is common to the northern parts of both the Old and the New Worlds; but the cedar waxwing—our bird—is found only in America, and the third waxwing is restricted to Eastern Asia.

Cedar waxwings breed over much of North America, from Quebec southward to northern Arkansas and North Carolina, and winter throughout nearly all of the states and south to Panama, but are very irregular and erratic in their annual and seasonal occurrence in much of their territory. Going about in flocks, except during the breeding season, these birds are seemingly attracted to any particular locality by the supply of food found there. In most parts of the South, where present, they are winter residents or transients, but they nest in some sections of the upper South.

MILITARY PRECISION IN FLIGHT

Waxwings are notable for the irregularity of their migrations and the cedar waxwings, in particular, for the lateness of their nesting season. In contrast with this irregularity is the precision of their flight. On the wing they look very much as if they had been drilled, each bird seeming to move its wings in time with the rest; a flock of cedar birds compared, for example, with a flock of blackbirds, looks very much like a company of regular soldiers by the side of a disorderly mob.

These birds are seldom seen on the ground, but fly, usually thirty or forty to a flock, and in close ranks—often in fives, sevens, or nines, and about on a level with the tree-tops.

The best time to watch for them is when the trees are bare and they can more easily be seen. A whole flock will sometimes alight in a tree and remain quiet for a long time, perhaps an hour or more. As they make very

CEDAR WAXWING
(*One-half natural size*)

Order—PASSERES   Family—BOMBYCILLIDÆ
Genus—BOMBYCILLA   Species—CEDRORUM
National Association of Audubon Societies

RED-WINGED BLACKBIRD

(Upper figure, Male; Lower figure, Female)

Order—Passeres   Family—Icteridæ

Genus—Agelaius   Species—phœniceus

National Association of Audubon Societies

little noise, one must depend on seeing, not hearing them. Such a flock recently stopped in a great tree on the campus at State College, Raleigh, and I timed their stay for over half an hour.

Just before the leaves came out last spring, a flock of twenty or more waxwings came into our garden. About eight or ten perched about the rim of the bird bath, and several others alighted on trees and shrubs about the garden—creating one of the most exquisite and interesting bird-bath pictures we have. They remained a long time, and then flew off. We did not see them again, but while they were there they added color and mystery and interest to a winter garden—and we counted ourselves fortunate that we had been "at home" for their visit.

"THE WELL-MANNERED BIRD"

"Dey's a well-mannered bird," say the colored people, who have noted the waxwings stroking each other's feathers, "billing," and passing a bit of food around from one to another. A worm or cherry will sometimes go the rounds of the flock, and back to the beginner, before being eaten. Some observers, however, believe this politeness only takes place when the birds have had all the food they want.

Though he is no songster, this waxwing has two peculiar calls, one a hushed whistle, and a more subdued call which Thoreau described as his "beady note"—a succession of short notes strung together.

The bird has several other names, including cedar bird and cherry bird, from its liking for those two fruits. Among the French Canadians it is also known as Recollet, from the color of the crest which resembles the hood of a religious order by that name.

Late nesting—almost as late as the goldfinches— these birds do not seem to think of settling down to homemaking until most of the other birds are through with their family cares.

In the North the nest is bulky, made of strips of bark, leaves, grasses, and sometimes mud. Where sheep are common, a bit of wool is often used in its construction. In the South, the few nests that have been observed seem to be smaller and more compact. Often they are in fruit or shade trees, and may be from five to twenty feet up. Both birds are said to bring material for the nest, and both aid in its construction. The three to five eggs are pale blue-gray or putty color, spotted with black or umber.

Perhaps because the waxwings have had such a long "play time," when they do nest they are devoted home-makers, assuming a protective attitude when their nest is approached. They are said to take turns at incubation —which takes fourteen days—and in feeding the young, which are first fed insects, and then, as they become older, some fruits.

A "MARKET-BASKET" FOR SHOPPING

A bird which uses its crop as a "market-basket" while shopping for insects, is this cedar waxwing. In *The Book of Bird Life,* Dr. Allen has a photograph of a cedar waxwing returning to its young with its "market-basket," or crop, full of food. Often, he says, these birds return to their nests with their necks bulging with a variety of small fruits and insects, most of them in a fairly good state of preservation. They are particularly fond of canker-worms and caterpillars.

Sometimes, in the spring, the waxwings are seen peck-ing at blossoms of fruit trees—the petals coming down in showers—but in reality the birds are after the tiny insects which infest the blossoms. It must be admitted, however, that these birds are also hard on the cherry and strawberry crops, but more than half of their food consists of wild berries, especially those of the cedar and wild cherries.

In August the waxwings are likely to be found near streams and lakes, where, from far up on a perch they sally forth, fly-catcher-fashion, in pursuit of insects, which they are adept at catching. At such times the flight is undulating and graceful, one moment the birds mounting high in the air for an insect, the next dropping down for one nearer the ground. At this time of year immense quantities of grasshoppers, moths, butterflies, crickets, crane-flies, scale-insects, bark-lice, and even a few snails are consumed.

XXIX

THE BLACKBIRDS

THE RED-WING

I hear you, Brother, I hear you,
  Down in the alder swamp,
Springing your woodland whistle
  To herald the April pomp!

You sound the notes of the chorus
  By meadow and woodland pond,
Till, one after another, up-piping,
  A myriad throats respond.

I see you, Brother, I see you,
  With scarlet upon your wing,
Flash through the ruddy maples,
  Leading the pageant of Spring.
                      —BLISS CARMAN.

ONE SHOULD walk along the marshes and ponds and streams, if he would see and hear the red-wing. While the red-wing is the best known member of the blackbird family in the South, it is known in far vaster numbers in the prairies of the upper Mississippi Valley. There the innumerable sloughs and ponds furnish such ideal nesting places that the territory has become the great breeding ground of the species. In the East, where breeding sites are fewer, the species is much less abundant.

The red-winged blackbird, about nine inches in length, is a handsome military looking bird whose glossy black plumage brings into greater relief his shoulder decorations—the bright red epaulets margined with pale yellow or buff. Apparently red-wing is aware how handsome he is, for he likes to alight on a bending reed, wings lifted to show his decorations, while he flutes his *o-ka-lees*. Besides his flute-like *o-ka-lee,* the male has a challenging note of *chut, chuck,* and a long shrill alarm note of *chee-e-e-e.*

The female is smaller and less conspicuous, having a blackish head and back streaked with rusty and buff, and she is without the red epaulets. Few recognize her unless she is seen with her mate. The young resemble the mother in color. The first winter the young male has orange shoulders and a brownish coat, not getting his glossy black coat and red shoulders until the second year.

The range of the widely distributed red-winged blackbird is eastern North America, except the Gulf coast and Florida, breeding from Nova Scotia and Quebec southward, and wintering mainly south of the Ohio and Delaware valleys. During the breeding season the red-wing is largely restricted to marshes, wet pastures, or low, boggy fields. Though he is accused of being a bigamist —or even worse—red-wing is a good protector of his one —or perhaps two or three—wives.

The nest is usually cleverly protected, either by marshy land or a bit of curving creek, or by being in an inaccessible spot. It is a thick pocket of coarse grasses and weed stalks, lined with grasses and finer rootlets, and is hung either between reeds over the water, or built near the ground over upright stems of a bush. When there is a marked difference in the range of the same species there is apt to be a corresponding variation in the nature of its nesting sites; so the red-wings living in reedy marshes weave their nests to the reed stems, while those in the adjoining alder growths place their nests in alder bushes.

The three to five eggs, laid usually in May, are pale bluish white, scrawled with blackish, especially around the larger end. As a rule there are two broods.

FEMALES FLOCK TOGETHER IN WINTER

Red-wings are sociable beings, nesting in small colonies, and when migrating north, especially, they will scrape acquaintance and travel with any other bird. The male red-wings (and they are in full song by then) often migrate three weeks in advance of the females. A peculiarity of the species is that the females seem to spend the winter in flocks composed of their own sex.

In February and March, in the South their numbers are greatly increased by northern-bound migrants. At this season, says Brimley, they feed largely in the fields of newly planted grain, probably doing some damage by eating the sprouting seeds, and some good by destroying cutworms and other noxious insects. After March, their numbers having been reduced to the resident population, the birds confine themselves rather closely to the low grounds.

In spring the red-wings like to follow the plowman, picking up grubs, worms, caterpillars. They are especially fond of canker-worms for feeding their young, and it is said they will sometimes fly half a mile to a known source for them.

Wilson, the early ornithologist, estimated that red-wings of the country destroy many larvae. They also eat the gypsy moth, forest tent-caterpillars, weevils, beetles, wire worms, grasshoppers, ants, bugs, and flies.

Unlike most birds, the red-wings never hop with both feet together, but move one foot after the other, just as we do, walking with long, stiff, awkward-looking strides.

The blackbirds belong to a distinctively American family, the *Icteridae,* and are most abundantly represented in the tropics, where the majority of the one hundred and fifty-odd known species are found, only nineteen advancing north of Mexico. They are medium-sized birds, intermediate in some respects between the crows on the one hand, and the finches on the other, but perhaps in most respects nearer the latter. With the exception of the orioles, they are gregarious after the nesting season, while some of the species nest in colonies and are found in flocks throughout the year. They differ markedly in habits, and are found living in country of every nature, from dry plains and marshes to the densest forest growth. Some species possess marked vocal ability, while the voices of others are harsh and unmusical.

THE RUSTY BLACKBIRD

Resembling somewhat the red-wing in size, flight, and song, but lacking the scarlet shoulder decoration, the rusty blackbird is known in many parts of the South in winter. Though in summer the adult female is a more brownish slate color than the male, in winter, while with us, both sexes are somewhat alike, having a more or less rusty-brown coat, which gives the birds their name. The pale yellow or whitish eye is also a distinguishing mark.

Breeding principally north of the United States, the rusty blackbirds' winter range is mainly south of the Ohio and Delaware valleys to the Gulf coast. In many parts of the South they are known as irregular winter visitors. They stay in wet pastures, along the borders of swampy woodlands, and even in woods and yards, where they feed on dogwood berries.

Usually they are seen in small flocks of fifteen or twenty, sometimes in company with their cousins, the red-wings. Their alarm note is a low *chuck*. The song resembles somewhat that of the red-wing, but it is far less musical, and it is interspersed with metallic splutterings and squealings.

The nest is of twigs and coarse grasses lined with finer grasses, either on the ground or in coniferous trees.

The four to seven grayish-green eggs are thickly blotched with brown.

The rusty blackbird's food consists of insects, including grasshoppers, beetles, caterpillars, weevils, as well as some grain and weed seeds. As the bird is in the South only in winter, it does no damage to our crops, and is a known enemy to the boll weevil.

XXX

THE MEADOWLARK

The cheerless remnant of the snow-drift lies
Along the fields, and there are wintry skies
Where chilling blasts assail thee, meadow lark.
I know not how you find subsistence here,
Among the withered herbs of yester-year:
I grieve for your uncertain day—but hark,
I hear your brave note calling, loud and clear.
—EDWARD R. FORD, in *Bird-Lore*.

THE MEADOWLARK, which isn't a lark at all, but a black-bird, likes best grassy plains and uplands covered with a thick growth of grass or weeds, and with near-by water.

In many localities the meadowlark has been classed as a game bird and shot, which, from the farmer's standpoint, is a mistake, for it is very useful as an insect eater, feeding on caterpillars, grasshoppers, cutworms, army worms, flies, wasps, the alfalfa weevil, and, in the South, the cotton-boll weevil. Though it is now protected everywhere by Federal regulations, this does not seem to make any difference to young Nimrods—or to older ones—who are frequently seen in and near our cities and suburbs, shooting these birds, as well as robins, thrushes, and even the beloved southern mockingbird.

The meadowlark's vegetable food consists of weed-seeds and grain, most of the grain being the waste grains of winter. In none of the stomachs examined by the government Biological Survey was there ever found a trace of sprouted corn. Some of these birds were taken, says the bulletin, while snow was on the ground; yet the stomachs showed numerous insects, proving how earnestly these birds work as "paying guests" even under the most adverse conditions.

Occasionally the novice in bird study confuses the meadowlark with the flicker. Both are large yellowish brown birds, with yellow under parts, and each has a black crescent breast decoration, the one on the lark, however, being more of a triangle. The meadowlark is streaked above, the crown is streaked with brown and black, and there is a yellow line from the bill over the eye. The outside tail-feathers are white. In the winter plumage the upper parts of both adult and young meadowlarks are more grayish brown, the under parts are duller, and the black crescent is veiled with buff. The bird is a little larger and plumper than the robin.

Belonging to the family *Icteridae*, the American black-birds, the meadowlark's range is eastern North America, breeding from Quebec southward. While not a highly migratory bird, most of those from the upper part of the range—that is, from Canada and the northern states, move southward, wintering from southern New England and the Ohio Valley to the Gulf states. Thus is added a vast number to the resident meadowlark population in our southern states.

The bulk of the migrants arrive in the South usually in the early part of October, and from then until April nearly every meadow and pasture is host to meadow-larks. Though these birds are largely confined to upland meadows during the breeding season, through the winter they may also be found in wet pastures and old corn and cotton fields. Often, during late plowing in the South, numbers of meadowlarks may be seen following the plow-man and feasting on grubs found in the fresh-turned soil.

From our sleeping porch, in the early mornings, we often see meadowlarks alighting in the tall pines at the edge of the woodland. In winter, when we tramp through

MEADOWLARK

Order—Passeres   Family—Icteridæ
Genus—Sturnella   Species—magna

National Association of Audubon Societies

BLUE JAY

Order—Passeres   Family—Corvidæ
Genus—Cyanocitta   Species—Cristata

National Association of Audubon Societies

the meadows beyond this woodland, the dogs which always accompany us, usually flush a number of meadowlarks, the birds rising with a whirring sound somewhat similar to bob-whites. They do not, however, all spring into the air at once, as the bob-whites do, nor do they fly in compact flocks as do other blackbirds.

The bird has a characteristic slow flight, proceeding by alternately flapping its wings and sailing, and when rising from the ground, the tail is usually spread, revealing conspicuously the white outer tail-feathers, which make the bird an easy target.

MORE MEADOWLARKS THAN FORMERLY

The meadowlarks are good examples of a species which, instead of decreasing, has increased with the coming of the white man and civilization. For, in the East and South especially, formerly there were great areas covered with virgin forests and the cleared meadows were few; so meadowlarks were restricted in their range. But as soon as the settlers began clearing the land and having pasture lands and meadows, the meadowlarks began to increase.

An affectionate couple are these birds, the male remaining near his mate and singing to her, and also providing food for her and the young. The nest is cleverly concealed on the ground under a tuft of grass or a clump of weeds and is made compactly of coarse grasses lined with finer materials. Often it is built where the grass is long enough to be drawn together, tent-like; and sometimes there is a long, covered vestibule leading to the nest, probably to conceal it from the keen eyes of hawks and crows. Nor do the birds come to the nest or leave it directly, but slip through the grass and leave from a different spot. If you examine one of these nests carefully, often you may discern several tiny paths leading from it in different directions.

The four to six eggs are a pure white ground color, spotted with reddish brown. The nesting period is May or June, and there may be two or three broods. It is interesting to compare the egg of the meadowlark, an *altricial* bird—whose young are born naked, or nearly naked, and helpless, and must be cared for by the parent birds—with that of the upland plover, a *precocial* bird. "*Precocial* birds, whose young are hatched in a much more advanced state than the *altricial* birds, necessarily lay larger eggs since development has to proceed farther in the egg and more yolk food has to be stored.

"The extreme in size of egg as compared with the size of the bird occurs among the shore-birds which lay but three or four eggs. Thus, the eggs of the upland plover are about twice the size of those of the meadowlark, though the birds are about the same size. *Precocial* birds like the grouse, which lay a large number of eggs, lay relatively smaller eggs than the shore-birds."[*]

The song of the meadowlark is a clear, sweet, plaintive whistle, which some interpret as *"Spring o' the year! Spring o' the year!"* while Van Dyke describes it as a "sad, sweet, slurred melancholy call that leaks slowly upward from the ground."

[*] A. A. Allen, *The Book of Bird Life.*

XXXI

THE COWBIRD, THE SLACKER OF BIRDDOM

Strange stalker of the pasture grass,
Whose presence nesting bird-folk fear,
All cares of family o'er you pass,
You lazy, feathered racketeer!
—R. W. G.

Too LAZY and shiftless to build her own nest and rear her own young, the cowbird—a parasite blackbird—may sometimes be seen sneaking through the trees and bushes in search of some nest left unguarded for a moment. In such a nest she will slyly lay her egg, and then slip off, leaving the cares of incubation and motherhood to the foster parent.

This bird is an acknowledged parasite and reprobate with no friends among man or bird. However, villain and delinquent as it is, any bird with the queer habits of the cowbird is of interest to the bird student.

The males, about eight inches in length, have glossy black plumage and a brown head and neck. The female is smaller and a dusky brown, lighter below. The cowbird's voice, like its habits, is harsh and ugly, a discordant *chuck-see, chuck-see.*

The bird gets its name from its habit of frequenting pastures where cattle are grazing; where large flocks feed on the insects stirred up by the cows as they graze. So close do the birds keep, right under the feet of the cattle, that seeing them one wonders how they avoid being stepped upon.

This reprobate bird breeds in the Atlantic coast states, mainly north of North Carolina, and inland to Texas and Louisiana. It winters from the Ohio and Potomac valleys (and sometimes farther north) to the Gulf coast and central Mexico.

A WORM'S-EYE VIEW OF THE PARASITE COWBIRD. IT IS AN OUTLAW, WITH NO FRIENDS AMONG EITHER BIRDS OR MANKIND. A LITTLE LESS THAN ONE-HALF NATURAL SIZE.

Bendire, in his *Life History of North American Birds,* lists over ninety-two species of birds that are imposed upon by the cowbird; the most frequent victims are the warblers, the vireos, and the song and the chipping sparrows. The cowbird is usually careful to choose a nest of a species smaller than herself, so that her egg (white, distinctly and evenly sprinkled with cinnamon), being larger than those that rightfully belong in the nest, gets more warmth and hatches sooner. The young cowbird grows rapidly and is vociferous in its demands for food. This results in the rightful nestlings often being smothered, crowded out of the nest, or starved.

Many cases are on record of the havoc and destruction wrought in other bird families by these parasite birds. One bird student who has made a special study of the havoc wrought by this bird over several seasons, has records of several hundred cases during his period of study.* In *Homing With the Birds* Gene Stratton Porter tells of her study of a flock of two hundred cowbirds on the banks of the Wabash River. She estimated that these birds were responsible for the deaths of six hundred birds of other species, while about four hundred more cowbirds were born to continue their havoc in other seasons.

And yet the young strangeling, reared by foster parents, usually at the cost of the lives of their own young, is an ingrate. As soon as fully reared it deserts these parents, and joins flocks of its own outlaw kind.

OCCASIONALLY THE COWBIRD IS OUTWITTED

Each female is believed to lay four or more eggs a year, but it is generally supposed that she lays only one egg in each nest. However, there are records of several cowbirds laying eggs in the same nest, which creates quite a problem for the imposed-upon bird. Bendire writes of an ovenbird's nest having been found which had seven of these eggs in it.

Some of the larger birds are able to push the unwanted egg out of the nest, but the yellow warbler, too small to do that, has a clever way of outwitting the parasite bird. Finding such an egg in her own dainty nest, this tiny bit of golden fluff calmly proceeds to build another floor to her nest, cleverly sealing in the cowbird's egg, then starts all over with her own laying and incubating. Such nests have been found with two or three floors in them, and a cowbird's egg sealed up in each space. There are even instances on record of four-story nests having been found.

* Alvin M. Peterson, *Nature Magazine*, October, 1933.

The cowbird has even been seen to remove an egg from the nest of a red-eyed vireo, and to drop its own in its place. If it is unable to find a nest, it will drop its own egg on the ground, and sometimes will even eat it. Reprobate and parasite, the cowbird is in every respect an outlaw of Birddom.

XXXII

THE PURPLE GRACKLE

Fust come the blackbirds, clatt'rin' in tall trees,
And settlin' things in windy congresses;
Queer politicians, though, for I'll be skinned
If all on 'em don't head against the wind.
—JAMES RUSSELL LOWELL.

NESTING in a crevice in the side of an osprey's, or a fish hawk's nest seems a queer place to build one's own home, but that is what the purple grackle, another of the blackbirds, has been known to do.

Usually they nest in a pine or some other coniferous tree. So adaptable are they, however, that if trees are not accessible, bushes, and more rarely, even a woodpecker's old hole may be made to do. The four to six eggs vary greatly in markings and in coloring, which may be anything from grayish white to rusty brown, spotted with black or chocolate. There is but one brood a year.

Though the birds are gregarious, and live in large flocks, when nesting time comes these flocks are decreased to smaller bands or colonies. They breed also in parks, occasionally on a college campus, and near buildings.

Also, they sometimes nest where food is not plentiful, and so are forced to make long journeys for the nestlings' food, which consists largely of insects.

Grackles are among the few of our land birds which live in flocks all the year. Gregarious birds, they even nest in colonies of from ten to twenty or more pairs. They are good but joyless parents, apparently looking after their young more from a sense of duty than of pleasure. Both parents share in the incubation.

[163]

"CROW BLACKBIRD"

In spite of its nickname of "crow blackbird" the purple grackle is not a crow, resembling it only in appearance and in some of its bad habits, such as corn and grain

WITH ITS YELLOW EYE AND ITS CRACKED AND REEDY WHISTLE, THE PURPLE GRACKLE IS AN UNCANNY BIRD. IT HAS NEVER LEARNED THAT SOMETIMES IT IS BEST NOT TO TRY TO SING. ABOUT TWO-FIFTHS NATURAL SIZE.

foragings and nest-robbing. It belongs, instead, to the *Icteridae,* the blackbird family.

The male grackle is an iridescent black, the color of the head and neck grading into the mingled purple and bronze tints of the body. The back has iridescent bars.

The belly is paler, the eye a light yellow, and from tip of bill to tip of tail the bird measures about twelve to thirteen inches. The female is smaller, and, though similar in color, is much duller.

This grackle is easily distinguished from other blackbirds by its large size, longer tail, and hoarse note—a harsh *chuck*.

The range of the purple grackle is the middle Atlantic coast region, and it breeds from southern New York south to the uplands of Georgia, Alabama, and eastern Tennessee. It winters mainly south of the Delaware valley, and seems to be equally at home in the rural districts, in small towns, or in cities.

During the winter, the southern resident birds have their numbers greatly increased by the birds from the northern part of the range.

The flight of the grackle appears labored, because of the bird's habit of "keeling" the tail-feathers, that is, folding them upward from the middle. This makes them easy to recognize on the wing.

Though not a songbird, the male grackle tries to be a troubadour, when—even in the bird world—"In the spring a young man's fancy lightly turns to thoughts of love." Then it is that he insists in making an attempt at singing, though the effort sounds like a rusty hinge creaking in the wind.

Sometimes, too, a whole group of grackles will feel this romantic urge and try to sing in concert, with the result that, while we admire their attempts, we should be entirely willing to have them give up and admit defeat.

Though they are accused of many sins, the examination of over two thousand stomachs of these grackles shows that one-third of their food consists of insects, most of which are injurious to agriculture. They also feed on snails, salamanders, crawfish, small fish, and occasionally on small birds. The grain they eat in fall and winter is largely waste found among stubble, but in summer and early fall they do some damage by eating grain and corn in the "milk" stage, or in the ear.

On the other hand, during the breeding season these birds do much good through the large amount of insects consumed in the feeding of their young. Also, during spring plowing, these "crow blackbirds" have the crow habit of following the plow in search of large grubs, of which they are particularly fond.

By midsummer, when the young are old enough, all begin to gather in flocks and roam about the countryside in search of good feeding grounds.

THE BRONZED GRACKLE

In the bronzed grackle (which may be a distinct species) the color of the head and neck is sharply defined from that of the body, which is not the case with the purple grackle. It has a more bronzed metallic luster, and lacks the iridescent bars on the back. This grackle is found in the South Atlantic coastal states mainly as a migrant, while in some sections of Tennessee it is known as a common winter resident, and in other parts as a migrant. South of New York it breeds only west of the Alleghenies, but in the Mississippi valley it is abundant, preferring to nest in the artificial groves and windbreaks near farms instead of in the natural timber which it formerly used.

The habits of the bronzed grackle are very similar in all respects to those of the purple grackle, but their notes differ, the song of the latter being louder and more musical than that of the purple.

THE BOAT-TAILED GRACKLE

This grackle, commonly called the jackdaw, is found along the coast, where it finds its living in the salt marshes or along the beaches, feeding mainly on small crabs, shrimps, and other sea-foods washed up by the waves. Rarely is it found far from water. Its notes are hoarse, forced whistles, or a rolling call. This grackle is a totally different species from the others.

XXXIII

THE BLUE JAY

I think when the fairies made the flowers,
To grow in these mossy fields of ours,
   Periwinkles and violets rare,
There was left of the spring's own color, blue,
Plenty to fashion a flower whose hue
   Would be richer than all and as fair.

So, putting their wits together, they
Made one great blossom so bright and gay,
   The lily beside it seemed blurred;
And then they said, ''We will toss it in air;
So many blue blossoms grow everywhere,
   Let this pretty one be a bird!''
          —Susan Hartley Swett.

''Much is forgiven Beauty'' is very applicable to that handsome, military-looking braggart, the blue jay. So much of color and action does this arrogant, swash-buckling bird add to our out-of-doors, especially in the drab days of late fall and winter, that we would not be without him if we could.

For, reprobate though he is, we could not spare him; none of us would really want to live in a jayless world. In casting up his accounts, while there is plenty on the wrong side of the ledger, there is some on the credit side, too. Though he is a bold and noisy enough fellow when he is roaming the woods with his companions in the fall and winter, he is quiet and cautious when near his own nest. And he is a good parent, devoted, it is claimed, to the point of death before he will desert his own.

The blue jay is around eleven inches in length, the upper parts grayish blue, brightest on wings and tail, which have many black bars and some white tips. The under parts are grayish white, and there is a black, crescent-like low collar. The high, pointed crest is blue and black. Male and female are indistinguishable.

Jays belong to the family *Corvidae,* which includes the crows and ravens, and is represented in all parts of the world except New Zealand. Of the two hundred species, twenty-one are found in North America.

Inhabiting wooded regions, they are resident throughout the year, except in the northern limit of their range, which extends over eastern North America westward to the plains and south to the Gulf. In the northern part of their range they are migratory, the northern birds adding their numbers to our native southern blue jays in winter.

As a family, the *Corvidae* show marked traits of character and possess much cunning and intelligence. Some scientists place them at the top of the avian, or "bird-family" tree.

Jays are both mimics and ventriloquists, and they have an apparently endless supply of whistles and calls of their own. One of the most attractive is rather flute-like, reminding one of a far-off sweet-toned bell. Jays can also imitate the notes of other species, especially those of the red-shouldered, the red-tailed, and the sparrow hawks.

"HOUDINI" OF BIRDS

Jaybird is also the Houdini of birds, a regular contortionist, who can twist himself into all sorts of queer shapes. He assumes one attitude for singing, another when he is on guard, and during his squeaks and squalls he often humps up, spreads his wings, drops his tail, and "sounds off," so that it is no wonder the poet wrote—

"Sometimes your piping is delicious
And then again it's simply vicious."

It is hard to have to admit that a bird as attractive as the blue jay is the reprobate that he is about other birds and their nests. For during his own breeding season, he seems to turn cannibal and sometimes eats the eggs or young of smaller birds.

But, even there, he is probably not so black as he is painted. Perhaps the fairest appraisal of birds and their good and bad habits is that given in the various government bulletins on birds. Nature writers and bird lovers are at times accused of being too sentimental or romantic-minded to admit that any bird can do wrong. But the surveys made by government scientists contain hard, cold facts. Birds are sent in to their laboratories from all parts of the country, and at different seasons, and the contents of their stomachs are examined by skilled scientists.

This is what they have to say of the blue jay: "As to the blue jays' reputation as nest robbers, special search was made for every possible trace of such material in the stomachs, and in six of the 530 examined were found the remains of birds and their eggs. This trait appears to be most pronounced during the jays' own breeding season." (This is true, also, of the owls, hawks, and other birds which sometimes feed on eggs and nestlings.)

Jays also eat some cultivated fruits, but their favorite vegetable food is mast: acorns, chestnuts, beechnuts. Some corn is eaten, but most of it is waste, though in the South there is a tendency for them to eat the corn when in the ear. However, in the southern states there seems to be less nest-robbing. Of 184 stomachs of birds from various parts of the South examined by the Biological Survey, only one contained eggs of another bird. Also, more insects are eaten in the South, and these include many of the most destructive pests, such as grasshoppers, caterpillar eggs, scale insects, and weevils.

On the credit side it may also be pointed out that the jays are foresters and planters, helping to clothe our waste spaces with green. For, in storing up nuts for leaner days, they often bury them, and these sometimes sprout and grow.

The jay's nesting season is in April and May. The rather large and untidy nest is interwoven of twigs and lined with rootlets. It is generally placed in a tree crotch from ten to twenty feet up. The four to six eggs are pale bluish green or brownish ash, thickly marked with varying shades of cinnamon brown. The young are born naked and helpless, and usually remain in the nest for about sixteen days.

In our woodland acre we hear the jays more often than we see them, although we frequently see a flash of blue streaking through the woods. As I write this, a jay comes to the "doughnut-tree" only a few feet away, and snatches off a great bite. Most of the other birds fly at his approach, but the small tufted titmouse—a distant cousin—stops at a near-by tree and loudly and vindictively voices his disapproval of the intruder. During the winter the jays occasionally come also to the kitchen feeding-shelf.

Jays are full of curiosity about other birds' affairs. They like to pry, and also to tease other birds, especially the owls and hawks, by imitating the cry of a wounded bird. Sometimes, however, the joke is turned on the joker, and the jays, who have aroused in the hawk hopes of a tasty meal, do not all escape in time, and a jay may himself become the "tasty meal."

Every southerner is familiar with the Negro superstition that jays are never seen on Friday. On that day they are supposed to go to the "Bad Place," and numerous are the plantation legends about why they go. In *Plantation Bird Legends* by Martha Young, the old negress "Witch Menee" says, "Hit's des de way one is hearn de tale," whether one likes the jays or not. Some say that Br'er Jay takes a splinter down every Friday so that old Mister Devil will have good kindling wood all the time. But others believe the trip is for a better purpose, and claim that Br'er Jay and all his family and kin go that way, each one totin' a grain of sand in his bill and dropping it in, with the good hopes of filling up that awful place. And if that is so, continues "Witch Menee," she for one doesn't care if he is a "bodacious" bird.

And so, even though we may agree with the Negroes, that the jay is a "bodacious" bird, still we should miss his color and antics from our woodlands.

XXXIV

THE CROWS

Then it is a distant cawing,
Growing louder—coming nearer,
Tells of crows returning inland
From their winter on the marshes.

Iridescent is their plumage,
Loud their voices, bold their clamour,
In the pools and shallows wading,
Or in overflowing meadows
Searching for the waste of winter—
Scraps and berries freed by thawing.
Weird their notes and harsh their croaking,
Silent only when the night comes.
                           —FRANK BOLLES.

So CLEVER and intelligent are the crows that it is said
Henry Ward Beecher once remarked that if men wore
feathers and wings, very few of them would be clever
enough to be crows.

They are, perhaps, the most intelligent of all our native birds—quick to learn and clever in action. Some
scientists place them with the jays at the top of the tree
of bird life. Young crows make excellent pets. They
are easily trained and taught tricks, but they are inclined
to become mischievous as they grow older. Mrs. Comstock tells of a pet crow that would steal all the thimbles
in the house, watching for them when sewing was laid
down, and burying them in the garden. This crow would
also nip the clothes-pins off the line, and bury them, until it became necessary to shut him up on wash-day.

Dr. A. A. Allen* tells of a tame crow that played with
his children and learned to talk, to play games, to tease,
and to teeter by himself; he even developed a sense of

* *The Book of Bird Life.*

humor.   When the children were not present this crow
would roll their balls and play their games by himself.
He was fond of teetering and would do this either with
the children or alone by running up one side of the see-
saw until it went down and then turning around and running up the other side.

THE MOST INTELLIGENT OF ALL OUR NATIVE BIRDS, THE CROW HAS BEEN
TAUGHT TO SPEAK, TO PLAY GAMES, TO TEASE, AND TO TEETER BY HIMSELF ON
A SEE-SAW.   ABOUT ONE-FOURTH NATURAL SIZE.

Crows learn a variety of sounds easily, and some have
been taught to imitate the human voice.   They belong to
the family *Corvidae,* which in America includes two subfamilies: the crows, ravens, and nutcrackers; and the
jays and magpies.   In the South we have neither the
magpies nor the nutcrackers, and the few ravens are
confined to the mountainous districts.

Though in the sunlight crows seem iridescent purple
or steel-blue, especially about the head and neck, their
plumage is mainly or entirely black, the under parts ap-
pearing duller than the upper parts.   They are com-

paratively large birds, around nineteen and a half inches in length, with wings much longer than the tail.

SOME BAD HABITS

From an economical standpoint, the crows, like the jays, have a bad reputation as robbers of other birds' eggs and young. To some extent this is sustained by facts, but, on the other hand, examination by the government entomologists, of large numbers of crows' stomachs proves they are not so black villains as they have been painted. They also make depredations on poultry yards, stealing eggs and newly hatched chicks. Another bad habit that has made them extremely unpopular is their fondness for corn, whether newly planted, just sprouting, in the "milk" or "roasting ear" stage, or in the shock. Their consumption of beneficial reptiles, frogs, and small toads also counts against them.

In the southern states there are sometimes depredations by crows on ripening watermelons; and also on apples, peanuts, pecans, and almonds, though they are less frequently injured. In defense of the southern crow, however, it should be pointed out that of 108 stomachs examined, the fragments of shell of a hen's egg found in one stomach supplied the only evidence of the objectionable trait of egg-eating, of which his northern brother is so often accused. No remains of wild birds or their eggs were found in any of these stomachs, nor was there much proof of the crow's fondness for corn.

SOME GOOD HABITS

However, his bad habits are offset to a great extent by his consumption of insects. About a fifth of a crow's diet is secured from the insect world, and among the pests destroyed are some of the most troublesome with which the farmer has to contend. Included among these are

May beetles and their destructive larvae, white grubs, of which the crow is particularly fond, grasshoppers, wireworms, cutworms, and caterpillars.

In the spring, numbers of crows may often be seen following the plowman and feasting upon grubs, larvae, worms, and field mice that appear with the freshly turned soil. The fact that no less than 656 different items have been identified in its food gives some idea of the bird's resourcefulness, and its possibilities for both good and harm.

As a carrion feeder the crow supplements the work of the buzzards and the gulls, especially along the river banks and tidal flats where dead fish, if left, would pollute the air.

The range of the common crow is the whole country, except here and there locally. In the states of the upper South crows are resident at all seasons, except in the higher mountains where ravens replace them to some extent. There are, however, large areas in the Gulf states of Florida, Alabama, Mississippi, and Louisiana, where crows are not common.

Raising one brood of from three to seven, with both parents sharing the incubation and the care of the young, crows are considered models among bird parents. Like their cousins, the noisy, rowdy jays, they are quiet and orderly in the vicinity of their own nests. In the South some begin nesting as early as February or March, though more nests are built in April and May.

The nest is usually in the top of a tall pine, cedar, or other tree, anywhere from twenty to sixty feet high, and is so placed that it is well concealed from below. The deep, bulky structure is of sticks lined with strips of grapevine bark, grasses, moss, and leaves. The eggs vary in color from pale bluish to olive green and are thickly spotted with dark brown; in rare cases they are even white with almost no markings. The young remain in the nest about three weeks, and even after that remain with the parents through the greater part of the summer.

Young crows are "mostly appetites" as Dr. Allen says. Experiments have showed that they require at least half their own weight of food each day merely to exist, and that they can easily consume the equivalent of their full weight each day.

"Many young crows—and other young birds—that are kept in captivity, are starved to death because their owners do not realize how much food is required. Though they do not eat much at a time, their digestion is so rapid that they require almost continual feeding, thus keeping the parent birds busy from morning to night."*

Crows are gregarious birds, and during the colder months as they resort to their nightly roosts, they often number up into the thousands. According to a government bulletin, this flocking is of considerable economic significance in that it results in the gathering together of large numbers of birds possessing some injurious habits. In the latitude of Washington, D. C., their roosts are well established by the end of September, and by mid-winter their combined southerly migration and gregarious habits have brought together in a comparatively small area the bulk of the crow population of North America. The upper South is within this area of great roosts, which reach their peak by January.

In the winter of 1919 a large roost was established just outside of Washington, and night and morning the vast hordes passed over our house. In the early morning they would go out from their roosts flying low, on the lookout for food, often making a journey of many miles. Their cawing was so loud that sleep was impossible dur-

* Allen, *The Book of Bird Life.*

ing the time of their passing. At night, on their return, they flew at a much greater height.

POST SENTINELS

When feeding in the fields crows invariably keep a sentinel posted at some high point from which he can quickly detect danger and warn the other birds. This post of honor and responsibility is always given to an older and experienced bird. And woe unto the hapless guard who may become careless, inattentive, or otherwise distracted while on duty! Then indeed do the other crows berate and punish him severely.

The government bulletin, from evidence that covers five years of survey and intensive study of the crow, states that its merits and shortcomings appear about equally divided. "While it would be unwise to give absolute protection, and thus afford the farmer no recourse when the bird is doing damage, it would be equally unwise to adopt the policy of killing every crow within gunshot.

"On game farms and preserves, about homes and gardens, and in suburban districts where it is desired to foster small birds, the crow population must be held in check."

THE FISH CROW

The fish crow is a common resident bird along the southern Atlantic and Gulf coastal states. It is migrant only at the extreme northern limit of its range, the Hudson River and Connecticut. Smaller than the common crow, measuring about sixteen inches in length, it resembles the crow in shape and coloring, and is distinguished from it mainly by its call. Its cracked, reedy notes resemble those of the young of the common crow, a hoarse *car*, sounding as if the bird had a cold in its head, instead of the familiar *caw* of the better known bird.

Though this crow is not confined to the coast, nor to the vicinity of water, still it is rarely found very far inland. Its nest and eggs are similar to those of the common crow, but the eggs are smaller. Usually where one nest is found, a search will reveal several others near by.

This crow gets its name from its habit. of feeding in shallow waters or along beaches and neighboring creeks and ponds. Its food is principally crabs, fish, and other animal food washed ashore by the waves.

The fish crow does not commit as many depredations on the farmer's crops as does the common crow, but it is credited with being an even worse robber of eggs and young nestlings. According to Brimley, it also plunders the heron and cormorant rookeries along our coast.

XXXV

THE WOODPECKERS—DOWNY

Downy came and dwelt with me
    Taught me hermit lore;
Drilled his cell in oaken tree
    Near my cabin door.

Architect of his own home
    In the forest dim,
Carving its inverted dome
    In a dozy limb.

So SAID John Burroughs, who lived intimately with Nature and wrote many delightful bird essays and poems.

Little black and white downy is the smallest and the most familiar of our woodpeckers and is common to many localities throughout the South, except in the highest mountain ranges, where the northern downy replaces him.

Downy, who makes a good Chief of the Tree Policemen, wears a trim uniform, the upper parts black with a whitish streak down the middle of the back, the under parts whitish; the black wing-feathers and their coverts are spotted with white; the middle tail-feathers are black, and the outer ones white barred with black. There is a white stripe both above and below the eye, and his badge of office is the vivid red patch on the back of his head. Chief Downy's night-stick, or club, is the powerful wedge-shaped bill. Mrs. Downy is similar in appearance, but lacks the scarlet on the head.

So many insects burrow into trees that Mother Nature has developed a highly specialized class of birds, the woodpeckers, to dig them out. Their strong bills,

DOWNY WOODPECKERS (MALE AND FEMALE) HAIRY WOODPECKER

Order—PICI   Family—PICIDÆ
Genus—DRYOBATES   Species—PUBESCENS AND VILLOSUS

National Association of Audubon Societies

RED-HEADED WOODPECKER
Order—Pici   Family—Picidæ
Genus—Melanerpes   Species—erythrocephalus
National Association of Audubon Societies

long, spear-like tongues, the peculiar structure of their feet, and their stiffened tails, are well adapted to this work.

Downy, in particular, is a business-like tree inspector in the way he goes about getting grubs. Bracing himself firmly with his strong feet and stiff tail, he throws back his head and drives powerful blows with his strong beak. When using this as a pick, he strikes hard, deliberate blows, but when drilling he strikes rapidly and not so hard, quickly making a small, deep hole leading to the burrow of the grub.

TONGUE A MARVELOUS MECHANISM

It would seem almost impossible for the downy to get the grub out of this small hole, but he can extend his long tongue far beyond the beak, and its tip is hard and thorny and covered with short backward-slanting hooks acting like a spear, which, when thrust into the grub, pulls it out easily. The slender bones that support this long tongue slide in a muscular sheath that extends around the back of the head and over the crown. Apparently, says Brimley, it is the contraction of these muscles which pushes the bones down and forward.

Since the food of the downy is where he can get at it all winter, he does not migrate, but is a permanent resident wherever found. Moreover, he is not built for long flights.

In contrast to the perching birds, all of which have three toes in front and one behind, so that they may easily grasp a perch and keep their balance, the foot of a woodpecker is especially adapted to creeping and climbing, having two toes directed forward and two backward, which assist it in clinging to an upright surface. For a woodpecker does not perch in the true sense; it rests against either a tree-trunk or a limb, even sleeping in such positions. Nor does it run about the tree trunks as do the nuthatch and the brown creeper.

Downy is no songster. His call note is a squeaky *peenk, peenk, peenk,* but though he belongs to a songless group, the woodpeckers have several ways of calling and signalling to each other. One method is to beat rapidly on a tree with the beak, which makes a rolling noise, each species doing its drumming in its own way.

"DRUMMING UP" A MATE

"Weeding out the lonesomeness" is how James Whitcomb Riley describes the drumming of the downy, as, with the coming of spring, the male selects a resonant limb of hardwood and there beats out a signal, "Wanted, a Wife." When he has found a limb that is sufficiently resonant, he may return to it, day after day. And after winning the lady he still drums for a time, to cheer her up during the cares of nesting.

For nesting, he drills a hole, usually in a partly decayed tree. His old holes are often taken over by other birds, but downy himself must have a fresh excavation each year. There are from four to six glossy white eggs, which are laid at the bottom of the hole on a bed of chips. The entrance hole is always a perfect circle and is about an inch and a quarter across.

One of the most interesting habits of the downy—and also of the hairy woodpecker—is the hollowing out of some old limb for a winter roosting cavity. It is somewhat similar to the hole made for nesting in the spring. As it is a roomy cavity, and as downy is a sociable bird in winter, often traveling in flocks with nuthatches, chickadees, and titmice, he often shares these snug winter quarters with them.

Downy is not, as some believe, a sapsucker. He does not bore holes in trees to drink the sap, but to get at the injurious grubs which live under the bark and which his sharp, barbed, sticky tongue is so adapted to reach. His food consists of some of the worst foes of orchard and woodland—ants, caterpillars, and other insects. Throughout the year downy is on duty all day long. He searches out the wood-boring beetles and their larvae in our forest trees; he finds the codling moths hibernating in our apple trees; he destroys the round-headed apple-tree borers which are so destructive to trees. Sometimes he varies this diet with a few berries of the dogwood, woodbine, or pokeberry. He even eats a few weed seeds occasionally.

No orchard should be without its downy woodpecker, but he does not like too trim a tree. Leave him a hollow limb or two. New, well pruned orchards may bear a better crop of fruit, but old, hollow trees bear a better crop of birds.

Downies are fond of suet and come to the feeding-station many times daily; if suet is kept out the year around, they will bring their young to feed upon it. My bird notebook reads: "All winter the male downy dined regularly, the female coming less often, but downy seemed indifferent to her. Towards spring, however, he began to notice her, and soon there was a courtship in our trees. The female was seen with him more often; then she disappeared, to reappear some weeks later with four baby downies, who resembled the parent birds.

"At first they would alight on a near-by tree and the parent bird, nipping off a bit of suet, would carry it to them. As they became larger they were coaxed to the tree itself, alighting above the suet, and backing down in awkward, jerky hops, keeping up an insistent crying and squeaking that only a mother downy could think beautiful, for it sounded like a saw going through a keg of nails. Once a baby downy calmly went to sleep on the trunk, using the toes and stiff tail to brace himself, and remained there an hour, letting us walk right up to him.''

Occasionally a young downy in juvenal plumage still has a trace of red on the head, but instead of being on the nape, it is forward, more on top of the head. All nestlings are *supposed* to have red on the crown, which in some cases, disappears very soon in the female. The past summer we had a young male with this red crown patch. We often saw him at the suet, being fed by a parent bird, usually the female.

Downy—a resident wherever found—belongs to the family *Picidae,* or woodpeckers, which occurs in all wooded parts of the world, except in the Australian region and in Madagascar. There are some three hundred and seventy-five known species, about half of which are found in the New World. Twenty-four species are found in North America, about ten or so in the South.

The hairy woodpecker is almost exactly like the downy, except that it is a third larger, the red patch of the male has a black ''parting'' through its middle, and the outer white tail-feathers are not barred with black, (see colored plate) and its notes are louder. Its habits are similar to the downy, though the hairy is a shyer bird, and in the South is found mostly in wooded lowlands. Its food habits are also similar to those of the downy.

XXXVI

THE RED-HEADED WOODPECKER

And now from yonder beech trunk sheer and sterile,
The rat-tat-tat of the woodpecker's bill.
—J. P. IRVINE.

THERE is nothing of protective coloring about the red-headed woodpecker, which is well named, as the whole head and neck of both adult male and female are a vivid, glowing crimson that readily distinguishes them from the other woodpeckers.

The belly, rump, and secondaries are white, the rest of the plumage a glossy blue-black. The bird is much larger than its Cousin Downy, being nine and a half inches in length.

More versatile than the other woodpeckers, the red-head eats small acorns as a staple food, and fruits and berries as do the berry-eating birds. It also flits along from stump to fence-post and catches insects on the wing, like the fly-catchers.

The red-heads are merry, frolicsome birds, with all sorts of tricks and manners. Some of them go through the antics of the jays. The woodpecker family, though songless, all have such jolly, laughing notes that they are sometimes called the "Laughing Family."

As a drummer the red-head wields a lively drumstick. And never is he at loss for a "drum." If there is no resonant dead limb at hand, he will drum on tin roofs and lightning rods, and he has even been known to get up quite a jazz concert by drumming on the wire of a barbed fence!

This particular woodpecker is a permanent resident in most of the South at all seasons, but its abundance seems to depend on local conditions. Wherever there are groves of oaks and beeches, there one will find the red-heads, for they like to go "nutting" as well as any small boy or girl, and they are particularly fond of beech-nuts.

PREFERENCE FOR CERTAIN LOCALITIES

As they are adaptable birds, changing their fare and habits somewhat with the seasons, they ought to be generally distributed; but instead they seem to show a choice for certain localities, and to be entirely lacking in others.

Those of the North are supposed to migrate southward for the winter, but this depends, apparently, not on the severity of the weather, but entirely on the abundance of food. Their movements are affected especially by the crop of beechnuts, of which they are particularly fond. Even though the weather was unusually severe they have been known to remain in large numbers in northern New York, when this food was plentiful.

On a motor trip through Kentucky some years ago we noted great numbers of red-headed woodpeckers. We saw so many we thought the red-head should have been the state bird, instead of the Kentucky cardinal, of which we saw but few. Kentucky is noted for its many beautiful beech groves, which probably accounts for the prevalence of red-heads.

Red-headed woodpeckers are also found in large numbers in the clearings in our mountains, where trees have been girdled so that they will die, thus opening up new fields. Hence the mountain saying, "As common as red-heads in a deadenin!"

These noisy, active birds have a loud, rolling, tree-toad-like call *ker-r-ruck, ker-r-ruck*. Unfortunately, the vivid red head and the white secondaries make them an easy target for bird enemies, hunters, and the small boy with an air-rifle or sling-shot.

Its nesting habits are common to those of the woodpecker family, the hole being dug in a dead tree or limb, or even in a telephone pole or flagstaff. Some years ago a pair even made their nest in the ball on the top of the flagstaff of the North Carolina State Capitol at Raleigh.

Evidently the male and female both believe in strict equality of labor, for both share regular turns in hollowing out a nest. This usually takes several days of rather constant labor, and the birds take "turn and turn about," the absent one returning promptly to work whenever the other calls before flying off.

THE COLOR OF EGGS

The eggs are laid in May. There are four to six, and, like all woodpeckers' eggs, they are round and glossy white, looking almost like porcelain.

In the earlier stages of their development all birds doubtless laid white eggs, and color is believed to have been acquired for purposes of protection, as most birds have departed from the ancestral habit of covering the eggs or laying them in covered situations, and most of them are now using more or less open nests. Therefore, where eggs are still laid in holes or hollow trees, they are usually white, and where they are laid in open nests they are generally protectively marked. Thus, the eggs of kingfishers, woodpeckers, and owls are white.

There are many exceptions to this rule: doves, for instance, lay white eggs in frail, open nests, but as both sexes incubate, the eggs are rarely exposed. Grebes lay white, or whitish eggs, in flat, open nests, but the eggs are usually covered before the parent bird leaves the nest.

On the other hand, chickadees, titmice, nuthatches, cliff swallows, crested flycatchers, and bluebirds usually nest in holes, and yet lay pigmented eggs.

In the South the red-headed woodpecker nests usually before the middle of May. Although the female is colored exactly like the male, the young are not colored like the parents—as in the case of the chickadee—but have the head and breast gray, streaked with black and white, and the wings barred with black. This makes for a little more safety for the young than if they had the vivid scarlet head and neck of their parents.

The red-head eats nearly twice as much vegetable food, mainly mast, as it does insect food. And being an eater of acorns, it has a hard, muscular gizzard. The insects that it eats, however, include many that are destructive, such as clover beetles, corn weevil, cherry scale, and seventeen-year cicadas.

On the other side of the ledger are the facts that it eats corn in the ear and some small fruits, and some ornithologists claim that it robs other birds of both eggs and birdlings. But other ornithologists say that this is a slanderous and untrue accusation, that it is more apt to be the occasional act of an individual bird and is not characteristic of the species as a whole.

XXXVII

THE FLICKER, THE BIRD OF MANY NAMES

> Tell me where you scare up
> Names for me like "Flicker," "Yarup,"
> "High-hole," "Yucker," "Yellow-hammer—"
> None of these are in my grammar—
> "Piquebois jaune," (Woodpeck yellow),
> So the Creoles call a fellow.
> Others call me "Golden-wings,"
> "Clape," and twenty other things
> That I never half remember,
> Any summer till September.
> —GARRETT NEWKIRK, in *Bird-Lore*.

THE FLICKER, or golden-winged woodpecker, is, as the poem states, a bird of many names. The habits, notes, colors, flight, and peculiarities of this well known bird are reflected in its popular names—some 124 in all—by which it is known throughout its range.

High-hole, yellow-hammer, yellow-shafted woodpecker, pigeon woodpecker, yarup, wake-up, clape, and wilcrissen are a few of the names.

At a distance this woodpecker is sometimes mistaken for the meadowlark. Both birds have somewhat similar coloring and markings; both have a black crescent breast decoration, and both feed on the ground—where no proper woodpecker is supposed to be.

Some twelve or thirteen inches in length, the flicker is one of the most handsomely colored and best known of the eastern woodpeckers, and attracts attention wherever seen. Nearly all old orchards are fortunate in containing a pair.

The head is ashy, with a red patch on the back. The

rump is white, and the rest of the upper parts are brownish barred with black; the lower parts are pinkish brown, shading into yellow, and there is a black crescent across the breast. (The meadowlark's breast mark is more V-shaped.) The under parts beneath the black crescent are heavily spotted with round black spots, and the shafts and under surface of the quills are a golden yellow. In flight, the white rump shows very conspicuously, and is one of the distinguishing marks of the bird.

The male is quite a dashing Lothario, having a handsome black *moustachio* extending on each side of the throat from base of bill. The female lacks this adornment. But the young flickers are unusual in that they resemble their fathers instead of their mothers. The young males, and even the young females, have the black *moustachio* of their father and wear it until their post-juvenal moult.

BIRDS OF MANY VOICES

The flicker is a bird of many voices as well as many names. In the early spring he makes himself known by a long, sonorous call *wick-wick-wick-wick* which Audubon called ''a prolonged jovial laugh.'' During the nesting season the call becomes a rapidly repeated and mellow *cuh-cuh-cuh*—as spring-like as the peeping of a frog, and in the autumn it is a vigorous, nasal *kee-yer, kee-yer*.

Like the other woodpeckers, the flicker beats a rolling tattoo in the spring. But, unlike the others, he is fond of feeding on the ground, ants forming a large part of his food. See a flicker working industriously on the ground, then go and investigate that particular spot, and invariably you will find an ant-hill.

Yellow-hammer's beak is more slender and curving than that of his brethren, and he has an extremely long, barbed tongue, which he uses to probe ant-hills. The

FLICKER

Order—Pici   Family—Picidæ
Genus—Colaptes   Species—auratus auratus
National Association of Audubon Societies

YELLOW-BELLIED SAPSUCKER

Order—Pici   Family—Picidæ
Genus—Sphyrapicus   Species—Varius Varius

National Association of Audubon Societies

flicker's tongue is capable of being extended more than any other woodpecker's. The sticky substance on the bird's tongue covers the little barbs, and thus he is able to catch a great many ants at a time.

Anyone who has been worried by ant-hills in a lawn will appreciate the fact that an examination of a flicker's stomach by the Biological Survey found that it contained five thousand ants. In contrast with the red-headed woodpecker, which, being largely an eater of acorns, has a muscular stomach, or gizzard, the flicker, being largely an eater of ants, has a weak, flabby gizzard.

Flickers are also fond of wild fruits and berries, such as the black gum, wild cherry, elderberry, dogwood, and frost grape, while in the South in winter they fairly swarm over the peanut fields.

As a suitor, this golden-winged woodpecker, as described by Burroughs, is an awkward, ridiculous fellow. The male, or two males, will alight on a limb in front of the female, and go through a series of amusing bowings and scrapings. Spreading the tail and puffing out the chest, he bends his body to the right and to the left, and utters a curious, musical call. The female looks on unmoved. Apparently she isn't particularly interested. Presently she flies away, followed by her suitor, and the little comedy may be repeated on another stump or tree.

SOMETIMES MAKE MANY HOLES

Flickers have a peculiar and wasteful habit of sometimes boring out a number of superfluous holes for nests high up (which accounts for the name of high-hole), in limbs, buildings, or hollow wooden columns; yet they use only one. Sometimes in order to enter unused buildings, such as houses, barns, or churches, the bird will, if necessary, drill holes through weather-boarding. Also, the bird is the only one of the woodpeckers which will use an old deserted nest. The hole may be anywhere from four to thirty feet up, and some are even as high as sixty feet. Flickers will also nest in bird boxes, if the boxes are made long and narrow and placed high up. When new holes are to be made, both male and female take turns at excavating, the work being done at odd times during the day.

The eggs, like all woodpeckers' eggs, are pure white, and vary greatly in number, usually from five to nine in a set. In the South nesting comes in April or the early part of May. As both birds assist in drilling the nest, so do both take turns in incubating, and each feeds the other while thus engaged.

Baby flickers are fed in the same way that baby hummers are, by regurgitation. The parent bird swallows the food and when it is softened sufficiently puts her beak far down into the baby's throat and pumps the food into it.

When the young are old enough to leave the nest, the mother tries to coax them out of the hole. Failing in this, she gives them no food for several hours, until, through hunger, they crawl out and to the upper branches, where the parents continue to feed them until they are able to care for themselves.

The flicker is among our protected birds, but that does not mean it is safe from the hunter's gun or the small boy's air-rifle. Several years ago we had a flicker that kept to our yard almost constantly. We learned its seasonal calls, and were particularly fond of its drumming. On the way home one day, my husband passed two young boys who had been trying out a new air-rifle. Proud young Nimrods they were, striding along with a dead flicker and a meadowlark as trophies of their skill.

We did not, of course, know positively that it was

our flicker. But we never saw our bird again. And when I called authorities to object about boys killing protected birds, I was told there were no funds to enforce the law, and that nothing could be done about it.

Evidently bird protection must come—not from laws which we have no means of enforcing—but from interest developed in birds, for, as Mrs. Comstock, mother of the Nature Study movement, said, "No boy or girl can become interested in the life history of a bird or animal and not become humane towards it."

XXXVIII

YELLOW-BELLIED SAPSUCKER, THE TIPPLER

A bacchant for sweets: " 'Tis nectar I seek!"
And he raps on the tree with his sharp-whetted beak;
And he drinks, in the wild March wind and the sun,
The coveted drops as they start to run.

He girdles the maple round and round
'Tis heart-blood he drinks at each sweet wound;
And his bacchanal song is the tap-tap-tap,
That brings from the bark its clear flowing sap.
　　　　　—EDITH M. THOMAS, in *Bird-Lore*.

THE YELLOW-BELLIED sapsucker is one of the few birds
whose intimacy we should discourage, for he is a woodpecker that has strayed from the paths of virtue—the
only woodpecker permanently injurious to trees. Instead of drilling a hole for the grub, he drills for a drink.

For the sapsucker is a tippler that has become too
fond of the sap of trees, and in drilling the numerous
little holes—often in regular lines—to catch the sap, he
sometimes girdles a limb or tree. When a great many
holes have been bored close together the bark loosens and
peels off, and the tree may die. The bird also does harm
by eating the cambium layer, through which flows the
sap which nourishes the tree. This cambium layer lies
just beneath the bast, or inner bark, and the bird, by
eating this bast, does even more harm. Unfortunately,
this woodpecker always prefers the youngest and most
vigorous trees.

AMUSING ANTICS

"It is amusing," says Anna Botsford Comstock, in
her *Handbook of Nature Study*, "to watch the sapsucker.

Using his bill as a pick, he makes the chips fly as he taps the tree; then he goes away and taps another tree. After a bit he returns to the first tree, and holding his beak close to the hole for a long time, sucks the sap, then throws his head back and 'swigs' it down with every sign of delirious enjoyment. The avidity with which these birds come to the bleeding wells which they have made has in it all the fierceness of a toper crazed for drink. They are particularly fond of the sap of mountain ash, apple, thorn apple, canoe-birch, cut-leaf birch, red maple, red oak, white ash, and young pines.'' In all, there are said to be about two hundred and fifty kinds of trees that are known to be attacked by the sapsucker.

On the trunk of a balsam tree on the campus at Guilford College, North Carolina, T. Gilbert Pearson counted over sixteen hundred of these miniature sap holes. In a recent article* on woodpeckers, Mr. Pearson writes of another tree in North Carolina which he kept under observation for fifteen years, and he believes that one sapsucker came to this tree for its food every winter and spring throughout the entire period. The tree became much swollen—as Nature struggled to overcome the damage done to it by this bird—and eventually died.

While some young trees are killed outright, loss is also caused by stains and other blemishes in the wood which result from sapsucker punctures. Often fungi or bacteria get into these holes causing decayed areas. Blemishes known as "bird pecks," are especially numerous in maple, hickory, walnut, oak, cypress, and yellow poplar. In the subsequent growth of the trees, these wounds sometimes cause "curly" or "bird's eye" wood.

Unlike most woodpeckers, this bird does comparatively little good and more or less damage.

* ''Woodpeckers, Friends of Our Forests,'' *The National Geographic Magazine*, April, 1933.

As the sap oozes out, many insects, including hornets, wasps, spiders, beetles, and flies, gather to feed on the sap. The sapsucker also eats these insects. Its tongue (shorter than that of any other of the woodpeckers) is not barbed like that of the others, but has a little brush at the end of it by which it can easily lick up great quantities of both sap and insects.

In spite of his iniquities, the yellow-bellied sapsucker is a handsome fellow. The male has the forehead and throat crimson, edged with black, with a black line extending back of the eye, bordered with white above and below. There is a large circular patch on the breast which is bordered at the sides and below with lemon-yellow. The female is similar to the male, sometimes but not always having the red forehead; but she has a white bib instead of a red one beneath her chin, and her outer tail-feathers have broken white bars.

The distinguishing mark of the sapsucker is that the red is on the front of the head instead of on the nape, as with the downy and the hairy woodpeckers. In flight, the broad, white stripes extending from the shoulders backward form a long oval figure which is very characteristic. The bird is eight and one-half inches long, or about one-fifth smaller than the robin.

GREATER MIGRANT THAN MOST WOODPECKERS

The sapsuckers rove farther north than most woodpeckers—sometimes going as far as Central Quebec—and winter as far south as Central America. Most of them spend the winter in the southern states, where they subsist mainly on berries, especially dogwood, holly, and frost grapes.

From Virginia to their breeding grounds in northern New York, New England, and Canada, and occasionally in the higher mountains of the Appalachians, they are seen only during migration, which occurs in late April or early May. Then the birds appear in two's and three's together, and are very bold in attacking shade trees, especially the white birch.

Their general breeding habits are similar to those of other woodpeckers. The nest is usually a hole in a dead or dying tree—though it may be in a living tree— often a birch, and may be as high as fifty feet. The enclosure is circular, and just large enough to admit the birds. The cavity is twelve to fifteen inches deep, the depth making for the safety of the young birds. From four to seven white eggs are laid.

When feeding their young, the sapsuckers are true flycatchers, snatching insects while on the wing. The young are somewhat similar to the adults, but with the crown dull blackish, the breast brownish gray barred with black, and the throat whitish.

"SAPSUCKERS' ORCHARD"

According to Pearson, if one will only search long enough when in the vicinity of the nest often he may find what is called a "sapsuckers' orchard." This is a small group of trees from which the birds get their living. Here the birds come many times every day to feed. New holes are added at intervals until the trees of their "orchard" become thickly pitted with them.

These "orchards" are frequented every summer for many years and when found may contain a dozen or more trees already dead. As the trees die, new trees are attacked. The young birds are brought to these trees by their parents when they are old enough to fly, and feed daily until the approach of winter drives the sapsuckers from their summer homes.

Here in the South, in their winter home—they come about September and leave in late April or early May

—the birds are rather quiet and inconspicuous. They like to keep a tree between themselves and an observer, and hence the bird is often better known by its work than by its appearance. But in their summer home, the birds are said to be noisy, rollicking fellows, chasing one another among the trees, and screaming at the top of their voices. Brewster describes their notes at this season as a clear, ringing *cleur-cleur-cleur-cleur,* while young and old utter a snarling cry not unlike the mew of a catbird.

A summary of a study made by the government Biological Survey states: "However strong seems the indictment against the sapsuckers, it must not be imagined that every tree pecked by them is doomed. On the contrary, they frequently work on a tree year after year without noticeably diminishing its vitality."

XXXIX

THE LESS COMMON WOODPECKERS

THE PILEATED

Bright carpenter of the deeper woods,
Whence comes your noisy skill
By which you hammer, cut and drill
In search of food—or, better still,
For place to sleep or nest?
—R. W. G.

Log-cock, woodcock, and cock-of-the-woods are some of the names by which the pileated woodpecker is known, especially in the South.

The individuals vary greatly in size, and may be from fifteen to nineteen inches in length, with a wing expanse of from twenty-five to thirty inches. The male pileated woodpecker is blackish brown above, with the whole top of the head scarlet, and the feathers lengthened to form a crest. A white stripe, tinged with yellow at the nostril, passes down the side of the neck. The throat is white, with a scarlet stripe at the base of the lower mandible, and the long, powerful bill is horn-color. The female is very similar, but without red on the forepart of the crown or at the base of the lower mandible.

The pileated woodpecker may still be found in heavily wooded sections throughout much of its range, which covers North America. In the less thickly populated parts of the country it is still not uncommon, and it is said that in the hummocks and cypress swamps of Florida it is sometimes found in numbers. It also inhabits heavily timbered swamps, river bottoms, and some mountainsides.

Using their chisel-like bills, these powerful birds make large, deep cavities in decaying logs and trees in search of larvae and wood-boring beetles.

In procuring their food, pileated woodpeckers have become very skillful as woodcutters, and half an hour after attacking a dead log or tree may have a pile of chips of which any woodcutter might be proud. Some of these chips are as large as, or larger than a man's hand. The neck muscles of woodpeckers are especially developed to enable the birds constantly to strike hard blows with their bills when digging in wood. Also they work steadily. If there was not some arrangement to absorb the shock of these repeated heavy blows of the bill, the brain, eyes, and ears would be definitely injured.

They also like many wild berries and fruits such as holly, dogwood, persimmon, tupelo gum, poison ivy, sumac, hackberry, and frost grapes, and the great birds look awkward and ungainly as they try to hold on to their perch and gather berries.

These woodpeckers are noisy birds, especially during the mating season and after the young have left the nest. The call is a long, rolling, sonorous *cow-cow-cow* repeated slowly many times. There is also a conversational note, a *wick-y-up* somewhat like that of the flicker.

SLOW, DIRECT FLIGHT

Although its flight is rather slow, it is unusually direct and, unlike that of most woodpeckers, is not undulating. It is in flight that the white underparts and the large white markings of its wings show most plainly. So conspicuous are these markings then that often, by means of them, one may discover the bird flying at a distance.

Like many cavity-nesting birds, this species uses holes to sleep in, usually excavating them in living trees,

PILEATED WOODPECKER

Order—Pici   Family—Picidæ
Genus—Phlœotomus   Species—pileatus
National Association of Audubon Societies

BELTED KINGFISHER

Order—Coccyges   Family—Alcedinidæ
Genus—Ceryle   Species—alcyon

National Association of Audubon Societies

often in black or sweet gum. Sometimes the same hole is used for several years, and occasionally two holes are bored in the same tree, with an opening between, to be used as a means of escape if the bird is hard pressed.

But though the same hole may be used for sleeping for several years, for nesting the birds must have a fresh one, though the cavities are often in the same tree. These holes may be from twelve to seventy-five feet up. Both birds assist in the work of excavating, but it is believed the female does the greater part. The three to five eggs are glossy white, and both birds take turns in incubating, which lasts eighteen days. It is said that when one bird wishes to leave the nest it will call the other, and then wait until it comes.

Hatched naked, the young (who are fed by regurgitation) are extremely helpless, and do not leave the nest until the wing-quills are well developed.

Never injurious to crops, the pileated woodpecker confines its attention largely to trees of the forest, where it renders valuable service in its consumption of destructive insects. Unfortunately, as a result of thoughtless shooting, and the desire for bills and crests for ornament, this great, interesting bird of our southern forests is growing steadily scarcer, until the day may soon come when the pileated, like the great ivory-billed woodpecker, will be almost extinct.

THE IVORY-BILLED WOODPECKER

The greatest of all woodpeckers in America, the ivory-billed, is almost extinct, or at least is on the verge of extinction. Larger than the pileated, being nineteen to twenty-one inches in length, with a wing expanse of thirty to thirty-three inches, this great bird was indeed king of the woodpeckers. Few living people have been fortunate enough to see one. It resembles somewhat the pileated, but the forepart of its head is blue, the back part and the crest scarlet. The great bill is ivory-color, giving the bird its name.

The ivory-billed has disappeared from most of its former domain in the low countries from North Carolina to southern Florida and eastern Texas. There are a limited number in the primeval forests of Louisiana and Florida, and possibly a few may remain in the swamps of Arkansas, Mississippi, and Missouri, although there have been no reports of their being seen there in years. The Louisiana Department of Conservation is trying to conserve its small colony of ivory-bills.

THE RED-COCKADED WOODPECKER

A woodpecker with nuthatch tendencies is the red-cockaded, for it frequently hangs head downward while feeding from the extremity of branches, and, according to Chapman, its call-note of *yank-yank* resembles that of the white-breasted nuthatch, though it is louder, hoarser, and not so distinct.

This woodpecker is a southern species, being found from eastern Texas northward to southern Virginia and southern Missouri. It is a bird of the great pineries of the South, and is seldom seen very far from them.

Between the hairy and the downy woodpeckers in size, the red-cockaded has a black back barred crosswise with white; white sides spotted with black, and a large conspicuous white patch on each side of the head. The male has a small tuft of scarlet feathers on each side of the back of the head.

While the cockaded nests in holes, like all good woodpeckers, it has some queer ideas about its home. It drills a hole in a living pine tree, but it is said that it usually chooses one in which the heart is dead. For two or three feet, both above and below the entrance hole, the bird makes numerous punctures through the bark, from which the resin flows, forming a sticky mass over the en-

THE RED-COCKADED WOODPECKER LIKES THE GREAT PINERIES OF THE SOUTH. REDUCED ABOUT ONE-THIRD.

tire area. This shows at a great distance, and is a give-away of the nest.

Though it is not definitely known why the red-cockaded does this, Brimley suggests it may be as a guard against the inroads of ants and squirrels. The nest is usually placed well up in the tree and there are two to five white eggs. Often the same tree is used year after year, though a new hole is usually drilled. Sometimes as many as seven or eight holes have been found in one tree.

Being somewhat gregarious, several pairs of the red-cockaded are often found together, though some writers believe these groups are formed by the parents and their brood. Frequenting mainly the upper branches and terminal twigs of pine trees, these birds feed chiefly on insects and seeds. Numbers of ants and the larvae of wood-boring beetles are consumed. Grasshoppers, crickets, caterpillars, and spiders are also eaten; also mast, comprised chiefly of pine seeds, and the seeds of magnolias, bayberry, and poison ivy. Considered beneficial because of destruction of ants and wood-boring beetles, these birds should be protected.

THE RED-BELLIED WOODPECKER

Sometimes called "zebra woodpecker" because of the zebra-like white stripes on its black back, the red-bellied woodpecker is a common bird in many woodlands of southern states.

The whole top of the head and back of the neck are bright scarlet, the middle of the belly and sometimes the breast is more or less tinged with red. The female is similar, but the crown is grayish ashy, the scarlet being only on the nape and nostrils.

Ranging throughout the eastern states and lower Ontario, the red-bellied is one of the most widely distributed woodpeckers east of the Rockies, and is known in most of the southern states at all seasons, but only in certain localities. In the Mississippi valley, and in the swamp lands bordering some of the rivers of the Carolinas it is often the most abundant woodpecker. Seemingly it prefers tall timber, especially deciduous trees, in the neighborhood of water. However, in some regions

BECAUSE OF THE ZEBRA-LIKE BLACK AND WHITE STRIPES ON ITS BACK, THE RED-BELLIED WOODPECKER IS SOMETIMES CALLED THE "ZEBRA WOODPECKER." ABOUT ONE-HALF NATURAL SIZE.

it is found in upland groves or orchards, and even about dooryards and gardens.

The nesting site is usually a decayed or hollow stump or tree; the softer varieties such as elm, poplar, willow, sycamore, and pine are apparently preferred, although telephone poles are occasionally used. The hole may range from twenty feet up, and is usually ten to twelve inches deep. The four to six eggs are white. There seem to be two broods a season, for we are told of nests in the same location in Alabama being occupied as early as April 16, and as late as July 27.* April or May is the usual nesting date.

Feeding upon both insects and vegetable matter, it eats ants, grasshoppers, eggs of cockroaches, and caterpillars, beechnuts, hazelnuts, and pecans. It also likes a little fruit, and some corn.

The call of the red-bellied is a hoarse *chuh-chuh,* but it also has a rolling *k-r-r-r-ring.*

* Howell, *Birds of Alabama.*

XL

THE BELTED KINGFISHER

He lives in a hole that is quite to his mind,
With the green mossy hazel-roots firmly entwined;
Where the dark alder-bough waves gracefully o'er,
And the sword-flag and arrow-head grow at his door.

. . . . .

O happy kingfisher! What care should he know,
By the clear pleasant stream, as he skims to and fro,
Now lost in the shadow, now bright in the sheen
Of the hot summer sun, glancing scarlet and green!
—MARY HOWITT.

As THE name implies, this bird is a great lover of fish, and in the pursuit of this food plunges headlong into the water. The prey is always carried in the long, strong beak. Shores of wooded streams, ponds, or lakes are the favorite haunts of the kingfisher, where he silently perches on a limb overlooking the water. There he keeps a sharp lookout for food or foe.

A handsome enough bird as to color, the kingfisher is awkward in shape, for with his large beak and head and long bristle-like crest—reaching back to the nape—the short tail, and small, weak-looking feet, he is badly proportioned. His upper parts are grayish blue; the throat, collar, and breast are white, with a grayish-blue band, or belt, across the under parts, which gives him the name of "belted" kingfisher.

The short, square tail, and the long, pointed wings are spotted or barred with white, and there is a conspic-uous white spot just in front of the eye. The straight, stout, sharp bill is longer than the head. The female is similar to the male, but is even more colorful, having a chestnut band beneath the gray-blue belt and below the wings.

Few birds wear their bright colors throughout the year, but the kingfisher, the red-headed woodpecker, the bluebird, the blue jay, the cardinal, and the purple finch are notable exceptions. The vast majority of birds shed their bright colors after the breeding season and do not gain them again until the following spring.

EXPERT FISHERMAN

A militant-looking bird, ever alert, the kingfisher sits on some favorite branch overlooking his domain. His keen sight catches the gleam of a fish and he darts down, plunging head first after his prey. Seldom does he fail, and when he reappears a wriggling fish is usually held in his powerful beak as he flies back to his perch. After beating his prey on a limb or branch until it is dead, the kingfisher swallows it head first, so that the fins will not prick his throat. Later, owl-like, he gulps up a ball or pellet of the indigestible scales and bones.

While in flight, if a kingfisher sees a fish beneath him, he can hover a second and then dive with the same accuracy as from a perch. He also dives into the edge of the sea after salt-water fish.

Unlike the fish hawk, or osprey, the kingfisher never grasps his victims with his feet, which are small and weak and of no use in clutching or holding prey. The foot is unusual, in that the third and fourth toes are joined together for half their length, an evolutionary development which is believed to be of aid to the bird in pushing out soil when excavating for a nest.

For the kingfisher nests in holes, usually tunneled by the birds in banks of streams or ponds. The opening may be from four to twenty feet deep, and ends in an enlargement. The tunnel may be straight, or it may wind about to avoid such obstructions as large stones or roots. The work is done by both birds, by means of their long, powerful bills, the loosened soil being pushed out by their peculiarly constructed feet. Aside from this, kingfishers have little use for their feet, which, through lack of use, have degenerated.

As the nest is usually quite difficult to excavate, it is often used again and again; the five to eight eggs are pure white, as are many eggs that are hatched in cavities. The breeding season is usually in May, and as the young are born naked and helpless, they grow slowly.

Both parents are kept busy catching small fish and other food for their nestlings, some observers believing the burden falls heaviest on the male. Frogs, grasshoppers, crickets, and even field mice are also in the kingfisher's menu.

YOUNG IN "QUILLS"

The young are born naked, and are unusual in that their first real feathers remain in the sheaths until full grown; so for a time the young kingfishers seem covered with quills. Towards the end, the transformation from quills to fluffy feathers takes place in a few hours. At this time the young birds are as brilliantly colored as are the adults, and even before they leave the nest the chestnut bands on the small females begin to show.

Economically, these birds belong to a group which does neither much good nor much harm. Their great value is in the interest they add to the borders of our streams, ponds, and other water-ways. Because they are considered destructive about fish hatcheries and trout streams, they are not protected by law. However, the harm they do is inconsiderable, and the charm they add to the out-of-doors for the nature-lover more than offsets the few fish they may consume.

Kingfishers are solitary birds, never traveling in flocks like the crows or jays, and only associating in pairs during the nesting season. Evidently they believe in "sovereign rights," for a pair may claim fishing rights to a half-mile of stream on either side of their nesting site, though they may range much farther afield in their search for food. They will drive other kingfishers away from their own "fishing grounds." There is also said to be neutral territory where several kingfishers may feed.

The bird is no singer, the notes being a harsh, discordant *kuk-kuk-kuk! crock-crock-crock!* The loud call echoing through the woodland can sometimes be heard for a considerable distance, and suggests a watchman's rattle. Nor, as with some birds, does the voice improve during the mating season; it remains as harsh, discordant, and rattly as ever. But, as everything about those we love sounds and looks good to us, the male's courtship rattle is probably very beautiful to Lady Kingfisher.

"HALCYON" BIRDS

Kingfishers belong to the family *Alcedinidae,* and are most numerous in the Malay Archipelago—"On the Road to Mandalay"—and the majority of the hundred and ninety-some known species are found in that part of the world. Of the seven American species, confined chiefly to the tropics, only one, our belted kingfisher, is found north of southern Texas. Its range covers much of North America and parts of northern South America, breeding from the Alaskan peninsula to our southern border and wintering from about Ohio and Virginia south to northern South America.

There are many legends about the kingfisher, though it is the European kingfisher—a much smaller and brighter-colored bird—about which they have gathered.

One is to the effect that these birds, called halcyons by the ancients, used the seven days before the shortest day of the year for building their nests, which were supposed to float on the water, and the seven days following, for the hatching of the young.

During this period of the "halcyon days" the ancients believed that the sea was always calm and hence the word "halcyon" came to be used as meaning calm, peaceful days out-of-doors.

The power of quelling storms was believed to have been conferred upon the kingfisher by Æolus, the wind god, who granted this dispensation when his loved daughter Halcyone, grieving deeply for her husband, Ceyx, threw herself upon his body in the sea, and both were immediately changed into kingfishers.

XLI

THE LOGGERHEAD SHRIKE, OR BUTCHER BIRD

I like
The shrike,
Because, with a thorn for a guillotine,
He does his work so well and clean,
A critic keen—
A practical bird
Whose common sense
Must be immense,
For, tell me, who has ever heard of such a thing
As a loggerhead shrike that tried to sing?
—THOMPSON, in *Bird-Lore*.

PERHAPS because he believes in being forehanded, and, when hunting is good, in keeping the larder well-filled against leaner days, the shrike, or butcher bird, impales his victims on a thorn, sharp twig, a splinter, or barb. Sometimes they are left there and apparently forgotten.

Or, as some scientists prefer to believe, this practice is simply because, while the shrike has the beak of a hawk or other bird of prey, he has not the right build nor such talons as enable true birds of prey to seize their victim and hold it securely while tearing it to pieces. And so he impales his prey, or forces it into a crotch or sharp crevice where it can readily be dissected.

Since scientists themselves are not agreed as to which is the correct version, you may take your choice. Dr. A. A. Allen, a national authority on birds, recently told me he thought both versions were partially right.

Like birds of prey and some other birds, the shrike habitually disgorges the indigestible part of its food after digesting the nutritive portion. The bones, feath-

LOGGERHEAD SHRIKE

Order—Passeres   Family—Laniidæ
Genus—Lanius   Species—ludivicianus

National Association of Audubon Societies

SCREECH OWL

Order—Raptores   Family—Strigidæ
Genus—Otus   Species—asio

National Association of Audubon Societies

ers, and hairs are rolled into compact pellets in the stomach before being disgorged.

The shrikes belong to the family *Laniidae*, and scientists are even disagreed as to their number, as they differ as to subfamilies. Only two—or three, if we consider the migrant shrike as a separate species instead of a subspecies of the more northern and migratory loggerhead shrike—occur in the New World.

In general, the loggerhead's range is from southern North Carolina to south Florida and west to Louisiana. Farming country, thin woods, and roadsides seem to be the favored territory of this shrike.

The northern shrike winters as far south as Kentucky and Virginia, and Brimley has one record of it from the coast of Carolina. The migrant shrike also winters from the middle states to Texas, Louisiana, and Mississippi. All the forms retire southward at the approach of winter.

"FRENCH MOCKINGBIRD"

The southern, or loggerhead shrike is a fairly large bird, a little smaller than the mockingbird, which it resembles somewhat in coloring and markings. It is gray above, white, sometimes tinged with grayish, below, and the wings and tail are black with white patches. There is a heavy black line through the eye, which is lacking in the mockingbird, and it has "a hawk's beak and a sparrow's feet."

Like the flycatchers and some of the hawks—or like a mediaeval robber baron in some ancient castle stronghold on the Rhine—the shrike does not go out in search of his prey, but waits for his victims to come to him, and then swoops down upon them.

A shrike's eyesight is marvelous. It is said he can see a grasshopper fifty yards distant. Like the flycatchers, he chooses a vantage point from which he can get an unobstructed view. It may be the top of a tree (never in the depths of a tree), fence post, telegraph wire, or housetop. From his perch he keeps a sharp lookout for mice, moles, lizards, shrews, beetles, and— I am sorry to say—small birds, though stomach analysis shows this food to be not common. The shrike has still another method of hunting. Like the crows, he sometimes sneaks upon his victim from the ground.

Once, while out on a field trip with some of my school children, I found a shrike's cache on a barbed wire fence which ran through a thick clump of bushes. There, impaled upon the wire barbs, were a field mouse and a bluebird. The little blue body was dried and dull looking —and I've disliked the shrike ever since.

Though he is sometimes mistaken for the mocker, and in the South is also known as the "French mockingbird," there is no resemblance in their songs. The northern shrike is a better singer than the loggerhead, whose notes are harsh and unmusical, but in spite of that, the bird occasionally persists in trying to sing. Perhaps he thinks practice will make perfect, but to most people his efforts usually sound like a series of harsh gurgles, squeaks, shrill pipes, and whistles that sound like a rusty, creaking hinge. But I suppose we should at least credit him with persistently trying to be a songster, for, the poet to the contrary, he *does* sometimes try.

In the far South mating begins in February, but it is a little later in the upper South. Usually the nest is not more than seven feet up, and is likely to be built in thorny hedges or scrubby trees, a thick-grown wild plum bush being a favorite place. It is made of strips of bark, small twigs, and vegetable fibers, lined with grasses, and the three to five dull white or creamy-white eggs are thickly marked with cinnamon brown or lavender.

The young birds are similar to the adults, but their entire plumage is more or less tinged with grayish brown. There are usually two broods a season.

In flight the shrike is strong and vigorous, and indulges in much wing-flapping, usually staying close to the ground until it approaches its lookout, when it suddenly rises upwards. As it never assembles in flocks, or seems to associate with other birds, the shrike is known as a solitary bird.

Although the loggerhead and other shrikes have acquired a bad reputation as eaters of small birds, in reality they eat very few. Insects of various kinds form the shrike's main diet, ordinary grasshoppers furnishing the great bulk. Mice and shrews are also eaten. In California, according to my husband, the western form of the loggerhead captures tarantulas and impales them on wild mustard stalks. As no one has a very keen desire for the company of tarantulas, there is probably no objection to this—except on the part of the tarantula.

Summarizing then, we may say that the southern butcher bird, or loggerhead shrike, eats a few birds and and some useful insects, but on the whole its diet is very much in its favor, especially in its consumption of grasshoppers, mice, and shrews. For its work as a consumer of noxious insects and rodents it is placed on the Bird Roll of Honor by the United States Department of Agriculture.

And, in sections where the loggerhead shrike is frequently seen, it adds to the interest of the landscape.

XLII

THE OWLS, NIGHT WATCHMEN OF OUR FIELDS
AND GARDENS

We are two dusky owls, and we live in a tree;
　Look at her,—look at me!
Look at her,—she's my mate, and the mother of three
　Pretty owlets, and we
Have a warm cosy nest, just as snug as can be.

We are both very wise; for our heads, as you see,
　Look at her—look at me!
Are as large as the heads of four birds ought to be;
　And our horns, you'll agree,
Make us look wiser still, sitting here on the tree.

And we care not how gloomy the night-time may be;
　We can see,—we can see
Through the forest to roam; it suits her, it suits me;
　And we're free,—we are free
To bring back what we find, to our nest in the tree.

—ANONYMOUS.

FOR LONG years the cry of "owl" or "hawk" has been synonymous with "Johnnie, get your gun"—and Johnnie did; and if Johnnie were a good shot, that was the end of the owl or the hawk.

And Johnnie proudly displayed his victim, ignorant of—or perhaps only indifferent to—the fact that while he might possibly have killed one of our few really bad owls or hawks, in all probability he had shot a valuable guardian of orchard or farmyard.

For the owls and the hawks are the policemen on the beats around orchards, woods, and farmsteads—and they even keep regular hours while on duty! The hawks keep watch during the day, and the owls are on guard at night and through the early dawn. During spells of extreme

[216]

cold weather, mice and rabbits often gnaw the bark of young trees, sometimes killing them, and many a mouse and young rabbit has been caught at this and at other devastating work, by an owl or a hawk.

HARD, COLD FACTS

Unfortunately, all the owls and hawks are lumped together as something evil to be exterminated, whereas, from the standpoint of the farmer, all except a very few really harmful ones should be given every protection.

As I have said before, there is no sentimentality about government bulletins on birds. Sometimes years of exhaustive study and research go into the making of a single bulletin. And these surveys relate the cold, hard facts.

According to a government bulletin, most of these "birds of prey" as they are called, "labor day and night to destroy the enemies of the husbandman, and are persecuted unceasingly, while that most destructive mammal, the house cat, is petted and securely sheltered to spread destruction among the feathered tribe. The difference between the two can be summed up in a few words—only three or four birds of prey hunt birds when they can procure rodents for food, while the cat seldom touches mice if she can procure birds or young poultry. A cat has been known to kill twenty young chickens in a day, which is more than most raptorial birds destroy in a life time."

Owls and hawks often swallow their small victims entire, and after the nutritious parts have been absorbed the indigestible parts such as hair, feathers, scales, and bones are rolled into a solid ball by the action of the muscles of the stomach. These balls, called "pellets" are ejected, or spit out, before more food is taken. If you find an owl's nest, look about on the ground beneath and you will be sure to see many of these little balls or pellets. The analysis of stomachs of owls and pellets taken from their roosts at all seasons, and from all parts of the country, are carefully summarized in the government bulletin on owls and hawks.

In this study these birds are divided into four classes, and are rated on their beneficial and harmful qualities:

1. Species wholly beneficial
2. Those chiefly beneficial
3. Those in which beneficial and harmful qualities about balance
4. Harmful species

Sometimes certain birds of prey belong to one or another class according to locality, for an owl or a hawk may be locally injurious because of scarcity of rodents, when it is not so classed in another section. A good example of this is the great horned owl. Most of the owls in the southern states come in the second, or "chiefly beneficial" class, which includes the screech, the barred, the barn, the long-eared, the short-eared, and the snowy owl.

An owl's eyes, like a cat's, are especially adapted for seeing in the dark; but, where the cat's pupil is elongated, the owl's is round. Unlike those of other birds, its eyes are in the front of its head, as in humans; but they are fastened into the sockets so tightly that it cannot roll them around at all. When an owl wants to see what is going on at the side, or in back, it simply turns its head, as though the head were on a pivot. I have seen a captured owl do this until it seemed as if there were danger of the bird's wringing its own neck!

The ears of an owl, like its eyes, are not on the side of the head, as in song birds, but in front. The ear-opening is large, and the hearing is so keen that the owl can hear the movements of tiny creatures. It is said that an owl probably can hear a mouse even farther than he can see it.

SILENT FLIGHT

It must be paralyzing to be a small mouse or bird or baby bunny and to see an owl, with eyes shining in the dark, slipping up on it on silent wings. For the owl's flight is noiseless; the feathers of the wings, instead of being stiff to the edge, have a soft downy fringe, which enables the bird to pass through the air without a sound.

Small birds are terrified at the sight of an owl—any owl. On the rare occasions when an owl ventures out of its hiding place by day, stupid looking and blinking and blinded by the bright sunlight, it is soon surrounded by a group of furious titmice, warblers, wrens, vireos, and even jays. Encouraged by numbers these small birds, instead of being paralyzed by fear, seem to remember only their hatred of this silent night prowler. Forgotten is their enmity to the jays, and all join in a chorus of vituperation against this common enemy. At such times the owl usually pays no attention to the birds, but sits apparently unmoved, or he may eventually take flight.

Owls are found in all parts of the world, about two hundred and fifty species being known, of which nineteen are found in North America. There are two owl families, the *Aluconidae,* or barn owls, and the *Strigidae,* which includes the horned and the hoot owls. Though they differ from each other in structure, the two families share certain characteristic habits.

Most of the owls are woodland birds, though a few species live on dry plains or grassy marshes, and some live in towers, steeples, barn lofts, or attics. Being nocturnal birds of prey, they feed mostly on small mammals, and so are of even greater value to the farmer than are the hawks.

XLIII

THE SCREECH OWL

"I will sing a song:
    I'm the owl."
"Sing a song, you sing-song
    Ugly fowl!
What will you sing about,
    Night in and day out?"
"Sing about the night:
    I'm the owl."
"You could not see for the light,
    Stupid fowl!"
"Oh, the moon! and the dew!
    And the shadows!—tu-whoo!"
                —GEORGE MACDONALD.

THE SCREECH OWL, also called gray owl, red owl, and
mottled owl, and in Louisiana the shivering owl, is one
of our most abundant owls, and is resident wherever
found. It is the smallest owl with ear-tufts, which, being
conspicuous, help to identify it. Though no longer than
a robin, this owl's large round head and thickset body
make it appear much larger.

The screech owl's plumage is an excellent example of
mimicry, or protective coloring. Perched on a limb, flat
against the tree trunk, its irregularly marked plumage
so resembles the bark of the tree that it is difficult for
the eye to discern the outline of the owl. Especially is
this so if the bird stretches, or "freezes," becoming rigid
and motionless like a limb or stump.

TWO PHASES OF COLOR

Strangely enough, this owl has two phases of coloring,
the extreme reddish brown, and the gray, and there is

occasionally a gradation of color between these two. These phases have nothing to do with age, sex, or season, and the two extremes may be found in the same brood.

The reddish-brown phase, or the red owl as it is sometimes called, has reddish upper parts finely streaked with black; and white under parts streaked with black and irregularly barred with reddish brown. In the gray phase, or the gray owl, the upper parts are brownish gray streaked with black and the under parts white, more finely and irregularly barred with black, and here and there touched with reddish. Both phases have light yellow eyes and toes partly covered with down.

The upper mandible of the beak ends in a sharp hook that can tear and rend flesh. The beak is partially concealed by the feathers of the face, which gives the bird a rather weird appearance. But it is the talons, rather than the beak, which the owl uses in striking at its prey, for the feet are strong and the sharp, curved claws seem built for grappling with a foe.

Besides small mammals, and, especially during its own nesting season, some young chicks or birds (very often English sparrows), the screech owl eats frogs, fish, crawfish, bats, night moths, spiders, grasshoppers, crickets, beetles, caterpillars, and even cutworms, those dreadful garden enemies that do their ruinous work during the night. Cutworms are especially damaging to young tobacco plants, often making resetting necessary; so the screech owl should have a special welcome in the South.

As he belongs to the group of songless birds, the male screech owl cannot woo his lady by his voice, but must resort to gesturing and posturing, and such bowings and scrapings, such wing-raisings and snappings of the beak as take place! His call is a weird wail, tremulous and long drawn out—blood-curdling, say some city dwellers who find the country a lonely place and the screech owl's call a disturbing thing.

But to the lover of the woods and the out-of-doors, who likes to hear Nature's voice in any of its forms, the weird, haunting wail of the screech owl is but a part of the music of the night. Thoreau, the great New England naturalist, said of their call, "I love to hear their wailing, their doleful responses, trilled above the woodside, reminding me sometimes of music and singing birds, as if it were the dark and tearful side of music, the regrets and sighs that would fain be sung. . . . They give me a new sense of the vastness and mystery of that Nature which is the common dwelling of us both."

Screech owls usually nest in holes, generally in hollow trees, often an abandoned flicker's nest being used. There is little or no nest—perhaps a few feathers, small chips, or leaves—often nothing at all, for Mrs. Screech Owl is a slack, untidy, housekeeper. The four to six, or sometimes eight, eggs, are very white and very round. Breeding begins in March or April.

Credited with being devoted lovers, both birds are attentive to the young. Mrs. Comstock says that sometimes both parents sit together on the eggs, a less lonely way of passing the long weary days of incubation. The young, when first hatched, are blind and covered with down, but the plumage they acquire before leaving the nest is regularly barred grayish, or reddish brown and white.

Like young crows, young owls are "mostly appetites," the parent birds not only feeding them all night, but also providing sufficient food for day feeding, when they do not hunt.

Many an owl's favorite home is an old apple orchard near a farm where small rodents will be plentiful, and the owner of such an orchard, if he has screech owls for tenants, should count himself favored, for the good they will do him in ridding the place of rodents is incalculable, for screech owls are non-migratory (except, perhaps, in the far northern part of their range). If they become attached to a location and are not persecuted, they are likely to remain and always prove themselves "paying" tenants.

Every bird lover should have a share in an old orchard. Not a neatly trimmed and pruned orchard which will bear a bountiful crop of apples, but an old orchard, with large, ancient, hollow limbs and other nesting sites, which will bear a wonderful crop of birds.

Such an orchard we had across from a country school where I once taught. When my father was a boy the orchard was the pride of the country-side, and bore apples that were shipped to great cities. But in our day the old orchard bore a far more interesting crop—flickers, downies, bluebirds, chickadees, wrens, orioles, cuckoos, owls, and hosts of other birds. The children named it "Birdland"—and there was our field laboratory right at hand, close enough for field trips at recess, noon hours, and before and after school.

XLIV

THE BARN, OR "MONKEY-FACED" OWL

When cats run home and light is come,
    And dew is cold upon the ground,
And the far-off stream is' dumb,
    And the whirring sail goes round,
    And the whirring sail goes round:
        Alone and warming his five wits,
        The white owl in the belfrey sits.
                    —ALFRED, LORD TENNYSON.

RECENTLY I heard one woman ask another, "What was all that commotion at your house early this evening? I saw John run out with his gun, and you and Junior follow."

"Oh, we heard an owl in the woods across the way."

"What kind of an owl?" I interrupted.

"Why, I don't know. Just an owl, but John grabbed his gun and ran out to try and get it, and Junior and I followed him."

"Did he get it?"

"No, we didn't find it. And Junior, who had taken his little gun, cried the rest of the evening. The poor child was so disappointed. He'd wanted to get an owl with his new gun."

It had never occurred to these people to find out about the owl first. No interest other than to kill was aroused in them.

Only one of our owls, the great horned, is listed in the third class, that in which the beneficial and harmful qualities about balance. And it couldn't have been the great horned, for he is not found in our suburban woodlands.

BARN OWL

Order—Raptores   Family—Aluconidæ
Genus—Aluco   Species—pratincola

National Association of Audubon Societies

SPARROW HAWK

Order—RAPTORES   Family—FALCONIDÆ
Genus—FALCO   Species—SPARVERIUS SPARVERIUS

National range of Audubon Society

In all probability it was one of our most beneficial owls, perhaps the most beneficial of all, the barn, or monkey-faced owl.

This owl is a southern species, rarely occurring with any regularity in the northern half of the eastern United States. Not only is it probably the most beneficial of all our owls, all analyses of its pellets showing that it eats numberless rats, mice, and other rodents, but only occasionally does it take a bird, or other useful animal. Consequently, it is of great value to the farmer, orchardist, and planter, and should be given complete protection everywhere. Instead, it is constantly facing persecution.

In the South Atlantic and Gulf states, the barn owl feeds extensively on the cotton rat, a mammal of destructive habits abounding in the bottom lands and near water. The common rat is also greedily devoured, as are all kinds of mice, gophers (in the West), and occasionally insects, and a small bird. But its diet is mainly mice and rats.

For years, states the government bulletin on owls and hawks, a pair of barn owls have nested in one of the towers of the Smithsonian Institution in Washington, D. C. At various times pellets, numbering hundreds and thousands, have been gathered from there and examined. In one summary of analyses, 97 per cent of the food eaten was mammals, 3 per cent birds, and a very few frogs. Probably the barn owl takes a smaller number of birds and useful mammals, than any other owl.

This owl belongs to the *Aluconidae,* the owl family, of which there are some twenty-five species and subspecies throughout the temperate and tropical regions. They differ from other owls in structure, but share with them the characteristics of the *Strigidae,* the second owl family. The barn owl breeds from New York (rarely) south to the Gulf states and southern Mexico, but it is distinctly a southern species.

ALSO KNOWN AS "MONKEY-FACE"

This owl is a peculiar looking bird, with a monkeyish face, triangular in outline. The general color of its upper parts is yellowish buff, with small black and white markings, and the under parts vary from white to pale bright tawny with numerous black spots. The facial disk, which gives it the monkeyish appearance, is narrowly margined by reddish buff, and the legs are long and slender. The bird measures eighteen inches.

Seldom seen during the day, the barn owl, when it is found, is frequently considered some odd animal, half bird, half monkey. Though rarely seen, it seems to be fairly numerous and rather widely distributed. Its notes are a wild, startling scream, and curious scraping and creaking notes and hisses.

Included in the barn owl's wide range of nesting sites are the cavities of trees, banks, cliffs, and, more frequently, the attics of deserted buildings, towers, and steeples. Often the nest is only the disgorged pellets of the parent birds, not a very comfortable or beautiful nest. The five to nine eggs are white, and are laid in April.

THE SAW-WHET OWL

About eight inches long, this owl is dark cinnamon brown above, with the head finely streaked and the back spotted with white; while the under parts are white, streaked with brown. The eyes are yellow, and the legs and feet feathered.

The small size, even smaller than the screech owl, and the absence of ear-tufts, distinguish it from others of the owl family. Breeding from about Central Canada to

Pennsylvania, it winters south to Virginia, casually to the Carolinas, and accidentally to Mexico.

While not exactly a migratory species, the saw-whet's wanderings in search of food during fall and winter are more or less irregular. It may be rather common at one time, and then not seen again for years, especially as it is nocturnal, staying in some retreat in the daytime. It is only rarely seen in the South.

The Florida burrowing owl, small, mottled, grayish brown with no ear-tufts and with legs and feet nearly naked, is locally abundant in its range, which is southern Florida.

XLV

THE BARRED, OR "HOOT" OWL

It was the owl that shriek'd, the fatal bellman,
Which gives the stern'st Good night.
—WILLIAM SHAKESPEARE.

Whoo-whoo-whoo-whoo-whoo, to-whoo-oh wails the barred owl, or the hoot owl, as it is often named for its call.

The absence of "horns" or ear-tufts, the large dark eyes, and the deep, questioning voice make this owl easy to distinguish from the others of the family. The upper parts are grayish brown, each feather with two or three whitish bars; the under parts are white, tinged with buff; the breast is barred (which gives the bird one of its names) and the sides and belly are broadly streaked with brownish. The tail has six or eight whitish bars, and the legs and feet are feathered nearly to the nails. The bird measures about nineteen inches.

One of the larger of the common species in eastern North America, this owl inhabits large tracts of woodland, and is generally resident wherever found. A lonely sort of fellow, its dismal hoot may be heard more or less throughout the year, but more frequently during the nesting season. Under favorable circumstances, it can be heard half a mile. Usually the call is heard during the early part of the night, and again just before sunrise; occasionally they call during the day. On moonlight nights, however, they sometimes hoot through the night.

Sometimes rival males try to *out-whoo* each other, and if one is fortunate enough to be within hearing distance

—and provided one enjoys owl calls—one may be treated to quite an owl concert.

The barred owl's range extends from southern Canada to Kansas and Georgia; in North Carolina it is a common resident throughout the state.

THE BARRED OWL IS A LONELY SORT OF FELLOW WHOSE DISMAL HOOT MAY BE HEARD OCCASIONALLY THROUGH THE NIGHT. ABOUT ONE-FOURTH NATURAL SIZE.

YOUNG OWLS GROW SLOWLY

The nest is usually in a hollow tree, though sometimes an abandoned crow's, or hawk's nest is used. A recent article in *Bird-Lore* tells of a nest and young, being found in a box in a tree; so these birds may occasionally be induced to nest in boxes that are made sufficiently large. The two to four eggs are white and round, and are usually laid in March or early April. Owls and hawks as a rule rear but one brood a year, but the young grow slowly and require a large amount of food.

Like most species of owls and hawks, this one feeds mainly on small mammals, mice, rats, and other rodents furnishing a large part of its menu. Occasionally it gets a bird, and even less often a young chick, but on the whole mice are its outstanding diet, and it is generally conceded that the barred owl does far more good than harm.

This is in contradiction to the reputation that the barred owl has, especially with the older writers, who accuse it of being very destructive to poultry and game. However, as it is the half-grown fowls which roost among trees and bushes that generally fall prey to this owl, it is suggested that if farmers will shut up their poultry at night, these depredations will largely cease.

Unfortunately, the barred owl is sometimes mistaken for the great horned owl, and is shot. In reality, there is not much resemblance between the two, except that both are owls.

Some owls, like the ants, believe in preparing for the proverbial rainy day, and in the cold days of fall, especially when rodents are plentiful during harvest—they often store up mice and other "owl-delectables" in hollow trees, against the leaner days when "good huntings" may not be so good.

XLVI

THE SHORT-EARED AND THE LONG-EARED OWLS

Unlike most other members of the owl family, the short-eared, or marsh owl, lives in open meadows or fields, large swamps, or marshes, rather than in dense woods.

Nor is this owl exclusively nocturnal. Unless the day is too bright, it may be seen flying more freely by day than any other owl. Having wings long in proportion to its body, its flight is easy and graceful, and like that of all owls, silent.

While most owls are inclined to be solitary—or at most go about in twosomes—the short-eared, which migrate, are often found in flocks of a hundred or more in winter. And there is still another difference. The short-eared owl nests on the ground, whereas most proper owls (except the barn owl) are supposed to nest in hollow trees, though a few do like to use the old nests of hawks or crows.

The adult male short-eared is a large yellow-brown owl measuring about fifteen inches in length. It is striped with darker brown, the stripes being narrower below. The adult female is similar, but the under parts are more richly yellowish buff. The ear-tufts of this owl are very short and close together and are often difficult to see, but its hearing is very keen.

This owl is not shy, and often one can creep up close to it before it takes wing, and even then it will sometimes alight on a slight elevation, where one can get a good view of it.

Were you traveling on a magic carpet—or any other kind of wishful conveyance—you might encounter the short-eared in almost any part of the world, provided you left Australia out of your itinerary. In North America the short-eared breeds irregularly from the Arctic zone to Indiana and Massachusetts, and winters from there south to Louisiana, Cuba, and Guatemala.

It nests—as we have already said—on the ground, either in a natural depression, under a log, or just in a tuft of grass. The slight nest may be comprised of a few sticks, soft grasses, and some feathers from the parents' breast. The four to seven eggs are white. Incubation is said to begin with the laying of the first egg, so that usually there are young and eggs in various stages.

Food and manner of feeding are similar to those of other owls, though it seems to consume an even larger number of mice. Fully 75 per cent of its food consists of mice; so the short-eared, which is listed by the government as belonging to the second class, or those "chiefly beneficial," should be given every protection.

THE LONG-EARED OWL

Unlike the short-eared, but like the screech owl, the long-eared is nocturnal in its habits, never hunting during daylight, but usually spending the day in small pine woods, alder swamps, thick willow copses, and, on rare occasions, in open spaces.

An unobtrusive bird, it is so quiet in its habits that one may live near its home for years without ever being aware of it. However, it is not wild and will sometimes allow close approach, but when it is conscious of being seen, it sits upright, drawing its feathers close to its body and erecting its ear-tufts until it resembles a limb or stub of a tree.

The long ear-tufts are its most conspicuous characteristic. The upper parts are dark brown, finely mottled with white and with some buff showing. The under parts are whitish buff and dark grayish brown, streaked on the breast and barred on the belly. It is a little under fifteen inches long.

Long-ear is also on the "chiefly beneficial" list, and is an industrious mouser, consuming also a large number of other noxious rodents, and molesting but comparatively few birds. Unlike most of its owl cousins, it does not nest in hollow trees, but usually takes over the disused nest of a crow, hawk, or squirrel. This is repaired and lined afresh, and in it are laid three to six round white eggs.

A bird of temperate North America, the long-eared breeds from central Canada south to North Texas, Arkansas, and Virginia, and winters from southern Canada to Georgia, Louisiana, and central Mexico. It is considered a rare winter visitor in most of the southern states.

XLVII

TWO BIG OWLS

Mourn not for the owl nor his gloomy plight;
  The owl hath his share of good;
If a prisoner he be in the broad daylight,
  He is lord in the dark greenwood.
  —BRYAN WALLER PROCTOR.

THE LARGEST and fiercest of our owls is the great-horned, sometimes called the "tiger of the woods" and the "eagle of the night." And because of its large yellow eyes and conspicuous ear-tufts, it is also known as the "cat owl."

The great horned's dismal hooting, a deep-toned *whoo, hoo-hoo-hoo, whooo, whooo,* is the most uncanny sound of the night. To get its full effect one should be alone in the woods on a dark, gloomy night, and also hear its rarer call, a loud, piercing scream, one of the most blood-curdling sounds heard in the woods. If that doesn't produce the shivers, then one is indeed made of stern stuff. So dreaded has this scream of the great-horned owl been, that it is said the Indians forbade the imitation of its call, fearing it would bring upon the tribe the enmity of the great owl.

According to Pearson, while some of these owl hoots would seem to frighten into hiding all game within hearing, they may be given for the purpose of helping to discover its prey. If the owl were trying to locate a rabbit which it had just seen a moment before, and which is crouching low hoping to escape detection, the sudden *hoot* might so startle the poor thing as to make it betray its exact location.

A great, dusky, twenty-two inch owl, the upper parts are mottled buff, brown, and black, and the under parts

THE LORD OF THE DARK GREENWOOD IS THE GREAT HORNED OWL. ITS DEEP-TONED, UNCANNY "WHOO-HOO-HOO" STRIKES TERROR TO THE HEARTS OF BIRD AND BEAST. ABOUT ONE-FOURTH NATURAL SIZE.

are the same colors, but barred. The ear-tufts are two inches long, the feet and legs feathered.

Inhabiting heavily forested and unsettled regions, the

great-horned is resident over the greater part of North and South America, though becoming more and more rare in thickly populated sections. In many of the less populated sections of the southern states, the great-horned is a fairly common resident.

NOT SO BAD AS REPUTED

The great-horned is the only one of our owls that destroys poultry and birds in any number, and it is our only owl that the government places in the third class, those in which "beneficial and harmful qualities about balance." It is placed there because, though it destroys poultry and birds, it also does a vast amount of good, and if farmers would shut up their chickens at night, instead of allowing them to roost in trees and other exposed places, the principal damage done by these owls would be prevented.

To the older bird writers, this judgment by government experts seems more than fair, even lenient. For the great-horned owl has a bad reputation, and so deep rooted is this opinion of him that it is instinctive in almost everyone to condemn and persecute him whether one really knows anything about him or not. In reality, the more recent opinion that the great-horned owl is not all bad has been reached as the conclusion of a long study by scientists of the government Biological Survey.

Hunting only at night, the great-horned preys indiscriminately on many forms of wild life, including game-birds, especially grouse and partridges, rabbits, and poultry, including turkeys and chickens. Scarcely any animal that is not larger than this owl, is safe from its attack. When hard-pressed for food it will even attack the odorous skunk—and not always does the owl come out of it unscathed. Also, even when food is plentiful, it is a killer, often killing several fowl, and just eating the heads. In the southern states, it captures many opossums and rabbits.

However, in the West, where the ranchers suffer from the depredations of gophers, ground squirrels, prairie dogs, rabbits, and other noxious rodents, the great-horned is really beneficial. Where these rodents are plentiful, it does not seem to attack poultry or other game birds to any extent, but where rabbits and squirrels, in particular, are scarce, it does make great inroads on fowls, especially those left to roost in the open.

In some sections it kills rats in large numbers; and also eats some insects, fish, and crawfish.

As among many of the owls, the female great-horned is larger than the male. We hate to admit it, but 'tis said that occasionally Lady Great-horned turns cannibal, and slays—and later dines on—her erstwhile lord!

The nest may be a hole in a tree, or, like that of the long-eared owl, in an abandoned nest of a crow, a squirrel, a hawk, or even an eagle. The two to three round white eggs are usually laid in February.

THE SNOWY OWL

No ear-tufts has this great white owl which in winter occasionally drifts down from remote, snowy wastes of the far North. Its head is almost as round as a large snowball; its large eyes are yellow; and the legs and feet are thickly covered with feathers. The bill and claws are black, but they are almost concealed by feathers.

This owl of far Arctic wastes is pure white, barred with dusky markings which are much more extensive in the female than in the male. It measures twenty-five inches.

Breeding from the Arctic to upper Canada, it winters from the Arctic coast to southern Canada and northern New Hampshire, and irregularly to the Middle States and Ohio valley. Occasionally a few stragglers are found as far south as Louisiana and Texas.

A day owl, the snowy can see quite well in sunlight, and most of its hunting is done in the hours of early morning and towards dusk. In its northern home it feeds chiefly on the lemming, a sort of clumsy, short-tailed field mouse, but in its wanderings it feeds on game-birds, especially if its favorite diet, mice, are not to be found. In some localities it feeds largely on rats. According to some observers, during its more southern wanderings it seems to be very partial to localities near water, especially barren sand wastes along the seashore, and marshy flats bordering bays and rivers.

The snowy owl's flight is smooth and silent, and is often long and rapid. By striking them down as the duck hawk does, it can capture ducks, pigeons, and even grouse on the wing.

The Biological Survey places this owl on the second, or "chiefly beneficial" list. On account of its size and strength it is capable of doing great good in destroying noxious mammals, and though it gets some water and game birds, the good it does overbalances the harm, and it should be protected.

Building its nest on the ground, this owl lines it with feathers before laying the two to three white eggs. The snowy owl's cries are said to be loud and dismal, sounding like the wind that sweeps over the great wastes of snow where it wanders.

XLVIII

THE SPARROW HAWK

On outspread wings a hawk, far poised on high,
  Quick swooping screams, and then is heard no more:
The strident shrilling of a locust nigh
  Breaks forth, and dies in silence as before.
                                    —J. P. IRVINE.

HAWKS, like buzzards, are graceful soarers, but while the latter are ugly birds when seen close up, the hawks are handsome-appearing then as well as when on the wing. When we see them "On outspread wing, far poised on high," they are likely to be hunting for mice in a field or meadow far below, for they have remarkable sight. From a great height a hawk seems able to discern a small creature moving in the grass far below, and can suddenly drop down upon it.

The vision of hawks is unique in that the birds are far-sighted when sailing back and forth policing their "beat" but, as they drop, the focus of the eye automatically and quickly changes, and by the time they reach the ground they are near-sighted, and can immediately pounce upon their prey.

Nearly two-thirds of the birds of prey inhabiting the United States are classed, by the Biological Survey, as being in the second, or "chiefly beneficial" class, for while they occasionally get small birds, game birds, and poultry, their food consists chiefly of mice and other noxious rodents which are injurious to all agriculture. Only two of our common species of hawks, the Cooper's and the sharp-shinned, habitually feed on birds and poultry.

The others are valuable aids to the farmers in keeping in check the small rodents so destructive to all forms of agriculture.

According to the Biological Survey, the hawks and owls complement each other. Like Jack Spratt and his wife, who, one eating the fat and the other the lean, between the two "licked the platter clean," the hawks and the owls, between them keep their "beat" clean. The hawks hunt by day and keep those rodents which feed by day in check, while the owls, whose eyesight is keenest during twilight and before dawn, capture nocturnal species. Again, owls are less migratory than hawks, and during the long winter most of them which are resident in the land of ice and snow, remain there to wage incessant warfare against the enemies of the orchard, garden, and harvest fields.

Hawks belong to the families *Falconidae* and *Accipitriidae* to which belong the "day-hunting" birds of prey, numbering some three hundred and fifty species distributed throughout the world. They are birds of strong flight, and they capture their prey on the wing by striking at it with their deadly sharp, curved claws. The short, hooked bill is used to tear the prey while it is held in the talons.

THE SPARROW HAWK

The sparrow hawk, the smallest and handsomest of the birds of prey, is also one of the most common. Though at times it attacks small birds and young chicks, examinations of stomach contents of many a sparrow hawk taken at different seasons and from different sections of the country, give it a pretty clean slate. Grasshoppers furnish the chief food of this hawk; mice, lizards, caterpillars, and terrestrial beetles are also consumed.

During late fall and winter these hawks feed more

and more on field mice and house mice, hunting the former in meadows and the latter about grain shocks and farm buildings.

Often this little hawk—for he measures only ten inches—may be seen hovering over meadows on rapidly moving wings, until, sighting a juicy tidbit, he swoops down upon it, and then returns to his favorite perch or look-out. From his call of triumph, an exultant, high-pitched *killy-killy-killy* uttered as he flies upward after a successful foray, the bird is often called the "killy hawk" especially by farm boys of the South.

Having much of the beauty of song birds, the male adult has a tawny back with a few black bars, whitish or tawny under parts spotted with black, and bluish and black wings. The chestnut tail has a broad band near the tip and the head is bluish with black markings on the side and a red spot on top. The female has back, wings, and tail barred with reddish brown and black, and black-streaked-with-reddish-brown under parts. Like most of the hawks, the sparrow hawk is large-headed and short-necked.

Its name is very inappropriate, for the bird has no resemblance to a sparrow in form or habits. Because of its chief food it might more properly be called grasshopper hawk.

Breeding throughout the United States, Canada, and northern Mexico, the sparrow hawk winters in the United States and south to Guatemala. A true falcon, though it may be found in the forest, it likes the more open country and usually nests in hollow trees. In our southern states the abandoned nesting cavity of the flicker is often used, and sometimes an old woodpecker's nest is taken over. Occasionally, however, nests may be found in crevices of rocks, holes in banks, and even in nooks about buildings. Sometimes these hawks kill birds, especially

English sparrows, and take over their nests, but most of us who have been constantly annoyed by English sparrows can find it in our hearts to forgive the hawks for these depredations.

There is no lining to the sparrow hawk's nest. The three to seven eggs vary greatly in color, and may be white, buffy, or pinkish buff, marked with irregular brownish spots and blotches.

All rapacious birds breed slowly, rearing only one brood a year, though if the first clutch of eggs is destroyed another will be laid. The breeding period usually begins about the middle of April, the period of incubation being about three weeks.

This beneficial bird is greatly warred upon, and in many localities has been practically exterminated.

XLIX

THREE GOOD HAWKS

Dimly I catch the throb of distant flails:
Silently overhead the hen-hawk sails;
With watchful, measuring eye, and for his
quarry waits.
—JAMES RUSSELL LOWELL.

IN FRONTIER days there was an old saying that "The only good Indian is a dead Indian." Similarly, to many people, the only good hawk is a dead hawk. There *are* bad hawks—two in particular—but there are also good hawks, and the red-shouldered and the red-tailed are among the latter. These two birds are so much alike in appearance and habits that they are often classed together.

The red-shouldered is the most abundant of our larger hawks, and has a grayish-reddish-brown back, and reddish shoulders; the head, neck, and under parts are spotted and cross-barred with rusty and white. The black or brownish tail is crossed with four or five white bars and has a white tip. From this tip to the tip of the bill, the bird measures nearly nineteen inches.

Its range is eastern North America from the plains to the Atlantic; it winters south to the Gulf coast, being a migrant in the more northern parts of its range. The loud scream, or call, *kee-you, kee-you, kee-you* as it sails high overhead is familiar to all bird lovers, though sometimes, when you think you hear the call, it may prove to be a blue jay mimicking the red-shouldered hawk.

Unfortunately, both the red-shouldered and the red-tailed, are commonly called "chicken" or "hen" hawks, and are popularly credited with being enemies to the farmer and poultryman, whereas in reality, though the red-tailed has been caught killing chickens, it is claimed that the red-shouldered hawk has never been known to kill a bird. Mice, snakes, frogs, fish, and grasshoppers furnish most of its diet, and it is said the red-shouldered is a veritable Frenchman in his love of frogs. Perhaps that is why most of the year it is a bird of the woods, liking particularly those woods with small streams, where it can fish for this favorite food.

The government bulletin on hawks and owls tells of a pair of these red-shouldered hawks which lived for several years within a few hundred yards of a poultry farm having eight hundred chickens and four hundred ducks, and the owner never saw these hawks attempt to catch a single fowl.

Both the red-shouldered and the red-tailed hawks are listed by the Biological Survey as belonging to the second class of "good hawks." When the farmer once realizes that these hawks are not his enemies, but his allies, he may be willing to grant them the protection they deserve.

The nest of the red-shouldered, like that of most of the hawks, is constructed of sticks and twigs, and may be from thirty to sixty feet from the ground. Apparently some pairs return year after year to the same location, either using the same nest, or building a new one. They are said to mate for life and to be happy in their home life.

About as large as hen's eggs, the two to three dull white eggs of the red-shouldered are sprinkled with brown. Most of these birds nest in April, and the young are covered with down, although they are helpless and are reared in the nest.

THE RED-TAILED HAWK

Like the red-shouldered, the red-tailed hawk also suffers from being incorrectly known as a "chicken" or "hen" hawk, when in general it equally deserves protection. Though larger than the former, being some twenty inches, it is very similar in appearance, but it has a more

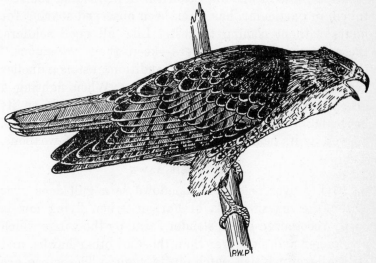

IT IS UNFORTUNATE THAT THE RED-TAILED HAWK IS INCORRECTLY KNOWN AS THE "CHICKEN HAWK." THE BIOLOGICAL SURVEY LISTS IT AS ONE OF THE "GOOD HAWKS." ABOUT ONE-FIFTH NATURAL SIZE.

reddish tail with a narrow black band near its end and a white tip, and the breast has a sort of black, irregular band across it. The female red-tailed—and also the female red-shouldered—is about three inches larger than the male. This hawk's call is a thin, long-drawn whistle which sounds like escaping steam.

These two hawks belong to the family *Accipitriidae,* which includes all the hawks except the true falcons (the sparrow hawk is a falcon). Abundant, widely distributed, and of striking appearance, the red-tailed is probably the best known of all the larger hawks. Not quite so particular about its food as the red-shouldered, when put to it through hunger it will eat carrion. Its usual food, however, is mice, frogs, snakes, crawfish, and insects. In the South it is particularly fond of the cotton rat, and in regions where rattlesnakes are abundant it also adds them to its menu.

Both these hawks are beautiful in flight, and the red-tailed, in particular, has often been observed soaring for hours without coming to rest. Like all good soldiers, these hawks—and all others—keep their "weapons," their talons, sharp and in good condition, just as a dueller keeps his sword sharp and shining. When fighting a larger animal, or man, a hawk will throw itself on its back and strike up at its opponent with its sharp claws, as well as its beak, but the talons are its chief weapons.

THE MARSH HAWK

Flying over fields and meadows as a gull does over water, the marsh hawk, or harrier, when flying low is easily recognized by its slender form, by the wings which are longer and slenderer than those of other hawks, and by the large whitish patch on its rump. The wings are adapted for a long, gliding flight.

The adult male measures nineteen inches and is pale bluish gray, the upper breast pearl gray, the lower belly white with reddish spots. The tail is silvery gray, irregularly barred with blackish. The female is larger and darker than the male and more heavily streaked; the young birds resemble her.

Essentially a bird of unwooded country, the harrier is a low-perching hawk, often alighting on the grass, or any slight elevation. Its abundance and wide distribution, its good habits, and its fondness for small rodents classify it as one of our most valuable hawks.

Winging its way over meadows, marshes, or prairie

lands, so indefatigable is this hawk in its pursuit of lizards, snakes, reptiles, frogs, grasshoppers, and especially mice, that it might well be called the "mouser hawk." Only occasionally does it offend by taking a small bird. It is of particular value in the prairie states, where it preys extensively on the gophers, which do such an enormous amount of damage to crops.

Known over most of North America, the marsh hawk breeds from Alaska to the southern border of the states. Over the more northern part of its range it is a migrant, and winters from the Ohio valley and New York south to Cuba and Colombia.

Having no love song—its screeching notes being its only voice—it apparently substitutes acrobatic feats for song in its wooing. During this period the male may be seen "looping the loop" over the spot where the lady hawk of his choice may be perching. Sometimes he makes several loops in succession, great somersaults which any famous circus acrobat or Tarzan of the Apes might well envy.

Unlike most of the other hawks, which build high up in trees, the harrier builds its nest on the ground, in meadows, pastures, but more often in marshes. The four to six eggs are dull white or pale bluish white, and may be laid in May or June. Incubation is said to take nearly four weeks, and the young when hatched are covered with whitish down.

"The easiest way to find a marsh hawk's nest," says Dr. Allen, "is to listen for the returning male and then note from what spot the female flies up to meet him and take food from his mouth!"

L

TWO BAD HAWKS

Winter or summer what care I?
　　The tilled or the untilled plain?
My lot is cast in the blue abyss,
　　And the lordly sun's domain.
Over the broad champaign I float,
　　And over the sparkling sea;
I mount at will to the peaks of heaven,
　　And rejoice that I am free.
　　　　Ko, keeo, kilio, keeo!
　　I exult that I am free.
　　　　　　—DORA READ GOODALE.

THE TWO HAWKS responsible for the hatred and suspicion which farmers have for birds of prey as a whole, are the sharp-shinned and the Cooper's. These two villains of hawkdom are the ones which continuously raid poultry yards and war upon small birds. It is they, and not the red-shouldered and the red-tailed, which should be known as the "chicken" and "hen" hawks.

In appearance and habits these two bad hawks resemble each other, though the Cooper's is the larger of the two. With both, the female is much larger than the male.

The sharp-shinned is bluish gray in general, with a square, gray tail barred with blackish; the under parts are lighter, and barred with buff or reddish. The male is a little over eleven inches, the female over thirteen. The young birds are browner.

Breeding nearly throughout the United States and Canada, the sharp-shinned winter from the northern states south to Panama. In the fall, numbers of these hawks may be seen high in the air, migrating southward in a leisurely manner, and so following the southern flight of the smaller birds on which they prey.

Fearless, daring, and aggressive, they fly swiftly and rather low over open fields or through woods. Upon spying a fowl, a game bird, or a song bird, they make a sudden dash. For both the sharp-shinned and the Cooper's capture their victims not so much by long, swift pursuing flights in the open, as by rapid darts and quick turns, the victim being grasped before it is aware of a hawk's presence. They are even known to pursue their prey on foot, running through undergrowth.

Liking young "fryers" as well as any good southerner, if these hawks once make a successful raid on a poultry yard, they are likely to make daily visits—particularly if early broods are allowed to run at large—either until they literally clean out the farmer, or the farmer brings down the hawks.

Usually silent, it is only during the nesting period that the sharp-shinned utters a few peculiar notes. The nesting period is from April to June, depending on the locality, being earlier in the South and later in the more northern part of the range. The height at which the nest is placed varies from fifteen to forty feet. The three to six bluish-white or buff eggs are heavily blotched with chocolate. Both sexes share in the incubation, and in the care of the young.

THE COOPER'S HAWK

Looking like a larger edition of the sharp-shinned, the Cooper's hawk is an equally ruthless villain in feathers. Known also as blue darter, blue-tailed hawk, and chicken hawk, it is hated by man and bird under all three names.

By far the most harmful species, these hawks, because of their numbers and their fearlessness, are de-

structive both to poultry and to bird life. They are fond
of squirrels and chipmunks, but seem to have but small
appetite for rats, mice, reptiles, or the larger insects, so
delectable to other hawks. They are also fond of young
doves, and if there is a dove-cote in the vicinity of their
nesting or hunting grounds, well, it is just too bad—for
the doves, that is. The hawks find the arrangement very
satisfactory, indeed.

THE COOPER'S HAWK—A TRULY BAD HAWK—IS ALSO KNOWN AS THE BLUE
DARTER, THE BLUE-TAILED HAWK, AND THE CHICKEN HAWK, AND IS HATED
UNDER ALL THESE NAMES.   ABOUT ONE-FOURTH NATURAL SIZE.

Ranging over the whole of temperate North America,
and most of Mexico, the Cooper's is abundant in many
districts. The nest is often built in the main crotch of a
tree, or on a limb close to the trunk, and small sticks and
twigs are used in the construction. Sometimes the old

nest of a crow or other hawk is made to do service. Whatever or wherever the nest is, it is usually between twenty-five and fifty feet up.

In the southern part of the Cooper's range there are usually two to four eggs, whereas farther north there may be three to six. They are bluish white; sometimes lightly spotted with brownish. In the South the breeding season begins about the first of April; in the vicinity of New York, about the last of the same month.

These two hawks, the sharp-shinned and the Cooper's, are the only ones of our common hawks which are placed in the fourth, or "harmful group" by government classification. A third, the goshawk, only rarely wanders this far south, while the duck hawk, the "falcon" of the hawking days of olden times, is a really rare bird, here, as well as in many other parts of the country.

LI

THE VULTURES, NATURE'S
SCAVENGERS

Against the hazy sky
The thin and fleecy clouds, unmoving rest.
Beneath them far, yet high
In the dim distant West,
The vulture, scenting thence its carrion-fare,
Sails, slowly circling in the summer air.
—WILLIAM DAVIS GALLAGHER.

THAT "distance lends enchantment" is certainly true of the vultures, especially of the turkey buzzard. Sailing far overhead, on outstretched, immovable wings, then soaring in great spirals until lost to sight, it is a thing of grace and beauty. Seeing it thus, one longs for wings and the ability to glide through the blue with like ease and grace.

Seen close by, the great ugly head and neck naked and red, the wicked beak tearing at a gruesome meal of putrid flesh, the buzzard is awkward, uncouth, and repulsive. Much of its time is spent on the wing, so that we are likely to see the great bird sailing overhead hundreds of times to the rare occasions when we see it feeding at close range. This may be Nature's way of having the buzzard "put its best foot forward."

The wonderful, soaring flight of vultures has long been a subject of study by inventors; the great birds are credited with being the inspiration of the American-invented airplane.

The wing of the vulture is an interesting example of a bird's adaptation. It is large, broad, and rounded, as are the wings of eagles and large hawks, and is adapted for soaring. At times the bird maintains itself in the air for hours without seeming to flap its wings. This aerial

TURKEY BUZZARDS ACT AS NATURE'S HEALTH OFFICERS IN KEEPING THE FIELDS AND BY-WAYS OF THE SOUTH CLEAN OF DECAYING ANIMAL MATTER. ABOUT ONE-SIXTH NATURAL SIZE.

glide is accomplished merely by the bird's taking advantage of the upward current in the air, and adjusting its wings accordingly.

Another interesting feature of the vulture is that in getting its food, the bird has degenerated from a predaceous habit to a diet of carrion.* Thus, while retaining its hooked bill for rending flesh, it has lost its powerful talons and the accompanying strength of limb through disuse, so that now the bird even springs from the ground with difficulty.

Turkey buzzards—and black vultures—are among the most familiar features of our southern landscapes, and one of the first typically southern things pointed out to the stranger. So familiar are they that a description is scarcely needed. The buzzard is chiefly black, tinged with brown, its head and neck red and completely bare of feathers, the base of the bill also bright red. The bird is about thirty inches in length.

The range of turkey buzzards is sparingly from New York and New Jersey southward, the birds becoming more common about Washington, and increasing in numbers further south. Their service as scavengers has made them invaluable to the South and in the Tropics, wherever sanitary conditions are bad, so that, until recently, they have been given every protection, both by law and by popular opinion. In some southern districts they seem to form a regular street-cleaning department.

Recently, however, some question has been raised as to the part vultures may play in spreading disease, such as hog cholera and anthrax. The United States Biological Survey, ornithologists, and other scientists have been investigating these charges for a number of years, and have found them to be greatly exaggerated, if not wholly without basis. Buzzards, like other birds, clean their feet, bills, and plumage of foreign matter, and examination of their stomachs has shown that all germs contained

* Allen, *The Book of Bird Life.*

in carrion eaten by them are totally destroyed in passing through their digestive organs. This has been established by the most careful microscopic examination of the excreta of buzzards that had been fed upon anthrax-infested and cholera-contaminated meat.

"On the other hand, anthrax spores are not destroyed in the digestive tracts of other carrion-feeding animals such as dogs, cats, chickens, opossums; nor of flies. All of these carriers are therefore more likely to spread the germ than are buzzards. This is also proved by the fact that cholera is often prevalent in regions where there are no buzzards or vultures."

Vultures belong to the family *Cathartidae,* and are a New World family of nine species, of which three are North American. Two of these are very common in the South. Within their range they are usually found wherever there is food, and, except during the nesting season, they are found in flocks, which each night return to a regularly frequented roost, usually a dead tree, or dead branch.

The vulture's vision is marvelous, and—the poet to the contrary—it is now generally believed that they find their prey more by sight than by smell. It is claimed they can see a snake or mouse on the ground from a height of half a mile. As their food is carrion, what a blessing it must be if they haven't delicate olfactory organs and can't smell their dinners, else they could not stomach the food they gulp down with such evident relish.

Various experiments have been tried to prove this. One I heard of was the placing of a dead sheep in a concealing thicket, and a sheep painted on canvas, in an open meadow. The vultures descended upon the canvas sheep, but failed to detect the smelly, but concealed real one near by.

Another experiment* to test their olfactory nerves was the taking of an alligator that had been dead several days and at night cutting it in halves. One-half was hidden by a piece of sacking; the other half placed in an exposed position thirty feet away. In the morning both the black vultures and the turkey buzzards were present in numbers. After finishing the exposed half, they jumped about after their usual fashion and actually stood upon the covered portion, but failed to discover it.

The turkey buzzard may build its nest in a slight depression in the ground, in the shelter of overhanging rocks, in a hollow tree stump, or among the limbs of an uprooted tree. The two or three eggs (more often but two) are creamy white, spotted with chocolate. The nesting period is usually in April or May, and both parents assist in the incubation, which is said to take two months.

Though born naked, the young soon acquire a white down which they retain for some time. If handled, the young birds are said to have the disagreeable habit of disgorging offensive matter. Indeed, the young are so unattractive that only a mother buzzard's heart could think them beautiful. After losing the infantile down, the immature birds are similar to the adults, but the head is covered with grayish-brown, fur-like feathers.

Buzzards, though classed with song birds under protective laws, have no song or notes, but only an occasional grunt, or hiss, when disturbed at the nest, or while feeding. The young, on the other hand, are sometimes very noisy.

After a rain, buzzards may sometimes be seen perching with their wings held spread-eagle fashion, as they dry their water-soaked plumage. It is said that during cold spells they are sometimes seen standing on chimneys taking advantage of the heat that rises with the smoke.

* Dugmore, *Bird-Homes.*

BLACK VULTURE

The South's only other member of the vulture family
is the black vulture, which is more abundant along sea-
coasts, and less common in the interior, than its near
relative, the turkey buzzard. It is also more often found
living in towns and cities than is the turkey buzzard. In
some southern cities, especially about the market-places,
the black vultures used to be so common that they were in
danger of being stepped upon while feeding.

The black vulture is shorter—being but twenty-four
inches long—and heavier than the buzzard, and it invariably wins any dispute with the latter. This vulture's
stretch of wing is not so great, and thus its flight is less
easy and graceful. The bird flaps its wings more often,
and this habit, in connection with its black head, and the
silvery under-surface of the wings, makes it distinguishable from the turkey buzzard.

Its range is more tropical than that of the turkey buzzard, or turkey vulture, and extends through the southern states and south to South America.

The nesting habits of both species are similar. The
black vulture's one to three pale bluish-white eggs are
spotted with chocolate, but its nesting season is earlier,
sometimes even in March.

LII

THE DOVES

O, gentle, feathered spirit of sadness,
  Why croonest thou thy mournful plaint,
    Now full, now faint,
  In all the summer gladness?
Has bird grief wrung thy little heart,
Or dost thou voice a minor part
  In Nature's harmony?
          —ALBERT W. SMITH.

THE MOURNING DOVE is the melancholy love-maker who so plaintively calls *Coo-o-ah-coo-o-o-, coo-oo*. Under favorable conditions it may be heard several hundred yards. Uttered slowly and tenderly, with much depth of feeling, this song would make one think that the dove was mourning a lost mate, instead of wooing her with a love-song.

It is this plaintive, melancholy *coo-oo*, with its throbbing refrain reminding one of the wind in the pine-tops, which gives the bird the name of "mourning dove" and makes it seem appropriate.

The sweet, haunting call may be heard from late winter until early September, which is our last record of it.

Another unique sound connected with the mourning dove, and which, once recognized, is never forgotten, is the whistling sound of the wings in rapid flight. This is due to the arrangement of the stiff wing-feathers. The flight of the passenger pigeon, on the other hand, is said to be noiseless.

The male mourning dove is grayish brown or fawn color above, glossed with bluish, the sides and back of

[258]

MOURNING DOVE

Order—COLUMBÆ   Family—COLUMBIDÆ
Genus—ZENAIDURA   Species—MACROURA CAROLINENSIS
National Association of Audubon Societies

KILLDEER

Order—LIMICOLÆ   Family—CHARADIIDÆ
Genus—ÆGIALITIS   Species—VOCIFERA

National Association of Audubon Societies

the neck being iridescent. The crown and upper part of the head are greenish blue, the breast has a metallic luster, the belly is cream buff, and there is a dark spot under each ear. The female's coloring resembles that of the male, but is duller and less iridescent. Both have a black bill and pink, or reddish, feet and legs, and are from eleven to thirteen inches in length.

Known over most of North America to Mexico and Guatemala, the mourning dove, belonging to the family *Columbidae*, winters from the Ohio valley and North Carolina to Panama. It is most common in the temperate zone.

Doves are devoted mates, evidencing so great an attachment for each other that it used to be thought they mated for life. Through the spring season they are seen in pairs, but in the fall, after the nesting season is completed, they gather in flocks of varying sizes, and may often be seen frequenting fields of grain, and in the South, peanuts, returning to their roosts at night.

During the day they are often seen visiting a neighboring supply of fine gravel, which they consume in large quantities. For a bird's gizzard takes the place of teeth, and it is made of rubbery muscles and lined with a tough, wrinkled skin which can be peeled off (try it on a chicken's gizzard). This gizzard grinds up the bird's food just as our teeth do the food we eat.

DOVES DRINK DIFFERENTLY

Doves and pigeons drink differently from other birds. As this is being written a wood thrush is drinking at the bird bath, and keeps raising its head to swallow. When a dove drinks it keeps its beak in the water until its thirst is appeased. But though they enjoy drinking and bathing, and so like to be near water, apparently they do not care for a bird bath. At least we have never seen a dove at ours, though they nest in our woodland and are often seen about, and come to feed on cracked peanuts placed on the ground in an open space near the bath.

They enjoy dust baths, and occasionally we see them settling down in the dirt road in front of our house, where they thoroughly and leisurely dust themselves.

During the mating season doves often may be seen sailing in the upper air much after the manner of our smaller hawks.

Though mourning doves are credited with being such devoted couples, they are shiftless builders and house-keepers. Their nest is a mere flimsy platform of twigs usually placed on the horizontal limb of a tree, generally on a lower branch. Sometimes, but not often, it is in a stump or on the ground. The structure is so frail that often the two white eggs can be seen from below. As there is no rim to the nest, an observer often fears that the eggs will roll out or that the babies will tumble out— which sometimes happens. Poor little nestlings! They are born naked, and in the flimsy, unlined nest their poor little bodies must often be cold and bruised.

However, both birds share in the incubation, and the nest is seldom left exposed. The young are fed by re-gurgitation, on predigested food, sometimes known as pigeon's milk—from the crop of the parent. It is said that the parental instinct of mourning doves is very poorly developed, and that they readily desert their eggs or young in time of danger.*

Dr. Allen tells of an interesting experience in feeding the young. "Young mourning doves have swellings at the corners of the mouth which the old birds press when they interlock bills, to inspire the proper swallowing action of the young. I once tried to raise a crippled young dove and could not make it swallow anything, even that

* Allen, *The Book of Bird Life.*

which was forcibly put into its throat, until I discovered
the nervous adjustment between the swellings and the
throat muscles. After that it was easy, for I merely had
to touch the swellings and it was like pressing a button.
The little bird's mouth flew open and the throat com-
menced to work even before the food entered the bird's
mouth.

PREVENTS OVERFEEDING

"With all birds there is a nervous adjustment which
prevents overfeeding. Birds do not feed their young in
rotation, as one might expect, but ordinarily they feed
the hungriest one first and continue to feed him until
some other one gets hungrier and stretches its neck further and cries louder. This might result in overfeeding
the largest one but, fortunately, when the young bird has
had enough, its throat muscles refuse to work. (Think
how many tummy aches we might be saved, if we had
such throat muscles!) So after each feeding the old
bird looks down into the throat of the young one (the
young bird, if well, keeps its mouth open for food as
long as the parent is about), and if the last bug is not
promptly swallowed, she takes it out and gives it to one
of the other young."

Not only are doves shiftless nest builders; they seem
unable to make up their minds about a site. Even when
they build and lay one or two eggs, we are never sure they
will complete incubation. This is probably because the
parental instinct is so poorly developed. Once a pair
started to nest on the lowest limb of the great pine in
front of the house. Through a small pane in the front
door was framed a branch of pine and the nesting bird—
creating a delicate Japanese-like etching.

We were delighted. The nest couldn't have been
better placed for observation, and we even began going

out-of-doors the back way, so as not to disturb the birds. They evidently started brooding; then they decided they were not quite ready for house-keeping cares, and left. In a half-hearted manner they started two or three other nests before finally settling down in earnest. Though devoted to each other, apparently they do not believe that "home-keeping hearts are happiest." Several times in the years since, we have observed mourning doves looking over sites and starting building activities only to discard all.

Their food is practically all vegetable matter, over 90 per cent being principally seeds of plants, including grain, but largely troublesome weed seeds. They do not eat insects or other animal food. Although they eat some grains, they seldom disturb grain in the ear, except a little wheat, now and then.

Classed as game birds, in a recent year over seventeen thousand were killed by licensed hunters, making bird lovers hope the day will soon come when the hunting of these doves will be done with the camera and field glasses, rather than with a gun.

Even with hunting, however, these doves seem to be holding their own, and because of their different nesting habits, there is probably no danger of their becoming extinct as has their one-time cousin, the passenger pigeon.

THE PASSENGER PIGEON—AN EXTINCT BIRD

In our grandfather's time passenger pigeons were so numerous that they darkened the sky for miles during their great migratory flights. Their nesting sites, or colonies, sometimes covered territory several miles in length and width, and great branches were torn from trees by the weight of these roosting birds.

This habit of flying and nesting in enormous flocks, sometimes up in the millions, made them easy prey for the market hunters, who, relentless in their pursuit of these birds, had a large part in their extermination.

However, in spite of this persecution, some ornithologists believe that had the birds been adaptable to changing conditions, they might have survived. After the flocks became so small and scarce that it was no longer profitable to kill and market the birds, some few, at least, should have survived. The cause of their final extinction is not known.

THE GROUND DOVE

The ground dove, somewhat similar to the mourning dove in coloring, is smaller and has a shorter tail, and is less commonly known. Its range includes the southeastern states, its habitat being more southerly than the other dove's, and North Carolina being its northern limit. A few stray as far north as Pennsylvania and New York.

This small pigeon, a little less than seven inches in length, is a bird of the fields and open woods, and is sometimes found even in the quiet streets of small southern towns. It likes orchards and even gardens, and while it may nest on the ground, on tops of stumps, in grapevines, and trees, its favorite roosting place is thickly leaved orange trees. When hidden in their depths it sometimes *coos* so softly as to remind one of the wind blowing through an ancient Aeolian harp.

LIII

BOB-WHITE

There's a plump little chap in a speckled coat,
And he sings on the zigzag rails remote,
Where he whistles at breezy, bracing morn,
When the buckwheat is ripe, and stacked is the corn
    "Bob-white! Bob-white! Bob-white!"

Ah, I see why he calls; in the stubble there
Hide his plump little wife and babies fair!
So contented is he, and so proud of the same,
That he wants all the world to know his name.
    "Bob-white! Bob-white! Bob-white!"
                   —GEORGE COOPER.

IN SPRING, when he seems to know he is protected by law, bob-white often mounts a fence by the roadside and calls *bob-white; bob-white!* to his mate. If she seems indifferent to this call, he sometimes whistles a more plaintive one that sounds like *bob-white, poor bob-white!*

Bob-white's call is recognized and loved by all country and suburban dwellers fortunate enough to be within hearing distance. The name, as everyone who has heard it knows, comes from the loud and clear two-noted whistle of the male in the nesting season. On a still, clear day it can be heard a surprising distance.

After the nesting season is over, when the birds are in coveys, their notes are different—a sort of three-noted call, known as "scatter calls" to rally the flock.

Often, in late fall and winter, when we are walking through open meadows and past a tree-bordered branch down to Crabtree creek and the old mill-site, the dogs flush a covey, and the birds fly up on rapidly whirring wings to the cover of some bush or tree.

If the dogs run on, and I wait unobtrusively until all is quiet again, I can usually hear the scattered flock signaling to one another in soft, three-noted calls, *"Where are you? Where are you?"* they seem to ask.

BOB-WHITE IS LOVED BY ALL WHO ARE FORTUNATE ENOUGH TO BE WITHIN HEARING DISTANCE OF HIS CHEERY WHISTLE. ABOUT ONE-THIRD NATURAL SIZE.

Bob-white has a range from southern Canada to the Gulf, but he is far more common in the South. He belongs to the family *Odontophoridae,* or American quail, whose center of abundance is in the tropics. In eastern North America we have only one species—divided into one or two subspecies—our familiar bob-white, which is really not so much a North American bird as the northern representative of a Mexican type.

A bird of the farm, the garden, and the meadow, the

bob-white—also called quail and partridge—is a friend to man, and the most abundant and popular of game birds. Any bushy fence row serves as a retreat for its nest or winter shelter, for the bird is protectively colored. The rich brown, buff, and black plumage of its back harmonizes well with its surroundings, as do the white, black, and chestnut under parts. The male has a white throat and a white line over the eye; in the female, these markings are buff. The birds are about ten inches in length.

Relying on their protective coloring to escape detection, the birds take wing only as a last resort, when they rise on rapidly whirring wings and seek wooded cover, sometimes in dense pine forests. Bob-whites are a good example of the body construction of birds which do not fly far from home, and have heavy bodies and short, round wings which are capable of rapid flight for escape, but for a short period only. They could not sustain a long flight.

Contrast the build of bob-white, a home body, with long-distance travelers, such as the swallows, which have long, slender light-weight bodies and long, slender wings.

BOTH BIRDS INCUBATE

About the first of May bob-whites begin to pair, and rival males may sometimes be seen battling like young game-cocks for their mates. The nest, built on the ground, is of grasses, and is sometimes arched. In the South it may be found in cotton rows, in a field, by a roadside, under a shrub or log, in a fence row, or at the edge of a woodland. The white conical eggs usually number from eight to eighteen, though nests have been found containing as many as thirty or more eggs, but that is usually the result of two hens' using the same nest. The sharply pointed eggs are glossy white and are packed closely with the points downward. When the bird is off

the nest it is rather easy to find, the white eggs showing prominently, but when the hen is sitting, her color
blends so well into her surroundings that it is difficult
to see her. Sometimes, when she quits the nest, she covers the eggs with leaves. Often, too, Bob takes his mate's
place on the nest.

Bob-whites are prolific birds, nesting both early and
late. Sometimes when the hunting season opens, there
are young broods, or "squealers" just learning to fly.

THE "EGG-TOOTH"

Young bob-whites furnish a good example of the use
of the "egg-tooth." In getting out of the shell, young
birds help themselves by the "egg-tooth", a hard cal-
careous tubercle, or knob, which develops on the upper
mandible.* The bird in the shell uses this "tooth" to
peck the egg, for, as the bills of all embryo birds are very
soft, some such arrangement is necessary. Sometimes
this "egg-tooth"-lasts for several days after hatching,
and shows quite plainly. (Snakes and lizards have this
"egg-tooth" also.)

Some birds break the shell irregularly, but the quail
—and the grouse also—cuts a neat little door out of the
larger end of the egg, and out he steps, to view his small
world.

The hatching of the eggs usually takes place after
twenty-four days of incubation; the birds, being *precocial,* remain in the nest only until the downy plumage is
dried, though most observers agree that they are able to
run about at once. At the first signal of alarm the baby
chicks squat close to the ground and fade into the surroundings so quickly that it is hard to see them.

Even the older birds do the same thing, an entire
covey forming a little circle, heads outward. When they

* Allen, *The Book of Bird Life.*

do take alarm and fly, it is often with an explosive sound that reminds one of a feathered bomb-shell.

During the hunting season the birds seem to grow shyer; then later in the year, when cold drives them in search of food, they again become more fearless. As cold weather approaches they like to seek shelter in thickets and wooded bottom lands, in boggy alders, or in wild growth about fences, especially the old worm, or zig-zag fences.

Bob-whites roost on the ground, tail to tail, and with heads pointing outwards, in the form of a circle. Some-times, in the North, heavy snows overtake them, and their closely huddled forms are later found, frozen stiff.

One extremely cold winter, when we were living in northern Virginia, bob-whites came regularly to the kitchen door steps to feed on the grain I put out for the birds. But at Woodhaven, though they nest at the edge of our woodland, and in the neighboring orchards and meadows, and though we hear their calls unusually close, we have never seen them feeding in the yard.

Bob-white is a bird valuable in every way to the farmer. He destroys beetles, wire-worms, weevils, lo-custs, grasshoppers, squash-bugs, chinch-bugs, caterpil-lars, and many other insects. In winter he varies his diet with the seeds of many weeds, including some of the greatest pests to the farmer, such as crab-grass, sheep sorrel, smartweed, bindweed, pigweed, chickweed, rag-weed.

In a study made by Dr. Sylvester Judd, he concluded, by careful computation, that the bob-whites of Virginia and North Carolina consume annually, between Septem-ber 1 and April 30, 1,431 tons of weed seeds, and that from June 1 to August 31, they eat 340 tons of insects. Some allies to the farmer, those!

Bob-white also furnishes a tasty meal for the farmer's table, and his game qualities are such, that if the farmer gives him protection and leaves him a few uncultivated nesting sites, it may be possible to lease the land for hunting privileges. For this bird is the favorite of all game birds. But, for his own good, the farmer should see that the quail numbers are not too greatly depleted by hunters in any one year.

THE HOME-INCUBATED FAMILY

Deserted eggs can sometimes be incubated and the young raised in captivity. This was successfully demonstrated by friends of ours, Dr. and Mrs. T. J. Woofter of Chapel Hill. A neighboring farmer, in cutting his grass, did not see the bob-white's nest until the grass was cut, leaving it fully exposed to the sun and any enemies. It is believed by some that if a quail's nest is disturbed by man or animals, the hen will desert it.

The eight eggs were still warm, and Dr. Woofter took them home and placed them in a basket with an electric pad and a thermometer. The temperature was carefully kept at 100°. In about four days the young birds hatched, every egg being fruitful. Like baby chicks, the young birds ran around right away. All were healthy and active birds and would jump up to get grass seeds, worms, and other food.

However, there was one problem the Woofters had difficulty in solving. The young birds would not drink from a pan, or from any kind of container. Finally someone told them that quails drink by going through wet grass and sipping the dewdrops from the blades. So they experimented. Putting their hands in water, they'd let the water drip down from the ends of their fingers, and the young bobs would hop up and greedily sip the drops! The young birds lived for ten days, until one morning a strange young bob-white wandered into the pen. The newcomer, it was ascertained later, was diseased—and the disease spread rapidly among the little orphan flock, which, until then, had been husky, healthy birds. All died within eighteen hours.

LIV

KILLDEERS

When ice breaks up and brooks run free,
When killdeers cry: *"kill dee, kill-dee,"*
Then laughing Spring crowds Winter's trail
While killdeers cry and flit and sail.

The whole earth smiles beneath the sky
When killdeers flit and sail and cry.
—ALBERT·W. SMITH.

THE PLAINTIVE cry of *kill-dee, killdee* is a familiar sound to most farm boys and girls of Dixie, who affectionately shorten the bird's name to "killdee."

Although one of the best known of the shore birds, and in some sections seeming to prefer the vicinity of water, in the South the killdeer often visits farmyards and upland meadows, sometimes even nesting in pastures, cornfields, or cotton rows.

During the greater part of the year these birds are found in flocks, scattering as they feed in pastures or plowed fields. Like the crows and the grackles, killdeers, too, enjoy newly plowed lands, and follow the plow or cultivator in search of grubs and worms. But, though they frequent cultivated lands and gardens, they do not care for fields where grass or grain grows thickly or too tall, probably because it is difficult to run in such places; for the killdeer is a graceful, rapid runner, being fleet both on foot and in flight. The expression, "run like a killdee" is common in the South.

Noisy and restless, these birds do not permit too close an approach. Often we see them on the golf links, but though we try to creep up on them, we never succeed.

Soon they are on the wing, flying gracefully and swiftly, and uttering their plaintive, half-petulant *kill-dee, kill-dee*. To me, however, their call sounds more like a querulous, worried *dea-r, de-a-r*.

The adult killdeer is a ten-inch grayish-brown bird with two conspicuous black bands across the snowy breast and a white ring around the neck. The forehead, a spot behind the eye, the throat, and the belly are white. The bird is slender and has long legs.

Killdeers belong to the family *Charadriidae,* the plovers, of which there are some seventy-five or so species, only eight of which are found in North America. Though they resemble the true snipes somewhat, their much shorter and stouter bills are not fitted for probing, and so these birds obtain their food from the surface. This probably accounts for the fact that several of the species are as frequently found on the uplands as near the shore.

Breeding from Canada to Mexico, and wintering from New Jersey to Peru, killdeers are resident in most of the South throughout the year, but are far more common during migrations, when their numbers are increased by the migrants from the more northern parts of the range.

The nest, which may be near or far from the water, is but a shallow depression, scantily lined, if at all, with bits of grass or even pebbles. The four eggs are buffy white, spotted and scrawled with brownish. These eggs are pointed at the end and are so arranged in the nest that each egg points toward the center, which prevents rolling. If the eggs become disarranged, the parent bird will rearrange them again before sitting.

"BROOD SPOT"

In *The Book of Bird Life,* Dr. Allen has an excellent photograph of a killdeer about ready to incubate, and with the "brood spot" showing. This is the bare area on the middle of the breast, which, as time for incubation approaches, becomes suffused with blood, and is termed the "brood spot." Ducks and geese, which have practically no bare area on the breast, at this period proceed to pull out the down from that region so as to bring the eggs in direct contact with the skin.

The eggs of the killdeer, being those of a *precocial* bird, are large for the size of the bird and hence, before hatching, permit the development of large, strong legs and feet. The young chicks are adorable little downy fellows, and as soon as the down is dry they follow the mother in search of food. They run about all day long, until their wings become strong enough for flight.

A pretty, heart-warming sight is that of a mother killdeer followed by her four downy chicks. Though they skitter about, she watches them closely, uttering a warning or "brooding" cry, if danger seems to threaten. Then the baby chicks squat quickly, and remain perfectly still, their little bodies blending into their surroundings so perfectly that they seem to become almost invisible.

Sometimes the mother bird will try to lead an unwelcome intruder away from her eggs or young by feigning an injury. Floundering along, with one wing drooping helplessly, she will utter pitiful cries of distress. If she succeeds in drawing the intruder far enough away from the nest or the young, she miraculously recovers and flies off.

In some parts of the South, especially Alabama, the killdeer is the commonest and best known member of its family.* There, though it is comparatively rare along the coast, it seems to be more an upland than a shore bird, and is found generally throughout the in-

* *Birds of Alabama.*

terior, frequenting wet meadows, pastures, cultivated fields, as well as the shores of ponds and lakes.

The food habits of this bird are wholly harmless and very beneficial. It eats wireworms, cattle ticks, mosquito larvae, ants, white grubs, alfalfa and pine weevils, grasshoppers, and beetles, and is one of the worst enemies of the cotton-boll weevil.

As the killdeer's flesh is said to be inferior, it is of little value as a game bird; and as it preys so extensively upon insects that are annoying to man and injurious to his stock and crops, it should be removed from the list of game birds, and given every protection.

INDEX

(The italicized page number indicates the main description.)

[275]

A CATALOGUE OF SELECTED DOVER BOOKS
IN ALL FIELDS OF INTEREST

A CATALOGUE OF SELECTED DOVER BOOKS
IN ALL FIELDS OF INTEREST

AMERICA'S OLD MASTERS, James T. Flexner. Four men emerged unexpectedly from provincial 18th century America to leadership in European art: Benjamin West, J. S. Copley, C. R. Peale, Gilbert Stuart. Brilliant coverage of lives and contributions. Revised, 1967 edition. 69 plates. 365pp. of text.
21806-6 Paperbound $3.00

FIRST FLOWERS OF OUR WILDERNESS: AMERICAN PAINTING, THE COLONIAL PERIOD, James T. Flexner. Painters, and regional painting traditions from earliest Colonial times up to the emergence of Copley, West and Peale Sr., Foster, Gustavus Hesselius, Feke, John Smibert and many anonymous painters in the primitive manner. Engaging presentation, with 162 illustrations. xxii + 368pp.
22180-6 Paperbound $3.50

THE LIGHT OF DISTANT SKIES: AMERICAN PAINTING, 1760-1835, James T. Flexner. The great generation of early American painters goes to Europe to learn and to teach: West, Copley, Gilbert Stuart and others. Allston, Trumbull, Morse; also contemporary American painters—primitives, derivatives, academics—who remained in America. 102 illustrations. xiii + 306pp.
22179-2 Paperbound $3.50

A HISTORY OF THE RISE AND PROGRESS OF THE ARTS OF DESIGN IN THE UNITED STATES, William Dunlap. Much the richest mine of information on early American painters, sculptors, architects, engravers, miniaturists, etc. The only source of information for scores of artists, the major primary source for many others. Unabridged reprint of rare original 1834 edition, with new introduction by James T. Flexner, and 394 new illustrations. Edited by Rita Weiss. 6⅝ x 9⅝.
21695-0, 21696-9, 21697-7 Three volumes, Paperbound $15.00

EPOCHS OF CHINESE AND JAPANESE ART, Ernest F. Fenollosa. From primitive Chinese art to the 20th century, thorough history, explanation of every important art period and form, including Japanese woodcuts; main stress on China and Japan, but Tibet, Korea also included. Still unexcelled for its detailed, rich coverage of cultural background, aesthetic elements, diffusion studies, particularly of the historical period. 2nd, 1913 edition. 242 illustrations. lii + 439pp. of text.
20364-6, 20365-4 Two volumes, Paperbound $6.00

THE GENTLE ART OF MAKING ENEMIES, James A. M. Whistler. Greatest wit of his day deflates Oscar Wilde, Ruskin, Swinburne; strikes back at inane critics, exhibitions, art journalism; aesthetics of impressionist revolution in most striking form. Highly readable classic by great painter. Reproduction of edition designed by Whistler. Introduction by Alfred Werner. xxxvi + 334pp.
21875-9 Paperbound $3.00

VISUAL ILLUSIONS: THEIR CAUSES, CHARACTERISTICS, AND APPLICATIONS, Matthew Luckiesh. Thorough description and discussion of optical illusion, geometric and perspective, particularly; size and shape distortions, illusions of color, of motion; natural illusions; use of illusion in art and magic, industry, etc. Most useful today with op art, also for classical art. Scores of effects illustrated. Introduction by William H. Ittleson. 100 illustrations. xxi + 252pp.

21530-X Paperbound $2.00

A HANDBOOK OF ANATOMY FOR ART STUDENTS, Arthur Thomson. Thorough, virtually exhaustive coverage of skeletal structure, musculature, etc. Full text, supplemented by anatomical diagrams and drawings and by photographs of undraped figures. Unique in its comparison of male and female forms, pointing out differences of contour, texture, form. 211 figures, 40 drawings, 86 photographs. xx + 459pp. 5⅜ x 8⅜.

21163-0 Paperbound $3.50

150 MASTERPIECES OF DRAWING, Selected by Anthony Toney. Full page reproductions of drawings from the early 16th to the end of the 18th century, all beautifully reproduced: Rembrandt, Michelangelo, Dürer, Fragonard, Urs, Graf, Wouwerman, many others. First-rate browsing book, model book for artists. xviii + 150pp. 8⅜ x 11¼.

21032-4 Paperbound $3.50

THE LATER WORK OF AUBREY BEARDSLEY, Aubrey Beardsley. Exotic, erotic, ironic masterpieces in full maturity: Comedy Ballet, Venus and Tannhauser, Pierrot, Lysistrata, Rape of the Lock, Savoy material, Ali Baba, Volpone, etc. This material revolutionized the art world, and is still powerful, fresh, brilliant. With *The Early Work,* all Beardsley's finest work. 174 plates, 2 in color. xiv + 176pp. 8⅛ x 11.

21817-1 Paperbound $3.75

DRAWINGS OF REMBRANDT, Rembrandt van Rijn. Complete reproduction of fabulously rare edition by Lippmann and Hofstede de Groot, completely reedited, updated, improved by Prof. Seymour Slive, Fogg Museum. Portraits, Biblical sketches, landscapes, Oriental types, nudes, episodes from classical mythology—All Rembrandt's fertile genius. Also selection of drawings by his pupils and followers. "Stunning volumes," *Saturday Review.* 550 illustrations. lxxviii + 552pp. 9⅛ x 12¼.

21485-0, 21486-9 Two volumes, Paperbound $10.00

THE DISASTERS OF WAR, Francisco Goya. One of the masterpieces of Western civilization—83 etchings that record Goya's shattering, bitter reaction to the Napoleonic war that swept through Spain after the insurrection of 1808 and to war in general. Reprint of the first edition, with three additional plates from Boston's Museum of Fine Arts. All plates facsimile size. Introduction by Philip Hofer, Fogg Museum. v + 97pp. 9⅜ x 8¼.

21872-4 Paperbound $2.50

GRAPHIC WORKS OF ODILON REDON. Largest collection of Redon's graphic works ever assembled: 172 lithographs, 28 etchings and engravings, 9 drawings. These include some of his most famous works. All the plates from *Odilon Redon: oeuvre graphique complet,* plus additional plates. New introduction and caption translations by Alfred Werner. 209 illustrations. xxvii + 209pp. 9⅛ x 12¼.

21966-8 Paperbound $5.00

CATALOGUE OF DOVER BOOKS

DESIGN BY ACCIDENT; A BOOK OF "ACCIDENTAL EFFECTS" FOR ARTISTS AND DESIGNERS, James F. O'Brien. Create your own unique, striking, imaginative effects by "controlled accident" interaction of materials: paints and lacquers, oil and water based paints, splatter, crackling materials, shatter, similar items. Everything you do will be different; first book on this limitless art, so useful to both fine artist and commercial artist. Full instructions. 192 plates showing "accidents," 8 in color. viii + 215pp. 8⅜ x 11¼.   21942-9 Paperbound $3.75

THE BOOK OF SIGNS, Rudolf Koch. Famed German type designer draws 493 beautiful symbols: religious, mystical, alchemical, imperial, property marks, runes, etc. Remarkable fusion of traditional and modern. Good for suggestions of timelessness, smartness, modernity. Text. vi + 104pp. 6⅛ x 9¼.
                                                    20162-7 Paperbound $1.25

HISTORY OF INDIAN AND INDONESIAN ART, Ananda K. Coomaraswamy. An unabridged republication of one of the finest books by a great scholar in Eastern art. Rich in descriptive material, history, social backgrounds; Sunga reliefs, Rajput paintings, Gupta temples, Burmese frescoes, textiles, jewelry, sculpture, etc. 400 photos. viii + 423pp. 6⅜ x 9¾.   21436-2 Paperbound $5.00

PRIMITIVE ART, Franz Boas. America's foremost anthropologist surveys textiles, ceramics, woodcarving, basketry, metalwork, etc.; patterns, technology, creation of symbols, style origins. All areas of world, but very full on Northwest Coast Indians. More than 350 illustrations of baskets, boxes, totem poles, weapons, etc. 378 pp.
                                                    20025-6 Paperbound $3.00

THE GENTLEMAN AND CABINET MAKER'S DIRECTOR, Thomas Chippendale. Full reprint (third edition, 1762) of most influential furniture book of all time, by master cabinetmaker. 200 plates, illustrating chairs, sofas, mirrors, tables, cabinets, plus 24 photographs of surviving pieces. Biographical introduction by N. Bienenstock. vi + 249pp. 9⅞ x 12¾.   21601-2 Paperbound $4.00

AMERICAN ANTIQUE FURNITURE, Edgar G. Miller, Jr. The basic coverage of all American furniture before 1840. Individual chapters cover type of furniture— clocks, tables, sideboards, etc.—chronologically, with inexhaustible wealth of data. More than 2100 photographs, all identified, commented on. Essential to all early American collectors. Introduction by H. E. Keyes. vi + 1106pp. 7⅞ x 10¾.
                                    21599-7, 21600-4 Two volumes, Paperbound $11.00

PENNSYLVANIA DUTCH AMERICAN FOLK ART, Henry J. Kauffman. 279 photos, 28 drawings of tulipware, Fraktur script, painted tinware, toys, flowered furniture, quilts, samplers, hex signs, house interiors, etc. Full descriptive text. Excellent for tourist, rewarding for designer, collector. Map. 146pp. 7⅞ x 10¾.
                                                    21205-X Paperbound $2.50

EARLY NEW ENGLAND GRAVESTONE RUBBINGS, Edmund V. Gillon, Jr. 43 photographs, 226 carefully reproduced rubbings show heavily symbolic, sometimes macabre early gravestones, up to early 19th century. Remarkable early American primitive art, occasionally strikingly beautiful; always powerful. Text. xxvi + 207pp. 8⅜ x 11¼.   21380-3 Paperbound $3.50

CATALOGUE OF DOVER BOOKS

ALPHABETS AND ORNAMENTS, Ernst Lehner. Well-known pictorial source for decorative alphabets, script examples, cartouches, frames, decorative title pages, calligraphic initials, borders, similar material. 14th to 19th century, mostly European. Useful in almost any graphic arts designing, varied styles. 750 illustrations. 256pp. 7 x 10.   21905-4 Paperbound $4.00

PAINTING: A CREATIVE APPROACH, Norman Colquhoun. For the beginner simple guide provides an instructive approach to painting: major stumbling blocks for beginner; overcoming them, technical points; paints and pigments; oil painting; watercolor and other media and color. New section on "plastic" paints. Glossary. Formerly *Paint Your Own Pictures*. 221pp.   22000-1 Paperbound $1.75

THE ENJOYMENT AND USE OF COLOR, Walter Sargent. Explanation of the relations between colors themselves and between colors in nature and art, including hundreds of little-known facts about color values, intensities, effects of high and low illumination, complementary colors. Many practical hints for painters, references to great masters. 7 color plates, 29 illustrations. x + 274pp.
20944-X Paperbound $2.75

THE NOTEBOOKS OF LEONARDO DA VINCI, compiled and edited by Jean Paul Richter. 1566 extracts from original manuscripts reveal the full range of Leonardo's versatile genius: all his writings on painting, sculpture, architecture, anatomy, astronomy, geography, topography, physiology, mining, music, etc., in both Italian and English, with 186 plates of manuscript pages and more than 500 additional drawings. Includes studies for the Last Supper, the lost Sforza monument, and other works. Total of xlvii + 866pp. 7⅞ x 10¾.
22572-0, 22573-9 Two volumes, Paperbound $11.00

MONTGOMERY WARD CATALOGUE OF 1895. Tea gowns, yards of flannel and pillow-case lace, stereoscopes, books of gospel hymns, the New Improved Singer Sewing Machine, side saddles, milk skimmers, straight-edged razors, high-button shoes, spittoons, and on and on . . . listing some 25,000 items, practically all illustrated. Essential to the shoppers of the 1890's, it is our truest record of the spirit of the period. Unaltered reprint of Issue No. 57, Spring and Summer 1895. Introduction by Boris Emmet. Innumerable illustrations. xiii + 624pp. 8½ x 11⅝.
22377-9 Paperbound $6.95

THE CRYSTAL PALACE EXHIBITION ILLUSTRATED CATALOGUE (LONDON, 1851). One of the wonders of the modern world—the Crystal Palace Exhibition in which all the nations of the civilized world exhibited their achievements in the arts and sciences—presented in an equally important illustrated catalogue. More than 1700 items pictured with accompanying text—ceramics, textiles, cast-iron work, carpets, pianos, sleds, razors, wall-papers, billiard tables, beehives, silverware and hundreds of other artifacts—represent the focal point of Victorian culture in the Western World. Probably the largest collection of Victorian decorative art ever assembled—indispensable for antiquarians and designers. Unabridged republication of the Art-Journal Catalogue of the Great Exhibition of 1851, with all terminal essays. New introduction by John Gloag, F.S.A. xxxiv + 426pp. 9 x 12.
22503-8 Paperbound $5.00

A HISTORY OF COSTUME, Carl Köhler. Definitive history, based on surviving pieces of clothing primarily, and paintings, statues, etc. secondarily. Highly readable text, supplemented by 594 illustrations of costumes of the ancient Mediterranean peoples, Greece and Rome, the Teutonic prehistoric period; costumes of the Middle Ages, Renaissance, Baroque, 18th and 19th centuries. Clear, measured patterns are provided for many clothing articles. Approach is practical throughout. Enlarged by Emma von Sichart. 464pp. 21030-8 Paperbound $3.50

ORIENTAL RUGS, ANTIQUE AND MODERN, Walter A. Hawley. A complete and authoritative treatise on the Oriental rug—where they are made, by whom and how, designs and symbols, characteristics in detail of the six major groups, how to distinguish them and how to buy them. Detailed technical data is provided on periods, weaves, warps, wefts, textures, sides, ends and knots, although no technical background is required for an understanding. 11 color plates, 80 halftones, 4 maps. vi + 320pp. 6⅛ x 9⅛. 22366-3 Paperbound $5.00

TEN BOOKS ON ARCHITECTURE, Vitruvius. By any standards the most important book on architecture ever written. Early Roman discussion of aesthetics of building, construction methods, orders, sites, and every other aspect of architecture has inspired, instructed architecture for about 2,000 years. Stands behind Palladio, Michelangelo, Bramante, Wren, countless others. Definitive Morris H. Morgan translation. 68 illustrations. xii + 331pp. 20645-9 Paperbound $3.00

THE FOUR BOOKS OF ARCHITECTURE, Andrea Palladio. Translated into every major Western European language in the two centuries following its publication in 1570, this has been one of the most influential books in the history of architecture. Complete reprint of the 1738 Isaac Ware edition. New introduction by Adolf Placzek, Columbia Univ. 216 plates. xxii + 110pp. of text. 9½ x 12¾. 21308-0 Clothbound $12.50

STICKS AND STONES: A STUDY OF AMERICAN ARCHITECTURE AND CIVILIZATION, Lewis Mumford.One of the great classics of American cultural history. American architecture from the medieval-inspired earliest forms to the early 20th century; evolution of structure and style, and reciprocal influences on environment. 21 photographic illustrations. 238pp. 20202-X Paperbound $2.00

THE AMERICAN BUILDER'S COMPANION, Asher Benjamin. The most widely used early 19th century architectural style and source book, for colonial up into Greek Revival periods. Extensive development of geometry of carpentering, construction of sashes, frames, doors, stairs; plans and elevations of domestic and other buildings. Hundreds of thousands of houses were built according to this book, now invaluable to historians, architects, restorers, etc. 1827 edition. 59 plates. 114pp. 7⅞ x 10¾. 22236-5 Paperbound $3.50

DUTCH HOUSES IN THE HUDSON VALLEY BEFORE 1776, Helen Wilkinson Reynolds. The standard survey of the Dutch colonial house and outbuildings, with constructional features, decoration, and local history associated with individual homesteads. Introduction by Franklin D. Roosevelt. Map. 150 illustrations. 469pp. 6⅝ x 9¼. 21469-9 Paperbound $5.00

THE ARCHITECTURE OF COUNTRY HOUSES, Andrew J. Downing. Together with Vaux's *Villas and Cottages* this is the basic book for Hudson River Gothic architecture of the middle Victorian period. Full, sound discussions of general aspects of housing, architecture, style, decoration, furnishing, together with scores of detailed house plans, illustrations of specific buildings, accompanied by full text. Perhaps the most influential single American architectural book. 1850 edition. Introduction by J. Stewart Johnson. 321 figures, 34 architectural designs. xvi + 560pp.
22003-6 Paperbound $4.00

LOST EXAMPLES OF COLONIAL ARCHITECTURE, John Mead Howells. Full-page photographs of buildings that have disappeared or been so altered as to be denatured, including many designed by major early American architects. 245 plates. xvii + 248pp. 7⅞ x 10¾.
21143-6 Paperbound $3.50

DOMESTIC ARCHITECTURE OF THE AMERICAN COLONIES AND OF THE EARLY REPUBLIC, Fiske Kimball. Foremost architect and restorer of Williamsburg and Monticello covers nearly 200 homes between 1620-1825. Architectural details, construction, style features, special fixtures, floor plans, etc. Generally considered finest work in its area. 219 illustrations of houses, doorways, windows, capital mantels. xx + 314pp. 7⅞ x 10¾.
21743-4 Paperbound $4.00

EARLY AMERICAN ROOMS: 1650-1858, edited by Russell Hawes Kettell. Tour of 12 rooms, each representative of a different era in American history and each furnished, decorated, designed and occupied in the style of the era. 72 plans and elevations, 8-page color section, etc., show fabrics, wall papers, arrangements, etc. Full descriptive text. xvii + 200pp. of text. 8⅜ x 11¼.
21633-0 Paperbound $5.00

THE FITZWILLIAM VIRGINAL BOOK, edited by J. Fuller Maitland and W. B. Squire. Full modern printing of famous early 17th-century ms. volume of 300 works by Morley, Byrd, Bull, Gibbons, etc. For piano or other modern keyboard instrument; easy to read format. xxxvi + 938pp. 8⅜ x 11.
21068-5, 21069-3 Two volumes, Paperbound $10.00

KEYBOARD MUSIC, Johann Sebastian Bach. Bach Gesellschaft edition. A rich selection of Bach's masterpieces for the harpsichord: the six English Suites, six French Suites, the six Partitas (Clavierübung part I), the Goldberg Variations (Clavierübung part IV), the fifteen Two-Part Inventions and the fifteen Three-Part Sinfonias. Clearly reproduced on large sheets with ample margins; eminently playable. vi + 312pp. 8⅛ x 11.
22360-4 Paperbound $5.00

THE MUSIC OF BACH: AN INTRODUCTION, Charles Sanford Terry. A fine, nontechnical introduction to Bach's music, both instrumental and vocal. Covers organ music, chamber music, passion music, other types. Analyzes themes, developments, innovations. x + 114pp.
21075-8 Paperbound $1.50

BEETHOVEN AND HIS NINE SYMPHONIES, Sir George Grove. Noted British musicologist provides best history, analysis, commentary on symphonies. Very thorough, rigorously accurate; necessary to both advanced student and amateur music lover. 436 musical passages. vii + 407 pp.
20334-4 Paperbound $2.75

JOHANN SEBASTIAN BACH, Philipp Spitta. One of the great classics of musicology, this definitive analysis of Bach's music (and life) has never been surpassed. Lucid, nontechnical analyses of hundreds of pieces (30 pages devoted to St. Matthew Passion, 26 to B Minor Mass). Also includes major analysis of 18th-century music. 450 musical examples. 40-page musical supplement. Total of xx + 1799pp.
(EUK) 22278-0, 22279-9 Two volumes, Clothbound $17.50

MOZART AND HIS PIANO CONCERTOS, Cuthbert Girdlestone. The only full-length study of an important area of Mozart's creativity. Provides detailed analyses of all 23 concertos, traces inspirational sources. 417 musical examples. Second edition. 509pp.
21271-8 Paperbound $3.50

THE PERFECT WAGNERITE: A COMMENTARY ON THE NIBLUNG'S RING, George Bernard Shaw. Brilliant and still relevant criticism in remarkable essays on Wagner's Ring cycle, Shaw's ideas on political and social ideology behind the plots, role of Leitmotifs, vocal requisites, etc. Prefaces. xxi + 136pp.
(USO) 21707-8 Paperbound $1.75

DON GIOVANNI, W. A. Mozart. Complete libretto, modern English translation; biographies of composer and librettist; accounts of early performances and critical reaction. Lavishly illustrated. All the material you need to understand and appreciate this great work. Dover Opera Guide and Libretto Series; translated and introduced by Ellen Bleiler. 92 illustrations. 209pp.
21134-7 Paperbound $2.00

BASIC ELECTRICITY, U. S. Bureau of Naval Personel. Originally a training course, best non-technical coverage of basic theory of electricity and its applications. Fundamental concepts, batteries, circuits, conductors and wiring techniques, AC and DC, inductance and capacitance, generators, motors, transformers, magnetic amplifiers, synchros, servomechanisms, etc. Also covers blue-prints, electrical diagrams, etc. Many questions, with answers. 349 illustrations. x + 448pp. 6½ x 9¼.
20973-3 Paperbound $3.50

REPRODUCTION OF SOUND, Edgar Villchur. Thorough coverage for laymen of high fidelity systems, reproducing systems in general, needles, amplifiers, preamps, loudspeakers, feedback, explaining physical background. "A rare talent for making technicalities vividly comprehensible," R. Darrell, *High Fidelity*. 69 figures. iv + 92pp.
21515-6 Paperbound $1.35

HEAR ME TALKIN' TO YA: THE STORY OF JAZZ AS TOLD BY THE MEN WHO MADE IT, Nat Shapiro and Nat Hentoff. Louis Armstrong, Fats Waller, Jo Jones, Clarence Williams, Billy Holiday, Duke Ellington, Jelly Roll Morton and dozens of other jazz greats tell how it was in Chicago's South Side, New Orleans, depression Harlem and the modern West Coast as jazz was born and grew. xvi + 429pp.
21726-4 Paperbound $3.00

FABLES OF AESOP, translated by Sir Roger L'Estrange. A reproduction of the very rare 1931 Paris edition; a selection of the most interesting fables, together with 50 imaginative drawings by Alexander Calder. v + 128pp. 6½x9¼.
21780-9 Paperbound $1.50

Against the Grain (A Rebours), Joris K. Huysmans. Filled with weird images, evidences of a bizarre imagination, exotic experiments with hallucinatory drugs, rich tastes and smells and the diversions of its sybarite hero Duc Jean des Esseintes, this classic novel pushed 19th-century literary decadence to its limits. Full unabridged edition. Do not confuse this with abridged editions generally sold. Introduction by Havelock Ellis. xlix + 206pp. 22190-3 Paperbound $2.50

Variorum Shakespeare: Hamlet. Edited by Horace H. Furness; a landmark of American scholarship. Exhaustive footnotes and appendices treat all doubtful words and phrases, as well as suggested critical emendations throughout the play's history. First volume contains editor's own text, collated with all Quartos and Folios. Second volume contains full first Quarto, translations of Shakespeare's sources (Belleforest, and Saxo Grammaticus), Der Bestrafte Brudermord, and many essays on critical and historical points of interest by major authorities of past and present. Includes details of staging and costuming over the years. By far the best edition available for serious students of Shakespeare. Total of xx + 905pp. 21004-9, 21005-7, 2 volumes, Paperbound $7.00

A Life of William Shakespeare, Sir Sidney Lee. This is the standard life of Shakespeare, summarizing everything known about Shakespeare and his plays. Incredibly rich in material, broad in coverage, clear and judicious, it has served thousands as the best introduction to Shakespeare. 1931 edition. 9 plates. xxix + 792pp. 21967-4 Paperbound $4.50

Masters of the Drama, John Gassner. Most comprehensive history of the drama in print, covering every tradition from Greeks to modern Europe and America, including India, Far East, etc. Covers more than 800 dramatists, 2000 plays, with biographical material, plot summaries, theatre history, criticism, etc. "Best of its kind in English," New Republic. 77 illustrations. xxii + 890pp. 20100-7 Clothbound $10.00

The Evolution of the English Language, George McKnight. The growth of English, from the 14th century to the present. Unusual, non-technical account presents basic information in very interesting form: sound shifts, change in grammar and syntax, vocabulary growth, similar topics. Abundantly illustrated with quotations. Formerly Modern English in the Making. xii + 590pp. 21932-1 Paperbound $4.00

An Etymological Dictionary of Modern English, Ernest Weekley. Fullest, richest work of its sort, by foremost British lexicographer. Detailed word histories, including many colloquial and archaic words; extensive quotations. Do not confuse this with the Concise Etymological Dictionary, which is much abridged. Total of xxvii + 830pp. 6½ x 9¼. 21873-2, 21874-0 Two volumes, Paperbound $7.90

Flatland: A Romance of Many Dimensions, E. A. Abbott. Classic of science-fiction explores ramifications of life in a two-dimensional world, and what happens when a three-dimensional being intrudes. Amusing reading, but also useful as introduction to thought about hyperspace. Introduction by Banesh Hoffmann. 16 illustrations. xx + 103pp. 20001-9 Paperbound $1.25

POEMS OF ANNE BRADSTREET, edited with an introduction by Robert Hutchinson. A new selection of poems by America's first poet and perhaps the first significant woman poet in the English language. 48 poems display her development in works of considerable variety—love poems, domestic poems, religious meditations, formal elegies, "quaternions," etc. Notes, bibliography. viii + 222pp.
22160-1 Paperbound $2.50

THREE GOTHIC NOVELS: THE CASTLE OF OTRANTO BY HORACE WALPOLE; VATHEK BY WILLIAM BECKFORD; THE VAMPYRE BY JOHN POLIDORI, WITH FRAGMENT OF A NOVEL BY LORD BYRON, edited by E. F. Bleiler. The first Gothic novel, by Walpole; the finest Oriental tale in English, by Beckford; powerful Romantic supernatural story in versions by Polidori and Byron. All extremely important in history of literature; all still exciting, packed with supernatural thrills, ghosts, haunted castles, magic, etc. xl + 291pp.
21232-7 Paperbound $2.50

THE BEST TALES OF HOFFMANN, E. T. A. Hoffmann. 10 of Hoffmann's most important stories, in modern re-editings of standard translations: Nutcracker and the King of Mice, Signor Formica, Automata, The Sandman, Rath Krespel, The Golden Flowerpot, Master Martin the Cooper, The Mines of Falun, The King's Betrothed, A New Year's Eve Adventure. 7 illustrations by Hoffmann. Edited by E. F. Bleiler. xxxix + 419pp. 21793-0 Paperbound $3.00

GHOST AND HORROR STORIES OF AMBROSE BIERCE, Ambrose Bierce. 23 strikingly modern stories of the horrors latent in the human mind: The Eyes of the Panther, The Damned Thing, An Occurrence at Owl Creek Bridge, An Inhabitant of Carcosa, etc., plus the dream-essay, Visions of the Night. Edited by E. F. Bleiler. xxii + 199pp. 20767-6 Paperbound $1.50

BEST GHOST STORIES OF J. S. LEFANU, J. Sheridan LeFanu. Finest stories by Victorian master often considered greatest supernatural writer of all. Carmilla, Green Tea, The Haunted Baronet, The Familiar, and 12 others. Most never before available in the U. S. A. Edited by E. F. Bleiler. 8 illustrations from Victorian publications. xvii + 467pp. 20415-4 Paperbound $3.00

MATHEMATICAL FOUNDATIONS OF INFORMATION THEORY, A. I. Khinchin. Comprehensive introduction to work of Shannon, McMillan, Feinstein and Khinchin, placing these investigations on a rigorous mathematical basis. Covers entropy concept in probability theory, uniqueness theorem, Shannon's inequality, ergodic sources, the E property, martingale concept, noise, Feinstein's fundamental lemma, Shanon's first and second theorems. Translated by R. A. Silverman and M. D. Friedman. iii + 120pp. 60434-9 Paperbound $2.00

SEVEN SCIENCE FICTION NOVELS, H. G. Wells. The standard collection of the great novels. Complete, unabridged. *First Men in the Moon, Island of Dr. Moreau, War of the Worlds, Food of the Gods, Invisible Man, Time Machine, In the Days of the Comet.* Not only science fiction fans, but every educated person owes it to himself to read these novels. 1015pp. (USO) 20264-X Clothbound $6.00

LAST AND FIRST MEN AND STAR MAKER, TWO SCIENCE FICTION NOVELS, Olaf Stapledon. Greatest future histories in science fiction. In the first, human intelligence is the "hero," through strange paths of evolution, interplanetary invasions, incredible technologies, near extinctions and reemergences. Star Maker describes the quest of a band of star rovers for intelligence itself, through time and space: weird inhuman civilizations, crustacean minds, symbiotic worlds, etc. Complete, unabridged. v + 438pp. (USO) 21962-3 Paperbound $2.50

THREE PROPHETIC NOVELS, H. G. WELLS. Stages of a consistently planned future for mankind. *When the Sleeper Wakes,* and *A Story of the Days to Come,* anticipate *Brave New World* and *1984,* in the 21st Century; *The Time Machine,* only complete version in print, shows farther future and the end of mankind. All show Wells's greatest gifts as storyteller and novelist. Edited by E. F. Bleiler. x + 335pp. (USO) 20605-X Paperbound $2.50

THE DEVIL'S DICTIONARY, Ambrose Bierce. America's own Oscar Wilde—Ambrose Bierce—offers his barbed iconoclastic wisdom in over 1,000 definitions hailed by H. L. Mencken as "some of the most gorgeous witticisms in the English language." 145pp. 20487-1 Paperbound $1.25

MAX AND MORITZ, Wilhelm Busch. Great children's classic, father of comic strip, of two bad boys, Max and Moritz. Also Ker and Plunk (Plisch und Plumm), Cat and Mouse, Deceitful Henry, Ice-Peter, The Boy and the Pipe, and five other pieces. Original German, with English translation. Edited by H. Arthur Klein; translations by various hands and H. Arthur Klein. vi + 216pp. 20181-3 Paperbound $2.00

PIGS IS PIGS AND OTHER FAVORITES, Ellis Parker Butler. The title story is one of the best humor short stories, as Mike Flannery obfuscates biology and English. Also included, That Pup of Murchison's, The Great American Pie Company, and Perkins of Portland. 14 illustrations. v + 109pp. 21532-6 Paperbound $1.25

THE PETERKIN PAPERS, Lucretia P. Hale. It takes genius to be as stupidly mad as the Peterkins, as they decide to become wise, celebrate the "Fourth," keep a cow, and otherwise strain the resources of the Lady from Philadelphia. Basic book of American humor. 153 illustrations. 219pp. 20794-3 Paperbound $2.00

PERRAULT'S FAIRY TALES, translated by A. E. Johnson and S. R. Littlewood, with 34 full-page illustrations by Gustave Doré. All the original Perrault stories—Cinderella, Sleeping Beauty, Bluebeard, Little Red Riding Hood, Puss in Boots, Tom Thumb, etc.—with their witty verse morals and the magnificent illustrations of Doré. One of the five or six great books of European fairy tales. viii + 117pp. 8⅛ x 11. 22311-6 Paperbound $2.00

OLD HUNGARIAN FAIRY TALES, Baroness Orczy. Favorites translated and adapted by author of the *Scarlet Pimpernel*. Eight fairy tales include "The Suitors of Princess Fire-Fly," "The Twin Hunchbacks," "Mr. Cuttlefish's Love Story," and "The Enchanted Cat." This little volume of magic and adventure will captivate children as it has for generations. 90 drawings by Montagu Barstow. 96pp. (USO) 22293-4 Paperbound $1.95

THE RED FAIRY BOOK, Andrew Lang. Lang's color fairy books have long been children's favorites. This volume includes Rapunzel, Jack and the Bean-stalk and 35 other stories, familiar and unfamiliar. 4 plates, 93 illustrations x + 367pp.
21673-X Paperbound $2.50

THE BLUE FAIRY BOOK, Andrew Lang. Lang's tales come from all countries and all times. Here are 37 tales from Grimm, the Arabian Nights, Greek Mythology, and other fascinating sources. 8 plates, 130 illustrations. xi + 390pp.
21437-0 Paperbound $2.75

HOUSEHOLD STORIES BY THE BROTHERS GRIMM. Classic English-language edition of the well-known tales — Rumpelstiltskin, Snow White, Hansel and Gretel, The Twelve Brothers, Faithful John, Rapunzel, Tom Thumb (52 stories in all). Translated into simple, straightforward English by Lucy Crane. Ornamented with head-pieces, vignettes, elaborate decorative initials and a dozen full-page illustrations by Walter Crane. x + 269pp.
21080-4 Paperbound **$2.00**

THE MERRY ADVENTURES OF ROBIN HOOD, Howard Pyle. The finest modern versions of the traditional ballads and tales about the great English outlaw. Howard Pyle's complete prose version, with every word, every illustration of the first edition. Do not confuse this facsimile of the original (1883) with modern editions that change text or illustrations. 23 plates plus many page decorations. xxii + 296pp.
22043-5 Paperbound $2.75

THE STORY OF KING ARTHUR AND HIS KNIGHTS, Howard Pyle. The finest children's version of the life of King Arthur; brilliantly retold by Pyle, with 48 of his most imaginative illustrations. xviii + 313pp. 6⅛ x 9¼.
21445-1 Paperbound $2.50

THE WONDERFUL WIZARD OF OZ, L. Frank Baum. America's finest children's book in facsimile of first edition with all Denslow illustrations in full color. The edition a child should have. Introduction by Martin Gardner. 23 color plates, scores of drawings. iv + 267pp.
20691-2 Paperbound $2.50

THE MARVELOUS LAND OF OZ, L. Frank Baum. The second Oz book, every bit as imaginative as the Wizard. The hero is a boy named Tip, but the Scarecrow and the Tin Woodman are back, as is the Oz magic. 16 color plates, 120 drawings by John R. Neill. 287pp.
20692-0 Paperbound $2.50

THE MAGICAL MONARCH OF MO, L. Frank Baum. Remarkable adventures in a land even stranger than Oz. The best of Baum's books not in the Oz series. 15 color plates and dozens of drawings by Frank Verbeck. xviii + 237pp.
21892-9 Paperbound $2.25

THE BAD CHILD'S BOOK OF BEASTS, MORE BEASTS FOR WORSE CHILDREN, A MORAL ALPHABET, Hilaire Belloc. Three complete humor classics in one volume. Be kind to the frog, and do not call him names . . . and 28 other whimsical animals. Familiar favorites and some not so well known. Illustrated by Basil Blackwell. 156pp.
(USO) 20749-8 Paperbound $1.50

EAST O' THE SUN AND WEST O' THE MOON, George W. Dasent. Considered the best of all translations of these Norwegian folk tales, this collection has been enjoyed by generations of children (and folklorists too). Includes True and Untrue, Why the Sea is Salt, East O' the Sun and West O' the Moon, Why the Bear is Stumpy-Tailed, Boots and the Troll, The Cock and the Hen, Rich Peter the Pedlar, and 52 more. The only edition with all 59 tales. 77 illustrations by Erik Werenskiold and Theodor Kittelsen. xv + 418pp. 22521-6 Paperbound $3.50

GOOPS AND HOW TO BE THEM, Gelett Burgess. Classic of tongue-in-cheek humor, masquerading as etiquette book. 87 verses, twice as many cartoons, show mischievous Goops as they demonstrate to children virtues of table manners, neatness, courtesy, etc. Favorite for generations. viii + 88pp. 6½ x 9¼. 22233-0 Paperbound $1.50

ALICE'S ADVENTURES UNDER GROUND, Lewis Carroll. The first version, quite different from the final *Alice in Wonderland,* printed out by Carroll himself with his own illustrations. Complete facsimile of the "million dollar" manuscript Carroll gave to Alice Liddell in 1864. Introduction by Martin Gardner. viii + 96pp. Title and dedication pages in color. 21482-6 Paperbound $1.25

THE BROWNIES, THEIR BOOK, Palmer Cox. Small as mice, cunning as foxes, exuberant and full of mischief, the Brownies go to the zoo, toy shop, seashore, circus, etc., in 24 verse adventures and 266 illustrations. Long a favorite, since their first appearance in St. Nicholas Magazine. xi + 144pp. 6⅝ x 9¼. 21265-3 Paperbound $1.75

SONGS OF CHILDHOOD, Walter De La Mare. Published (under the pseudonym Walter Ramal) when De La Mare was only 29, this charming collection has long been a favorite children's book. A facsimile of the first edition in paper, the 47 poems capture the simplicity of the nursery rhyme and the ballad, including such lyrics as I Met Eve, Tartary, The Silver Penny. vii + 106pp. (USO) 21972-0 Paperbound $2.00

THE COMPLETE NONSENSE OF EDWARD LEAR, Edward Lear. The finest 19th-century humorist-cartoonist in full: all nonsense limericks, zany alphabets, Owl and Pussycat, songs, nonsense botany, and more than 500 illustrations by Lear himself. Edited by Holbrook Jackson. xxix + 287pp. (USO) 20167-8 Paperbound $2.00

BILLY WHISKERS: THE AUTOBIOGRAPHY OF A GOAT, Frances Trego Montgomery. A favorite of children since the early 20th century, here are the escapades of that rambunctious, irresistible and mischievous goat—Billy Whiskers. Much in the spirit of *Peck's Bad Boy,* this is a book that children never tire of reading or hearing. All the original familiar illustrations by W. H. Fry are included: 6 color plates, 18 black and white drawings. 159pp. 22345-0 Paperbound $2.00

MOTHER GOOSE MELODIES. Faithful republication of the fabulously rare Munroe and Francis "copyright 1833" Boston edition—the most important Mother Goose collection, usually referred to as the "original." Familiar rhymes plus many rare ones, with wonderful old woodcut illustrations. Edited by E. F. Bleiler. 128pp. 4½ x 6⅜. 22577-1 Paperbound $1.00

TWO LITTLE SAVAGES; BEING THE ADVENTURES OF TWO BOYS WHO LIVED AS INDIANS AND WHAT THEY LEARNED, Ernest Thompson Seton. Great classic of nature and boyhood provides a vast range of woodlore in most palatable form, a genuinely entertaining story. Two farm boys build a teepee in woods and live in it for a month, working out Indian solutions to living problems, star lore, birds and animals, plants, etc. 293 illustrations. vii + 286pp.

20985-7 Paperbound $2.50

PETER PIPER'S PRACTICAL PRINCIPLES OF PLAIN & PERFECT PRONUNCIATION. Alliterative jingles and tongue-twisters of surprising charm, that made their first appearance in America about 1830. Republished in full with the spirited woodcut illustrations from this earliest American edition. 32pp. 4½ x 6⅜.

22560-7 Paperbound $1.00

SCIENCE EXPERIMENTS AND AMUSEMENTS FOR CHILDREN, Charles Vivian. 73 easy experiments, requiring only materials found at home or easily available, such as candles, coins, steel wool, etc.; illustrate basic phenomena like vacuum, simple chemical reaction, etc. All safe. Modern, well-planned. Formerly *Science Games for Children*. 102 photos, numerous drawings. 96pp. 6⅛ x 9¼.

21856-2 Paperbound $1.25

AN INTRODUCTION TO CHESS MOVES AND TACTICS SIMPLY EXPLAINED, Leonard Barden. Informal intermediate introduction, quite strong in explaining reasons for moves. Covers basic material, tactics, important openings, traps, positional play in middle game, end game. Attempts to isolate patterns and recurrent configurations. Formerly *Chess*. 58 figures. 102pp. (USO) 21210-6 Paperbound $1.25

LASKER'S MANUAL OF CHESS, Dr. Emanuel Lasker. Lasker was not only one of the five great World Champions, he was also one of the ablest expositors, theorists, and analysts. In many ways, his Manual, permeated with his philosophy of battle, filled with keen insights, is one of the greatest works ever written on chess. Filled with analyzed games by the great players. A single-volume library that will profit almost any chess player, beginner or master. 308 diagrams. xli x 349pp.

20640-8 Paperbound $2.75

THE MASTER BOOK OF MATHEMATICAL RECREATIONS, Fred Schuh. In opinion of many the finest work ever prepared on mathematical puzzles, stunts, recreations; exhaustively thorough explanations of mathematics involved, analysis of effects, citation of puzzles and games. Mathematics involved is elementary. Translated by F. Göbel. 194 figures. xxiv + 430pp. 22134-2 Paperbound $3.50

MATHEMATICS, MAGIC AND MYSTERY, Martin Gardner. Puzzle editor for Scientific American explains mathematics behind various mystifying tricks: card tricks, stage "mind reading," coin and match tricks, counting out games, geometric dissections, etc. Probability sets, theory of numbers clearly explained. Also provides more than 400 tricks, guaranteed to work, that you can do. 135 illustrations. xii + 176pp.

20335-2 Paperbound $1.75

Mathematical Puzzles for Beginners and Enthusiasts, Geoffrey Mott-Smith. 189 puzzles from easy to difficult—involving arithmetic, logic, algebra, properties of digits, probability, etc.—for enjoyment and mental stimulus. Explanation of mathematical principles behind the puzzles. 135 illustrations. viii + 248pp.

20198-8 Paperbound $1.75

Paper Folding for Beginners, William D. Murray and Francis J. Rigney. Easiest book on the market, clearest instructions on making interesting, beautiful origami. Sail boats, cups, roosters, frogs that move legs, bonbon boxes, standing birds, etc. 40 projects; more than 275 diagrams and photographs. 94pp.

20713-7 Paperbound $1.00

Tricks and Games on the Pool Table, Fred Herrmann. 79 tricks and games—some solitaires, some for two or more players, some competitive games—to entertain you between formal games. Mystifying shots and throws, unusual caroms, tricks involving such props as cork, coins, a hat, etc. Formerly *Fun on the Pool Table.* 77 figures. 95pp.

21814-7 Paperbound $1.25

Hand Shadows to be Thrown Upon the Wall: A Series of Novel and Amusing Figures Formed by the Hand, Henry Bursill. Delightful picturebook from great-grandfather's day shows how to make 18 different hand shadows: a bird that flies, duck that quacks, dog that wags his tail, camel, goose, deer, boy, turtle, etc. Only book of its sort. vi + 33pp. 6½ x 9¼. 21779-5 Paperbound $1.00

Whittling and Woodcarving, E. J. Tangerman. 18th printing of best book on market. "If you can cut a potato you can carve" toys and puzzles, chains, chessmen, caricatures, masks, frames, woodcut blocks, surface patterns, much more. Information on tools, woods, techniques. Also goes into serious wood sculpture from Middle Ages to present, East and West. 464 photos, figures. x + 293pp.

20965-2 Paperbound $2.00

History of Philosophy, Julián Marias. Possibly the clearest, most easily followed, best planned, most useful one-volume history of philosophy on the market; neither skimpy nor overfull. Full details on system of every major philosopher and dozens of less important thinkers from pre-Socratics up to Existentialism and later. Strong on many European figures usually omitted. Has gone through dozens of editions in Europe. 1966 edition, translated by Stanley Appelbaum and Clarence Strowbridge. xviii + 505pp. 21739-6 Paperbound $3.50

Yoga: A Scientific Evaluation, Kovoor T. Behanan. Scientific but non-technical study of physiological results of yoga exercises; done under auspices of Yale U. Relations to Indian thought, to psychoanalysis, etc. 16 photos. xxiii + 270pp.

20505-3 Paperbound $2.50

Prices subject to change without notice.
Available at your book dealer or write for free catalogue to Dept. GI, Dover Publications, Inc., 180 Varick St., N. Y., N. Y. 10014. Dover publishes more than 150 books each year on science, elementary and advanced mathematics, biology, music, art, literary history, social sciences and other areas.